TWAYNE'S WORLD AUTHORS SERIES

A Survey of the World's Literature

Sylvia E. Bowman, Indiana University
GENERAL EDITOR

RUSSIA

Nicholas P. Vaslef, U.S. Air Force Academy
EDITOR

Alexander Pushkin

(TWAS 82)

TWAYNE'S WORLD AUTHORS SERIES (TWAS)

The purpose of TWAS is to survey the major writers —novelists, dramatists, historians, poets, philosophers, and critics—of the nations of the world. Among the national literatures covered are those of Australia, Canada, China, Eastern Europe, France, Germany, Greece, India, Italy, Japan, Latin America, New Zealand, Poland, Russia, Scandinavia, Spain, and the African nations, as well as Hebrew, Yiddish, and Latin Classical literatures. This survey is complemented by Twayne's United States Authors Series and English Authors Series.

The intent of each volume in these series is to present a critical-analytical study of the works of the writer; to include biographical and historical material that may be necessary for understanding, appreciation, and critical appraisal of the writer; and to present all material in clear, concise English—but not to vitiate the scholarly content of the work by doing so.

Alexander Pushkin

By WALTER N. VICKERY

University of North Carolina

Twayne Publishers, Inc.   ::   New York

For Anne Virginia

Preface

While most Russians and students of Russian literature unhesitatingly rate Pushkin as Russia's greatest poet, his merits have been insufficiently recognized outside his own country. The reasons for this are several, and they have a direct bearing on the peculiar difficulties confronting the writer who would attempt to present Pushkin to the non-Russian reader. The main obstacle to Pushkin's rise to fame abroad has been the language barrier: until recently the Russian language, compared with French, German, English, Italian, or Spanish, has been studied and known by relatively few people. This barrier has not prevented the rise to fame of Tolstoy, Dostoyevsky, Turgenev, or Chekhov; ill-served at times by their translators, these writers have nevertheless secured for themselves positions of pre-eminence—thanks to the fact that they wrote in prose. Pushkin, who also wrote in prose but whose principal claim to fame is as a poet, has been, in this limited respect only, less fortunate than a Tolstoy or a Dostoyevsky; for the loss incurred in translation must, with a few possible doubtful exceptions, inevitably be more damaging in poetry than in prose. And in Pushkin's particular case this unavoidable problem has been aggravated by the manner of his writing. His style is characterized by an unobtrusiveness and self-restraint which in the original are among his chief assets. Such virtues are not, however, easy to convey in translation. If, in spite of the difficulties, this introductory essay on Pushkin's life and work can be instrumental in giving something of the flavor of the original and some idea of Pushkin's greatness, it will have fulfilled a worthwhile task.

While Pushkin has suffered abroad from neglect, he has not gone unscathed at the hands of his fellow countrymen. Full tribute must be paid to Russian and, in particular, Soviet scholars for their invaluable achievements in collecting and documenting materials on Pushkin's life and works. This cannot, however, blind one to the fact that their critical judgments (often echoed in Western scholarly works) have been all too often at fault. It is not merely that the position occupied by Pushkin as Russia's national poet has led to adulation, for superlatives are not in themselves necessarily harmful. More important, this adulation, combined with a one-sided theoretical approach, has caused emphasis to be placed on qualities which either are nonexistent or are irrelevant to a critical appreciation of Pushkin as a poet, and has at the same time obscured some of those qualities which are essential to such appreciation.

The avowed intent of this essay—to provide an introduction to Pushkin—argued against an overly polemical tone; on the other hand, it would obviously have been purposeless to compose a synthesis of viewpoints which I do not share. It is my hope that the present volume may serve a purpose not only in introducing the new reader to Pushkin but also in stimulating fresh inquiry and discussion among those already acquainted with Pushkin and Pushkin criticism.

I have attempted to treat Pushkin in two ways. I have attempted to provide as much background information as space permitted: information relating to such things as Pushkin's development, his literary environment, the influences he experienced, his writing of individual works, and the findings of previous literary scholarship. Secondly—and this has been my principal aim—I have attempted to arrive at some sort of critical appreciation of Pushkin's work, to define what Croce would have called its fundamental theme, or themes, to interpret as far as possible Pushkin's poetic personality.

I would like to express my gratitude to the Baring Trustees for permission to produce two translations by the late Maurice Baring: "The Prophet" and "Remembrance." The remaining translations are my own. In some cases I have been tempted to rhyme. More often I have sought only to reproduce roughly the English equivalent of Pushkin's Russian meters. In all cases I have been conscious of my inability to approach the original.

Considerations of space have obliged me to be selective. Pushkin connoisseurs will readily spot the omissions. I have, in general, omitted Pushkin's unfinished works and his historical and critical writings, and have been paid only perfunctory tribute to his literary prose. The decision to be selective was prompted by the fear that all-inclusiveness could turn a monograph of this type into something approaching a catalogue and by the hope that, in devoting greater space (often required by the need to translate or recapitulate) to Pushkin's most famous works, I could the better give to the non-Russian reader some sort of feeling of what Pushkin was about.

The debts of gratitude incurred in the writing of this book are too numerous to cover. Discussions with both colleagues, at home and abroad, and students have been immeasurably helpful. For their assistance in making ready the manuscript, I wish to express my sincere thanks to Mrs. Kathleen Charlton and Miss Geraldine Neish. I cannot say enough in thanking Professor Nicholas Vaslef for his careful and understanding editing. A very great debt of gratitude goes to my wife—for her help in the writing and her patience with the writer.

Contents

Chronology

1799   Born May 26 (old style) in Moscow.

1811   Enters lycée in Tsarskoe Selo, near Petersburg.

1813   Writes earliest surviving verses.

1815   Reads his "Memories in Tsarskoe Selo" at a lycée examination in the presence of the poet, Derzhavin.

1817   Finishes lycée. Appointed to the Ministry of Foreign Affairs.

1817- Lives mainly in Petersburg. Achieves fame for liberal
1820   verses.

1820   Completes *Ruslan and Lyudmila*. Transferred compulsorily out of Petersburg. Permitted to travel with Raevsky family in the Caucasus and Crimea (May-September).

1820- Lives mainly in Kishinev. Writes *The Prisoner of the Cau-
1823   casus* (1820), *Gavriiliada* (1821), *The Fountain of Bakhchisaray* (1821-23); starts work on *Evgeny Onegin* (1823).

1823   Transferred to Odessa.

1824   Writes most of *The Gypsies*. Dismissed from the service and ordered into exile at Mikhaylovskoe, near Pskov.

1824- Exile at Mikhailovskoe. Completes *The Gypsies* (1824),
1826   *Boris Godunov* (1825), *Count Nulin* (1825). Decembrist Revolt, December 14, 1825. Requests reprieve from exile (May, 1826). Pardoned by Nicholas I (September 8, 1826).

1826- Bachelor existence mainly in Moscow and Petersburg.
1831

1828   Investigated with regard to authorship of *Gavriiliada* (August-October). Writes *Poltava*.

1829   Travels without authorization to the Army of the Caucasus and receives reprimand.

1830   Engaged to Natalia Nikolaevna Goncharova (May 6). Obliged by cholera epidemic to remain at Boldino, near Nizhny Novgorod (September-December), where he writes *The Tales of Belkin, The Little House in Kolomna,* the "Little Tragedies," numerous lyrics, and completes (almost entirely) *Evgeny Onegin.*

1831   Marriage to Natalia (February 18). Moves with bride from Moscow to Tsarskoe Selo to Petersburg. Writes *The Tale of the Tsar Saltan.* Is accepted in the service as historiographer.

1831-   Married life spent mainly in Petersburg. Four children
1837   born.

1831   Completes *Evgeny Onegin.*

1833   Elected member of the Russian Academy. Travels to Orenburg and Kazan, to collect materials for his history of Pugachev. Stays October-November at Boldino, where he completes *The Bronze Horseman, The History of Pugachev,* and *Angelo.* Also writes two further "tales in verse." Appointed *Kammerjunker* (December 30) which he deeply resents.

1834   Writes *The Queen of Spades.* Fails with his request to be retired. Writes *The Tale of the Golden Cockerel.*

1835   Request for temporary retirement refused.

1836   Completes *The Captain's Daughter.* Receives (November 4) anonymous "diploma" designating him a member of the "Order of Cuckolds." Challenges d'Anthès. Duel averted.

1837   January 10: D'Anthès marries Pushkin's sister-in-law; continues to court Pushkin's wife. January 25: Pushkin writes insulting letter to d'Anthès' adoptive father. January 26: receives challenge to duel. January 27: Is mortally wounded in duel with d'Anthès. January 29: Dies. February 6: Pushkin's remains sent out to Svyatogorsky Monastery and he is buried.

CHAPTER 1

Early Poetry and Ruslan and Lyudmila

I Early Influences: The Lycée and Petersburg

PUSHKIN was born in Moscow on May 26, 1799 (old style), the second of three children. Of importance for his future development was his lack of a close relationship with his parents, particularly his mother, who made no attempt to conceal her preference for his younger brother. What adult affection the boy did receive seems to have come from his maternal grandmother and the family nurse. Of importance for Pushkin's literary development was the fact that both his father, Sergey Pushkin, and uncle, Vasily Pushkin, were writers, the latter in particular enjoying quite a reputation among contemporaries. Young Pushkin was, therefore, exposed from a very early age to a literary atmosphere and to the presence of literary ambitions. The most distinguished men of letters used to gather at his father's house, and Pushkin had free access to his father's library, which contained, among other things, a good collection of French literature. By the time he was twelve years old, the future poet had read widely for his age, though without systematic guidance, had tried his hand at writing poetry (his earliest verses, which do not survive, were apparently in French), and had almost certainly conceived the ambition of making his name as a poet.

Pushkin came of the old Russian aristocracy (he was proud to be able to trace his family tree back six hundred years), but the family had by Pushkin's time lost almost all its onetime wealth. These two factors, consciousness of his aristocratic lineage and lack of money, were to have a decisive influence on the poet's life.

In 1811, at the age of twelve, Pushkin was entered in the newly founded lycée at Tsarskoe Selo, near Petersburg. The lycée was designed to give what was understood to be a broad, liberal education to young boys, especially," in the words of its charter, "those destined for high administrative posts in the state service." The education was free. Pushkin became one of the first class of thirty pupils.

Pushkin spent six formative years at Tsarskoe Selo. He was not one of the more popular members of his class, but he did make some lifelong friendships and, like many of his classmates, always looked back on his lycée days with tenderness and a certain nostalgia. He had strong personal likes and dislikes, and other people tended to react fairly strongly toward him—positively or negatively. He was of a lively disposition, but uneven in mood. His teachers varied in their assessment of his scholarship, but the most generally held view was that Pushkin was more gifted than he was diligent, and that he was unwilling to make an effort in subjects that did not appeal to him—for example, ethics, political philosophy, history. Acknowledged, on the other hand, were Pushkin's proficiency in French language and literature and, above all, his brilliance in all things relative to his native language. In particular, he established himself as the outstanding poet in a class that numbered among its members no less than six aspiring poets.

Before he left Tsarskoe Selo his talent and promise had received recognition from such distinguished writers as Batyushkov, Zhukovsky, Karamzin, and the aged Derzhavin, the dean of the Russian poets at the time. He had also had the opportunity, along with his fellows, of gaining firsthand some idea of what adult life might be expected to hold in store. During their last years in the lycée, Pushkin and his classmates were received as guests in the houses of some of the residents of Tsarskoe Selo (it was thus that Pushkin became an intimate of the Karamzin household). They also established friendly relations with some of the hussar officers stationed there, through whom they learned something not only of drinking and wenching, but also of the philosophical and political ideas that were beginning to stir the youth of those years. Chaadaev, the philosopher, was a hussar officer at the time, and it was at Tsarskoe Selo that Pushkin struck up his lifelong friendship with him.

On leaving the lycée in 1817, with little or no desire for any of the more conventional careers, but eager for poetic fame, Pushkin received a civil service appointment in the Ministry of Foreign Affairs, and after two summer months on his mother's estate, went in September 1817 to live in Petersburg. Freed of the restraints of Tsarskoe Selo, he now set himself to lead the dissipated life of a young blood.

He was short, about five feet-three inches tall, solidly built, dark complexioned and with dark curly hair which he had inherited from an Abyssinian forebear. He could not not be described as handsome, but he had considerable charm. At this youthful stage he was much exercised by the art of love in the Ovidian sense; but he was always too emotional by nature to restrict himself cold-bloodedly to the tactics and techniques of seduction, and his heart was constantly vulnerable to falling in love. He also indulged, like many of the younger sets, in late-night partying, actresses, and brothels. All this was natural enough. Yet one cannot escape the impression that Pushkin's escapades were partly motivated by a desire to cut a figure. Meanwhile, Pushkin was writing and his ideas were developing.

Pushkin's early verse attempts (up to 1817) reflect fairly faithfully the literary currents of the day. These were extremely confused, the more so since the early nineteenth century was a period of rapid cultural change. To attempt to summarize the prevailing situation is inevitably to oversimplify. No generalization, it seems, is safe; it immediately brings to mind an exception to the rule. With these reservations, it is nevertheless possible to say that in Russia the dominant influence was still the literature of France of the seventeenth and eighteenth centuries.

French Classicism, which in the eighteenth century, had received a strong admixture of Sentimentalism, was actually approaching disintergration. By Pushkin's day the glories of tragedy and of the ode were bowing to a preference for comedy, comic epic, and the more trivial genres such as the epigram and the madrigal. The Roman and Greek heroes of Corneille and Racine had yielded place to nymphs, fauns, shepherds, and shepherdesses; forcefulness was less sought after than elegance; and passion had been supplanted by either a wistful melancholy or a cynical and hedonistic eroticism. That is one side of the picture, but there is another.

It must be recognized, for example, that even in its seventeenth-century heyday, Classicism had found place for comedy, for the trivial genres, for elegance, and for eroticism. It must be remembered, too, that such eighteenth-century epics—and surely there can be no more classical genre than the epic—as Voltaire's

Henriade and Kheraskov's *Rossiada* were written in response to a growing interest in the past culture and past history of individual nations or peoples—an interest which is legitimately regarded as an outgrowth or concomitant of Romanticism. In effect, the seeds of Romanticism can be seen in Voltaire. In speaking, therefore, of the dominance in Russia of French Classical literature, we must bear in mind the extreme complexity of the situation, of which the following dates will serve to remind us: Macpherson's first "Ossianic" poems were published in 1760; Rousseau, the great precursor of Romanticism, died in 1778; Herder published his *Volkslieder* in 1778–1779; Goethe's *Werther* came out in 1774; Chateaubriand's *Atala* was first published in 1801; and, while Pushkin wrote his first extant verses in 1813, Benjamin Constant's *Adolphe* had already been written four years earlier. There were, in fact, several tendencies simultaneously at work and the European literary situation was far from clear-cut.

For Pushkin, at any rate, it was the Classical and Sentimental traditions that provided the first formative influence: among French writers Voltaire especially, and also Parny; in Russian Derzhavin to some extent, Zhukovsky certainly, and, most compatible of all at this stage, Batyushkov's Epicureanism. Also of importance is the "hussar" poetry of Denis Davydov. Pushkin's early poems are mostly "occasional pieces." The themes are typical enough of his age and upbringing. The joys of love and drinking occupy a prominent place. Anacreon, Eros, and Bacchus are treated with sympathy, the glories of war are compared unfavorably to the delights of love, and the poet seeks to avoid the loud sounds of the world, the ambitious quest for glory. Solitude in nature, calm, idleness, contemplation, reading, friendship, and love are the things his heart craves, and he hastens to enjoy his epicurean delights, to gather his rosebuds, for old age and death lie ahead—a thought which scarcely afflicts young Pushkin very deeply, though he mentions it more than once.

A lighthearted voluptuousness makes itself felt in some of these early poems. In one dedicated to a snuff-addicted beauty, the poet wishes he were a piece of snuff—on the chance that he might get to roll down her bosom, under the dress; another, describing Zeus' seduction of Leda, concludes with the admonition: "Learn from this example, beautiful maidens; on summer evenings beware of the water in the deep grove."

The epigram was a literary weapon that Push used throughout his life. Here is an early sample (1814):

> Artist promised us a tragedy
> That would make everyone in the hall howl with pity
> And shed copious tears.
> We awaited this great play.
> And now we've seen it and there's no denying:
> It is impossible to describe its merits,
> Artist really did succeed in writing
> A thoroughly pitiful play.

Pushkin also tried his hand at the more "official" type of poem that stems from the tradition of the eighteenth-century panegyric ode. His "On the Return of the Emperor-Tsar from Paris in 1815" is a patriotic outburst, abundant in its praise of Alexander I in the struggle against Napoleon.

In a rather different vein are three imitations of Ossian. These include descriptions of Northern nature (caves, rocks, gloom, mists, and moonlight) not found in Pushkin's other poems written at the same time. They tell short stories, two of them with unhappy endings. The poems are somewhat stilted and do not evoke a very Celtic atmosphere. Their slight importance lies mainly in the fact that they indicate some interest on Pushkin's part in Ossianic themes, an interest transmitted from Parny.

An important genre for Pushkin was the friendly verse epistle, sometimes merry and humorous, sometimes more serious, even sad. The verse epistle could be written to some anonymous and fictitious addressee, but more often it was destined for a specific friend and provoked by a specific occasion. Pushkin wrote several for other inmates of the lycée. The fact that these epistles were in effect personal letters gave them a lack of pretentiousness and a stylistic simplicity which were not characteristic of some of the other genres in which Pushkin was undergoing his apprenticeship (e.g., his "On the Return of the Emperor-Tsar from Paris in 1815"). The fact that simplicity was to become one of Pushkin's cardinal virtues lends to these early epistles an added significance.

In 1816 a new note is sounded in Pushkin's writing— that of melancholy. Up to this year, though there had been, we have seen, references to death, such thoughts, one feels, went only

skir ʔp; they were literary rather than personal. In 1816 some-
thiʃseems to have occurred in the life of the adolescent poet
(hʃecᴣme seventeen that year). In this and the following year,
hʃ ꝼroⱱ a series of elegies in which the theme of unhappy love
constᴣⱡly recurs. Now, he tells us, the friendship of his com-
panioⱷ no longer brings comfort; his lyre lies idle, he sits in
silentʃsorrow at the feast; he is unable to forget; for him there
can Ꝿe no happiness. This repeated mention of lyres and feasts
maꝼ strike one as something of a poetic mannerism—and some
oꝼ the more melancholy pronouncements may to some people
sound exaggerated—but there is no doubt that in these 1816-17
poems Pushkin was expressing a genuine and deeply felt emotion and, as a poet, he was for the first time acquiring the language of passionate feeling. The following short poem, "Desire,"
is an example of this mood:

> Slowly my days drag by
> And each instant multiplies in my sad heart
> All the woes of unhappy love
> And stirs up dreams that are madness.
> But I am silent; unheard is my complaint;
> I shed tears; tears are a comfort;
> My soul, the prisoner of longing,
> Finds in them a bitter joy.
> O! life's hour run on, I've no regret,
> Disappear in darkness, empty specter;
> Dear to me is the torment of my love;
> No matter that I die, but let me then die loving.

Meanwhile, the over-all effect on Pushkin of the influence of
such writers as Voltaire, Parny, and Batyushkov was to encour-
age in the young poet tendencies which are really a part of his
own poetic nature: a lively wit; an eye for the *mot juste* and the
epigrammatic turn of phrase; the careful subordination of emotion to the restraints imposed by intellectual thought and high
technical standards; the demands of craftsmanship; harmony,
measure, and balance as opposed to exaggeration and one-sided-
ness; a strong feeling for reality; the noble virtue of poetic
common sense; brevity and concision; simplicity. These attributes of Pushkin's mature works can be seen developing in his
early writings.

It should be noted that Pushkin's first efforts as a poet coin-

cided with a period of lively debate in Russian literat
the first two decades of the nineteenth century there w
difference of opinion as to the correct path of develop
the literary language. The need for development was clea
been brought about by the impact of Western European
and by the advent of post-Classical literary trends. If Ru
literature were to hold its own on an equal footing with o
European literatures, then it would have to devise methods
expressing concepts and shades of thought and feeling it ha
never felt the need of expressing before. Furthermore, the
eighteenth-century Classical literary language of Lomonosov and
even Derzhavin must, in order to meet the demands of the early
nineteenth century, he brought closer to the norms of everyday
speech. How were these goals to be achieved? The alternative
solutions offered divided Russian intellectuals into two sharply
opposed camps.

There were those, the traditionalists, who insisted that inno-
vations should be made by coining new words from Old
Slavonic, the language of the church, which had already profoundly influenced the Russian language and which remains
even today a productive influence. On the other hand, there
were those, including the foremost writers of the time, who
maintained that the solution lay in borrowing lexically and syn-
tactically from abroad, in particular from French and German.
For the former, foreign borrowings constituted an erosion and
corruption of the purity of the language; for the latter, words
coined from Old Slavonic appeared clumsy, artificial, and far
removed from the norms of everyday speech.

From today's viewpoint, the whole issue is remarkably dead,
and it is with difficulty that one recognizes the intensity of emotion that it once generated. Both solutions—coining and borrowing—were in part adopted. But the traditionalists, though their
purist demands were probably beneficial for the development of
modern Russian, were on the whole fighting a losing battle. It
was the "Westerners" who, for the most part, carried the day.

The literary society which served as a focus for the "Westerners" was known as *Arzamas*. During his lycée days, Pushkin had
conceived the ambition of being elected a member. And indeed,
the ambition was fulfilled in the fall of 1817. But for various
reasons *Arzamas* went out of existence in 1818. Thus the poet's

actual rticipation in the society was not of great significance.
How the fact that for several years he had been at heart a
men f this society, his general alignment with the "Western"
grou nd the influence of Batyushkov and other "Westerners"
were 's already noted, of consequence for his literary develop-
men

stalled in Petersburg in September 1817, Pushkin continued
to write the same types of short poem that had exercised him during his lycée years. But in Petersburg a new influence was soon
reflected in his poetry—that of political liberalism or radicalism.
Pushkin's awareness of the intellectual and political ferment that
was agitating the young generation of the aristocracy actually
dates back to the end of his stay in the lycée. It was Chaadaev
at Tsarsgoe Selo who was, as it were, the original mentor of
Pushkin's intellectual awakening. But it was the brothers A. I.
Turgenev and N. I. Turgenev in Petersburg who were more than
anyone else responsible for the strongly liberal anti-authoritarian
streak that now developed in Pushkin's political attitude.

It should be borne in mind that, in the years following Napoleon's defeat, political discontent was rapidly taking on a definite
shape throughout much of Europe. In Russia the young people
were forming secret societies. Heavily involved in these societies
were members of the generation that had made the campaign
West to Paris, in particular junior army officers. Their ranks were
in the next few years augmented by contemporaries of Pushkin's,
and at least two of his classmates were to be found guilty for the
part they played in the abortive Decembrist Revolt of 1825. The
members of the secret societies varied among themselves in the
degree of their political radicalism. While the institution of serfdom came under criticism, the more generally felt opposition
was to the principle of unlimited autocratic rule. Some would
have been satisfied with a constitutional monarchy, while others
were belligerently anti-monarchical, in some cases to the point
of advocating regicide. Pushkin himself, though he wished to
become a member of the secret societies whose presence he was
perfectly well aware of, was never asked to join. This is sometimes attributed to a desire on the part of the members to avoid
involving a poet who was rapidly winning national acclaim. The
more substantial reasons, as given by I. I. Pushchin, Pushkin's
classmate and very close friend, later exiled to Siberia for his

part in the Decembrist plot, were, however, different: Pushkin's impulsive nature did not make him a good security risk, and in any case, Pushkin's Petersburg activities—in particular his willingness to court the favor of the conservative aristocracy—raised the question as to whether his liberalism was maintained consistently enough to make him totally reliable.

Reliable or not, Pushkin's emotions during these years in Petersburg (1817-20) were with the liberals. The verses he wrote to support the liberal cause were, since they could not be published, circulated in manuscript form from hand to hand till they were known to many by heart. It was these verses, combined with a certain ostentatious anti-authoritarianism in his behavior, that were in 1820 to bring him to the attention of the authorities and to cause disciplinary action to be taken against him.

Pushkin's most famous liberal poems of this period were three: his "Ode to Freedom," "Christmas Fairy Stories," and "The Countryside." The "Ode to Freedom" was written late in 1817. In form, it belongs to the tradition of the eighteenth-century ode. The ode was most often employed for panegyric purposes, to celebrate or commemorate military victories or such civic events as a monarch's arrival in Moscow or Petersburg; but it was also used didactically—to complain or warn against civic injustice. Derzhavin had written several odes inveighing against such abuses as tyranny and administrative corruption. Radischev, who had been exiled to Siberia by Catherine II, had written an ode with the same title as Pushkin's: "Freedom." Consequently, Pushkin was following a well-established literary genre which left no doubt as to his purpose. The poem is linked with the eighteenth-century tradition not only in form but in the political ideas it propounds. It is not rabidly anti-monarchical. It is directed, rather, against the tyrannical abuse of unbridled power: "Tremble you tyrants of the world!/And you degraded slaves, give ear,/Be strong, take courage and arise!" The poem is particularly severe on Napoleon, "horror of the world, nature's shame, a rebuke to God on earth," who was sent to scourge France for the lawless execution of Louis XVI. Louis XVI himself is seen as innocent. But his predecessors, for whose crimes Louis XVI was called to answer, abused their powers. And in Russia the tyranny of Paul I led to his assassination. The moral is that abuse of power by the monarch must lead to lawless

acts and crimes perpetrated by his subjects; the monarch has no
absolute God-given rights; he must himself answer to Law:

> Rulers! Crown and throne are given
> You not by Nature, but by Law;
> You stand above the people, but
> Above you is the eternal Law.

Only when the monarch makes himself subservient to the Law
will he be able to count on the support of his free people and
will there be peace and security. The poem concludes with the
warning:

> Learn, O tsars, today this lesson:
> Not punishments and not rewards,
> Nor prison roof nor holy altar
> Can save; trust not, O tsars, in these.
> Be you the first to bow your heads
> Beneath the sure shield of the Law;
> Then will the peoples' peace and freedom
> Forever stand and guard the throne.

"Christmas Fairy Stories" follows a French tradition of verses
written at the year's end to comment satirically on the political
events of the past year. It is a personal attack on Alexander I,
for whom Pushkin always felt a strong antipathy. Poland, which
was under Russian rule, had been granted a constitution, and in
his speech at the opening of the Polish Parliament in March
1818, Alexander had promised to extend the constitutional form
of government throughout the remainder of the Russian Empire.
Pushkin's short poem, written in December 1818, expresses the
skepticism widely felt at that time as to the good faith of the
Tsar's political promises. It also contains an unflattering reference to Alexander's participation in the reactionary Holy Alli-
ance with Prussia and Austria.

"The Countryside," written in 1819, is an attack on the institution of serfdom. It opens with an idyllic description of the
countryside. Here, far from the vulgar crowd and the aberrations
of the city, the poet happily seeks solitude, peace of mind, truth,
and inspiration. But no, it cannot be. For amid this beautiful
scenery he is horrified to observe scenes of violence and degra-
dation. Here he sees the peasant deprived by force of the fruits
of his labor; here gaunt Slavery, bent over the plow, lashed by

whips, drags itself to the grave along the furrows belonging to the pitiless owner; here no one dares to hope or wish; here young girls grow up beautiful only to satisfy the miscreant's whim; and here young boys are taken from their father's home to serve unhappily in the owner's household. The poet wishes ardently that his voice could move men's hearts. He wonders, in conclusion, whether he will ever see "the people unoppressed, and slavery banished at a wave of the Tsar's hand."

It will be seen that Pushkin's mood at this time was not consistently rebellious. Although "The Countryside" constitutes a strong and emotional attack on serfdom, it is to the Tsar that Pushkin looks for a solution. The story has it that Alexander I, on reading this poem, asked to have conveyed to Pushkin his thanks for "the noble sentiment that inspired his work." Again, the "Ode to Freedom" can legitimately be interpreted as an attack not on the monarchy as such but on the tyrannical abuse of monarchical power. But there was, on the other hand, the highly personal "Christmas Fairy Tales." There were, too, in circulation a number of politically loaded epigrams, some of which were certainly written by Pushkin, although others may have been wrongly attributed to him. There was the fact that Petersburg had gradually come to regard Pushkin as the voice of liberalism. And there was Pushkin himself who seemed at times to take delight in truculently and ostentatiously calling attention to his impatience with established authority. Finally, there was the increasingly suspicious and repressive attitude of the regime. These were the principal factors which led in 1820 to the official decision to curb Pushkin's activities.

For a time it seemed that Pushkin was in danger of being exiled to Siberia. But various people (among others, Karamzin; Zhukovsky; Pushkin's former lycée principal, V. V. Engelhardt; and even Count M. A. Miloradovich, Military Governor of Petersburg, whose official duty it had been to interrogate Pushkin concerning his subversive poetry) interceded on the poet's behalf with the Tsar, and a more moderate form of punishment was agreed upon. On leaving the lycée, Pushkin had, we recall, received an appointment with the Ministry of Foreign Affairs, and during his Petersburg years Pushkin had remained officially, although not, it seems, very actively, attached to the Ministry. The decision was now taken, rather than exiling Pushkin, to use

his official position with the Ministry of Foreign Affairs in order
to transfer him away from the capital. It will be remembered
that Russia had invested six years of free education in Pushkin
and looked for dividends from both him and his classmates. The
attitude officially adopted to Pushkin's liberal writing and rebellious conduct was thus one of chagrin and disappointment alle-
viated by the hope that the misguided youth would mend his
ways and employ his undoubted talents more appropriately.
This is precisely the tone taken in a letter from Pushkin's
superiors in Petersburg to his new superior in the south, General
I. N. Inzov:

This letter, General, is to place the young man under your command
and to solicit for him your benevolent protection. Permit me to give
you some of the facts about him. After an extremely unhappy childhood, young Pushkin left his paternal home without feeling any regrets. His heart, devoid of all filial affection, could feel only a passionate desire for independence. As a student, he quickly showed
signs of possessing an extraordinary genius. He made rapid progress
at the lycée, his intellect was admired, but his character seems to
have received little attention from his teachers. He entered the world
endowed with a fiery imagination but lacking completely those inner
feelings which serve as a substitute for principle until such time as
experience has completed our education. There are no excesses to
which this unfortunate young man has not given himself over, just
as there is no perfection he could not attain through the great excel-
lence of his talents. . . . Certain poems, especially an ode to freedom,
have brought Monsieur Pushkin to the attention of the government.
Beautiful in conception and style, this poem reveals dangerous principles stemming from the modern school of thought or, rather, from
that anarchical system which people deliberately misrepresent as the
system of the rights of man, liberty and the independence of peoples.
. . . Monsieur Pushkin seems to have mended his ways, at least if we
can believe his tears and promises. At least his protectors [Karamzin
and Zhukovsky] believe that his repentance is sincere and that by
sending him out of Petersburg for a while, giving him work and surrounding him with good examples, it will be possible to make of him
an excellent servant of the state or at least a first-class writer. . . .

The letter was approved by the Tsar. The decision to send
Pushkin away from the capital was not entirely unwelcome to
the poet. He was not well suited to dissipation, and the life

he had been leading was not calculated to satisfy his more
serious spiritual needs. As he himself confided in a letter of
March 1820 to his fellow poet and lifelong friend, P. A. Vyazemsky, "Petersburg is suffocating for a poet. I crave new horizons."
Pushkin had, in fact, more or less consciously courted official
displeasure, prompted either by some inner need to see himself
chastised or by the desire to provoke a mandatory removal.

Pushkin was given one thousand roubles for travel expenses.
He left Petersburg on May 6, 1820, and traveled south, joining
General Inzov in Ekaterinoslav (now renamed Dneprope-
trovsk). A little more than one month before he left Petersburg,
Pushkin completed his first major long poem, *Ruslan and
Lyudmila.*

II   Ruslan and Lyudmila

Ruslan and Lyudmila is a comic epic consisting of six cantos,
written in freely rhymed iambic tetrameters. The story, situated
in ancient Kievan times, tells of the ravishing of Ruslan's bride,
Lyudmila, by a magician; of Ruslan's adventurous quest for her;
and of his eventual success in recovering her. It was probably
started while Pushkin was still in the lycée, but the main work
was done during his Petersburg years (1817-20); the poem was
basically finished by the time the young poet was transferred
to the South.[1] An examination of the plot shows that the principal narrative ingredients were culled from two literary traditions: the Russian epic (*bylina*) and the fairy tale. But the whole
bent of the poem is neither heroic nor folkloristic. On the contrary, heroism and fairy tale magic are consistently ridiculed and
subjected to irony. *Ruslan and Lyudmila* harks back to the
tradition of Voltaire's *La Pucelle* and, beyond that, to the Italian
Renaissance poetry most eminently represented by Ariosto's
Orlando Furioso.[2]

Pushkin's decision to try his hand at comic epic was partly
a response to the pressures of the Russian literary scene at that
time. Everywhere in Europe, the advent of the Romantic movement coincided with a heightened national self-consciousness
and with an increased interest in the national past. Symptomatic
of this interest were the revival of the ballad and the newfound
enthusiasm for folklore. And no less important in this context

was bound to be the national epic. Among the *Arzamas* group, to which Pushkin even in his lycée days belonged in heart, there existed the consciously felt desire to produce a national epic.

But interest in the national epic did not make it any easier to write one. K. N. Batyushkov attempted to write a poem on Ryurik, the Scandinavian founder of the dynasty which ruled Kiev and, later, Muscovy. But Batyushkov's muse was not of epic caliber, and he conceded resignedly: "Clearly, when I die, I shall still be pregnant with my *Ryurik*."[3] Equally ill-suited to the epic task was Zhukovsky's introspective sentimentalism. His *The Twelve Sleeping Maidens* should, perhaps, be excluded from this discussion: in genre it comes closer to the ballad than the epic, and for another thing, its origin is German rather than Russian. But his plan for *Vladimir*, taking its title from one of the first great rulers of Kiev, a truly national theme, remained no more than a plan.[4] Thus the problem remained unsolved. Pushkin chose not to rise to the challenge. His response, dictated by the strong influence on him of Voltaire's skepticism and wit, was to write a non-epic, a comic epic, which was in effect a mockery of nationalistic epic aspirations and of the otherworldly, mystically inclined Romanticism of Zhukovsky. *Ruslan and Lyudmila* is in fact, partly, a friendly polemic aimed at Zhukovsky. Several incidents and characters are taken from Zhukovsky's projected *Vladimir*, and in his fourth canto Pushkin recapitulates ironically the plot of *The Twelve Sleeping Maidens*, casting vague doubts on the latters' chastity and introducing in his own poem, by way of contrast, twelve maidens who were the reverse of chaste.

But the significance of *Ruslan and Lyudmila* is certainly not limited to the negative achievement of making it virtually impossible for anyone else to dare write a serious epic. On the contrary, *Ruslan and Lyudmila* is a brilliant masterpiece in a vein and genre in which Pushkin was at his best. And Zhukovsky was wise and kind enough to recognize this by giving to his young rival a portrait of himself with the inscription: "To the victorious pupil from the vanquished master on that most important day on which he completed *Ruslan and Lyudmila*. Good Friday, March 26, 1820."

Unfortunately, *Ruslan and Lyudmila* is sometimes treated by Russian critics as Pushkin's first step toward a poetic rapproche-

ment with the people, the *Volk* (*narodnost'*), "the young
poet's first attempt to create a national poem (*poema*)."[5] This is
completely false. Certainly, it is not difficult, as already indicated, to point to various component parts of Pushkin's narrative as deriving from the Russian epic or fairy tale traditions. To
maintain, however, that these components lend to the poem
a national or folkloristic character is to fail completely to understand the poetic use to which they are put. Clearly, a given
incident can in one context be regarded as "popular," while in
another context the same incident may have quite a different
impact. The epic and the fairy tale normally presuppose a certain ingenuousness, a degree of naïveté—real or assumed—
whereas the comic epic, which takes lightly what the epic and
fairy tale take seriously, normally presupposes a degree of sophis-
tication. The use to which Pushkin puts his epic and fairy tale
elements is precisely the highly sophisticated use to which they
were put in the comic epic of Voltaire. By the same token, the
epic and the fairy tale tend to be oriented somehow toward the
outdoors. The epic hero of chivalry may feast beneath a roof
and sleep, sometimes, in bed; but his main activity, apart from
single combat and ordinary battlefield duty, seems to consist in
pricking endlessly over plains and through forests. The fairy
tale, though it may be situated in the hearth and home, is insis-
tently aware of the surrounding woods from which sprites and
spirits are wont to intrude on human habitations.

In *Ruslan and Lyudmila* the knights do indeed dutifully prick
over the plains; but the whole poem is oriented toward the
indoors, toward the drawing rooms of Petersburg, toward the
young girls of Petersburg society, and toward Pushkin's male
friends in the sense that he shares with them his pleasure in the
poem's erotic passages and in the effect that these passages are
allegedly calculated to have on the young female hearts of
Russian society. Just as *Orlando Furioso* acquires its tone from
the sophisticated men and women of the court at Ferrara to
whom it is addressed, so the entire orientation of Pushkin's
poem is determined by his audience. His dedication runs as
follows:

> For you, the rulers of my heart,
> For you, you beauties, you alone,
> I have in hours of golden leisure

> Recorded with a truthful hand
> The fantasies of times gone by;
> Accept, I beg, this flippant work!
> While I, demanding praise of none,
> Am gladdened by the hope, sweet hope
> That, fluttering with love, some maid
> May perhaps take a stealthy look
> At these my sinful tales in rhyme.

The dedication goes a long way toward defining the tone of the work.

One important feature of *Ruslan and Lyudmila* is the author's tendency to break off the narrative and digress. This feature he shares with such predecessors as Voltaire and Ariosto. In its simplest form the author's digression may be merely a mechanical device enabling the author to temporarily abandon his narrative at a point of high suspense and switch to another episode: "But now, my friends, what of our maid?/Let's leave these heroes for a while;/I will return to them quite soon. . . ." But clearly the author's digression has a very wide range of possibilities. It can involve the author's relationship with the reader, the author's attitude to his characters, his attitude to life, and his personal experiences. Through the digression, the author can in fact create a whole new focus for the events he describes and impose on his work the imprint of his own subjective poetic personality. Pushkin was later (in *Evgeny Onegin*) to learn to exploit more fully the possibilities of the digression. Meanwhile, his mastery of the technique is in evidence as early as *Ruslan and Lyudmila*. The dedication (quoted above) conveys something of the flavor of these digressions. Here is one more example:

> Ah me, how sweet my princess is!
> Her character has great appeal:
> She has feeling, she is modest,
> And faithful to her wifely love,
> And slightly flighty . . . What of that?
> That makes her all the more delightful.
> New charms she constantly reveals
> Which captivate our willing heart;
> Say: can Lyudmila be compared
> To stern, severe, austere Delphira?
> The one was given by fate the grace

> To charm our hearts and hold our gaze;
> Her smiles and the sweet things she says
> Kindle in me the flame of love.
> The other's skirts belie the truth:
> More apt would be mustache and spurs!
> Blessed the man for whom at eve
> In some deserted trysting place
> Lyudmila mine all eager waits,
> Prepared to tell him of her love.
> But blessed too, believe me, he
> Who from Delphira runs away
> Or, even better, never knew her.

One function of this type of digression is clearly to give a contemporary dimension to events which purportedly lie in the legendary past.[6]

Ruslan and Lyudmila opens in one of the conventional settings of Russian epic. Vladimir, Prince of Kiev, is presiding at a feast. The feast is to celebrate the wedding of his daughter, Lyudmila, to Ruslan. The feast is gay, but not so the erotically minded Ruslan, who "Impatient tugs at his moustache,/While every second seems an hour." Equally unhappy are Ruslan's three unsuccessful rivals: Rogday, a bold warrior; Farlaf, a loud-talking, boastful coward; and the extremely passionate Ratmir. At last the feast is over and the bride is led to her bridal chamber. Ruslan's long-awaited moment is at hand: "Love's gifts are readied, and the clothes/That jealous shield Lyudmila's charms/Fall to the lush carpet-strewn floor. . . ." But at this point there is a flash and a crash and, lo, Lyudmila is gone, snatched away by some mysterious, magic hand. The angry father, Prince Vladimir, summons his court and promises Lyudmila and half his kingdom to the man who rescues her. Ruslan and his three rivals ride out together and then split up and begin their search. Various adventures befall them. One of the more amusing of these concerns the passionate Ratmir, who arrives toward dusk at a castle inhabited by twelve beautiful maidens. He is made welcome, disrobes and receives a fragrant Russian bath at the hands of the semi-nude maidens, in the course of which his desires are so stimulated that he forgets Lyudmila. In a voluptuously described scene, reminiscent of Ariosto, Ratmir is visited that night by one of the maidens. He remains for a while in the castle living carnally with his delightful temptresses, but eventually he is rescued from these seductions by his love for a pure shepherdess. He becomes a fisherman and, full of contentment, settles down to a simple pastoral life with his one true love.

Lyudmila's ravisher is the evil magician, Chernomor. He carries her through the air to his enchanted castle. But his advanced age renders him incapable of working his vile will—which does not prevent the author from giving an amusing and fairly intimate description of Chernomor's lascivious but unavailing attempts.[7]

Meanwhile, guided by a benevolent old magician, Finn, Ruslan is pursuing his adventuresome way toward his imprisoned Lyudmila. Finn's life story, which he relates to Ruslan, is one of the more entertaining episodes. As a shy youngster herding sheep in his Finnish Northlands, Finn falls in love with the beautiful Naina. Eventually he brings himself to declare his love. But Naina replies with indifference. "Shepherd, I don't love you!" Driven by his grief, Finn now becomes a Viking marauder; for ten years he and his bold seafaring companions fight, kill, and loot. He returns home full of passion, pride, and plunder. But Naina tells him with indifference: "Hero, I don't love you!" For Finn there is one last resort—to live in the depths of the forest and to master the arts of magic in order to obtain power over Naina. For many lonely years he pursues his studies. At last he is ready. He pronounces the incantation and invokes the spirits.

> And in the forest dark
> A thunderbolt crashed down to earth,
> A magic whirlwind shrieked and wailed,
> The ground shook, quaked beneath my feet—
> And lo, before my eyes appeared
> Gray-haired, decrepit, an old hag,
> With wildly gleaming sunken eyes
> Hunchbacked, her senile head awag. . . .

Finn's single error has been his failure to take into account the effect on Naina's charms of the long years—forty—during which he has been completing his apprenticeship in magic. For, indeed, the old hag is none other than Naina and, alas, Finn's magic arts have prevailed—only too well. Naina is aflame with passion. Finn relates:

> A ghastly grin contorts her mouth,
> While in sepulchral, croaking tones
> The ugly crone declares her love.
> How much I suffered you can guess!
> Shaking I stood, with downcast eyes;
> Coughing and wheezing on she went
> Mouthing her noisome passions's plea:
> "Yes, now, I've learned to know my heart;
> I understand, true friend, that it
> For passion's tender joys was born;
> My senses now awake, I burn,
> I am consumed with love's desires . . .
> Come let us clasp each other close . . .
> Oh, darling, I grow faint with love . . ."

Finn escapes Naina's clutches and flees, pursued by accusations and threats.[8]

Aided by Finn, Ruslan eventually overcomes Chernomor and regains Lyudmila. He survives a treacherous attack from Farlaf who is acting under Naina's directions—for she too has learned the arts of magic. He saves Kiev from its besiegers and lives happily with his bride.

Looking back on *Ruslan and Lyudmila* in 1830, and recalling its generally favorable reception, Pushkin remarked: "No one even noticed that it is cold."[9] If by "cold" Pushkin meant that his poem calls into play a relatively narrow range of emotions—not including those which tug deep at our heartstrings—then he was right. But therein lies the particular charm of *Ruslan and Lyudmila*. Pushkin carries us with him into an unreal and delightful poetic world of cheerful unconcern. He employs the techniques normally associated with this particular genre: wit, irony, bathos, occasional buffoonery, and eroticism. And, in keeping with the tradition and its essentially realistic vein, he subjects to gentle ridicule such basically "serious" matters as chivalry, hand-to-hand combat, sorcery, abduction, passion, and love. But the reader's delight derives only in part from seeing these things exposed to the shafts of Pushkin's wit; it derives more from the fact that these normally serious things are unsubstantial and, as it were, without gravity in the make-believe world of fantasy that Pushkin has created.[10]

Ruslan and Lyudmila is a poem of lightness and fun, an escape from reality, rendered beautiful by the perfection of its poetry. In a sense it is "cold," limited in emotional range, and less ambitious in terms of its appeal to the human spirit than many of Pushkin's subsequent works, but it does succeed fully in what it sets out to do, and in its own modest way it is as fine as anything he ever wrote.

CHAPTER 2

Southern Exile:
The "Southern Poems" and Gavriiliada

WHEN Pushkin arrived in Ekaterinoslav, he appeared to be sick. General Inzov, who was throughout his relationship with Pushkin to prove himself an understanding, tolerant, indulgent and almost paternal superior, lost no time in showing his kindheartedness. One of his first acts was to allow Pushkin leave. It so happened that at the time of Pushkin's sickness, a certain General N. N. Raevsky, a hero of the 1812 war, and his family passed through Ekaterinoslav on their way to the Caucasus and the Crimea. Since the Raevskys were accompanied by a doctor, Pushkin was entrusted to their care. Thanks to Inzov's generosity, Pushkin was able to experience three of the most memorable and significant months of his life. From the end of May into September he traveled and lived as a member of the Raevsky family. The superb scenery of the Caucasus made a deep impression on him and was reflected in his poetry. At the same time, under the guidance of members of the Raevsky family Pushkin became acquainted with the work of Byron, who was immediately to exert an important influence on the Russian poet.

Reluctantly leaving the shores of the Black Sea, Pushkin returned to place himself once more under the supervision of Inzov, who had in Pushkin's absence been transferred to Kishinev (near what is now the Rumanian border). For the next three years, Kishinev was Pushkin's home, and though the city was in many ways unappealing to him, he had every reason to be grateful for the patient and kindly good will of his superior. This became doubly clear to him when in July 1823, he was transferred to the more entertaining city of Odessa only to find that it was quite impossible to get along with his new superior, the Governor-General of Novorossiya, Count M. S. Vorontsov. Their mutual antipathy was instinctive, wholehearted and, for a variety of reasons, inevitable; but, undoubtedly, it was aggravated by the attentions Pushkin lavished on Vorontsov's wife. It was, indeed, probably more than anything else, Pushkin's persistent and indiscreet courtship that led Vorontsov to decide to get rid of him. For an adroit bureaucrat it was not particularly difficult to find a pretext, and the Governor-General was in fact able not only to have Pushkin removed from Odessa but to engineer his dismissal from the Ministry of Foreign Affairs. On July 30, 1824, now officially an exile, Pushkin set out on a specifically prescribed route for his mother's estate in the Pskov area. He was to live under the direct supervision of his father. The four years since leaving Petersburg, the years of his so-called Southern exile, had been productive. They had seen him well launched into what was to become his best-known poem, *Evgeny Onegin* (discussed in Chapter 5). During this same period he had surreptitiously written his brilliantly blasphemous *Gavriiliada;* he had written a number of excellent shorter, lyric poems (discussed along with his other lyrics in a later chapter); and—what most sets the tone for the period—he had nearly completed his three "Byronic" or "Southern" poems: *The Prisoner of the Caucasus, The Fountain of Bakhchisaray,* and *The Gypsies.*

I Byronism and the "Southern" Poems

The dominant influence in European letters around 1820 was probably that of Byron. To the modern-day reader this still comes as something of a surprise. We are apt to forget that no less a writer than Goethe once held him in high esteem. We are apt to feel the subsequent decline in his reputation was deserved. And though in the last two decades Byron's star has once again risen, it is mainly his later works, *Beppo* and above all *Don Juan,* that arouse the admiration of today's reader. Yet it was, on the contrary, his earlier poems, *Childe Harold* and the "Eastern tales," that first brought him fame and fixed his image in the eyes of Europe. The reasons for this have little to do with literary merit. They lie, rather, in the fact that Byron exploited two strong cultural preoccupations of his contemporaries: their interest in a certain type of personality, and their eagerness for the exotic and the primitive. Just as Goethe's *Werther* had once shaken Europe and produced a rash of suicides precisely because it was so perfectly in tune with the mood of the times, so

Byron's early work gained its tremendous success precisely because it touched exactly the right chord for Byron's day and age. In this sense, Byronism was more than the mere total of Byron's early writings; it summed up an entire attitude, an outlook on life.

Byronism was not, of course, new with Byron. It embodied the profound disquiet, the melancholy, the Weltschmerz of the Romantic age. It spoke with the voice of liberal protest against tyranny. It questioned the accepted values of a hypocritical and corrupt society. And to an age mesmerized by the figure of Napoleon, it offered, in place of mediocrity and conformism, the appealing and exciting spectacle of the Byronic hero. Byronism thus constituted a sort of focus for a number of widespread dissatisfactions and aspirations. And the Weltanschauung it represented became closely associated with the name of the British poet because it was so clearly expressed in some of his writings and because it appeared to many of his contemporaries to be personified in his life and character.

To attempt a brief description of the Byronic literary hero is to court the dangers of oversimplification and caricature. Nevertheless, this hero, as he appears in the appropriate works of Byron, may be said to have the following principal characteristics: he is proud, aristocratic, highly individualistic, romantic; he is profoundly disillusioned by life; he feels in conflict with society; he feels superior to society; although his conduct may be antisocial and he inspires awe and fear in others, he possesses a basic underlying nobility of character; he seems to be marked down by Fate and has suffered some irreparable misfortune at some time in the past (an unhappy love affair or some unspecified injustice perpetrated against him); as a result of this misfortune his view of life has become warped, his emotions atrophied; he brings tragedy to the woman who loves him; and he is portrayed against some primitive, exotic background.

Two examples, both relevant to this study of Pushkin, must suffice. In *The Giaour,* the first of Byron's "Eastern tales," the hero had at sometime in the past fallen irrevocably in love with the beautiful Leila. Leila had been a member of Hassan's harem. But this could not deter the hero, and when Leila had responded to his love, she had been duly killed by Hassan. The hero had then killed Hassan. At the poem's end he is living in a monastery, wearing monk's clothing, but apparently an unbeliever. For the monks he is an object of awe and fear:

> Dark and unearthly is the scowl
> That glares beneath his dusky cowl:
> The flash of that dilating eye
> Reveals too much of times gone by. . . .
> But sadder still it were to trace
> What once were feelings in that face. . . .
> The close observer can espy
> A noble soul, and lineage high. . . .

In *The Corsair* the hero, Conrad, is leader of a pirate band:

> That man of loneliness and mystery,
> Scarce seen to smile, and seldom heard to sigh;
> Whose name appalls the fiercest of his crew. . . .
> He cared not what he softened, but subdued;
> The evil passions of his youth had made
> Him value less who loved—than what obeyed.

He has been the victim of man's duplicity: "His heart was formed for softness—warped to wrong,/Betrayed too early, and beguiled too long. . . ." His one redeeming feature, his last hold on human feelings, is his love for Medora. But now he must leave Medora behind on the pirate island. An attack is expected by Seyd and, to anticipate this, Conrad and his men attack and set fire to Seyd's palace, gallantly saving the lives of the harem inmates. Seyd counterattacks. Conrad and his men are overwhelmed by superior numbers, and Conrad is made prisoner. One of the harem women, Gulnare, who is "Extreme in love or hate, in good or ill . . ." falls in love with him, kills Seyd, and escapes with him, though she knows he cannot love her, for he loves Medora. Conrad is appalled by her crime. He returns to the island to find that Medora is dead! He disappears.

So much for this brief glimpse into two of the "Eastern tales." This talk of pirates and harems, the melodramatic language and the exaggerated character traits of the heroes: all this is more likely to amuse than engross the modern reader. Byron himself did not take it seriously. But for Pushkin, this was in 1820 heady stuff, and the appeal of the Byronic hero was strong.

In some respects Pushkin came to Byron prepared. Byronism was not altogether a new graft, rather it was an organic development. Something of the Byronic mood can be discerned in the melancholy outpourings of Pushkin's 1816-17 elegies.[1] And in 1820 the events of his personal life made him particularly receptive to the appeal of Byronism. The dissatisfactions of Petersburg life—including, it is often thought, an unhappy love affair—had induced in Pushkin that pessimistic frame of mind which is an essential part of the Byronic outlook. The Russian poet's liberalism made it natural for him to look on Byron with sympathy. His exile—Byron too was in a way an exile—had caused him suffering, given him a sense of injustice, and created the feeling of a rift between himself and society. He was visting the Caucasus and the Crimea which rivaled in their exoticism Byron's Eastern Mediterranean. He was confronted with the living example of one of the Raevsky sons, Alexander, who had cast on himself the Byronic mantle and did everything to ape Byron's manners and personality. And he was encouraged by the Byronic enthusiasms of various members of the Raevsky family, and helped by their knowledge of the English language. Everything, in fact, conspired to create an identity of mood with Byron. There was, finally, one further factor which should not be overlooked: for Pushkin, who was always a craftsman and always interested in trying his hand at new genres, Byron's themes and techniques opened up entirely new poetic horizons, and the Russian poet embraced eagerly the chance of exploiting the newfound potential.

The Prisoner of the Caucasus, the first of the "Southern" poems, was written during the latter half of 1820 and the first months of 1821. Written mainly, like *Ruslan and Lyudmila,* in free-rhyming iambic tetrameters, it consists of a dedication, two "parts," and an epilogue (777 lines altogether). The mood of the author is made clear from the start—in the dedication to N. N. Raevsky, one of General Raevsky's sons and a good friend to Pushkin from the Petersburg days. Pushkin here speaks of his "exiled lyre," of "love's painful dream," and of the "sad days of separation." He sees himself as "innocent," the "victim of calumny" (calumny is twice mentioned), and he talks of "betrayal." His gloom, sense of persecution and feeling of self-pity predominate: "Early I knew sorrow, persecution suffered early." In fact, the author identifies very closely, as we shall see, with his melancholic hero.

The story is simple. At the outset the wild Circassian hillsman of the Caucasus are sitting around in their village talking. Their talk, which is, inevitably, of war, horses, and women, is interrupted by the return of a Circassian bringing in an unconscious Russian prisoner. The Russian revives and remains in the village, in chains. He awakens the love of a Circassian maid and for a time appears to respond to her untutored, passionate advances. But no. The past is too strong for him. Haunted by a previous unhappy love, he has lost his emotional spontaneity, his ability to feel, and he cannot return the love of this child of nature. She understands his predicament (the initial language barrier between them appears to break down as the poem proceeds and, presumably, as the Russian extends his stay in the Circassian village). For a while the hero is left to his solitude. Then, one night, the maid comes to him, saws through his chains, and bids him flee. Greatly moved, the Russian begs her to flee with him. But:

> No, Russian, no!
> Bitter for me what once was sweet;
> Life I have known, have felt its joys.
> And all has vanished, without trace.
> Can it be so? You loved another!
> That one go seek, and find, and love....
> Farewell! Forget my pain and grief,
> Give me your hand—for the last time.

A last embrace, and the hero swims the river to freedom. As he climbs the far bank, he hears a splash in the water and a groan. True to her passionate, violent nature, and to the Romantic tradition, the Circassian maid has drowned herself.

The Prisoner of the Caucasus contains some excellent descriptions of nature and of the Circassian way of life. These passages exemplify the anti-urbanism, the delight in nature's more exotic aspects and wilder manifestations, and the tendency to glorify human primitivism, which are so typical of the Romantic outlook. The Circassians are depicted as more generous, more cruel, more passionate than their more civilized, decadent, and corrupt counterparts; whatever the vices and virtues of these primitive hillsmen, their emotions are uninhibited, wholehearted, and in-

stinctive. This picture stands in direct contrast with the character of the civilized hero, on whom the poem focuses.

The Fountain of Bakhchisaray, the second "Southern" poem,
was begun in the spring of 1821, the main work was done in
1822, and the final revision took place in the fall of 1823. The
poem, consisting of 578 lines, is, once again, written in freely
rhymed iambic tetrameters. In this work also the background is
exotic, and the hero finishes in a state of apathy induced by his
ill-starred love. The main differences in plot, compared with
The Prisoner of the Caucasus, are that the women (here there
are two of them) play a larger role and that the traits of the
Byronic hero have here been attached not to a "civilized" European, but to a Tatar Khan—to someone, therefore, who is himself
part of the exotic background.

The poem opens with Girey, the Tatar Khan, brooding in
menacing and sorrowful silence in the midst of his servile court.
He has fallen in love with Maria, a Polish girl, recently captured
by the Tatars, and Maria, sorrowing in captivity, knows nothing
of love or passion, and has no feeling for Girey. Awed by his
love, the fearsome Khan will not force his attentions on Maria;
he even permits her to sleep apart from the other women and
the vigilant eunuch is not allowed to enter her room. Meanwhile, Zarema, the passionate Georgian girl, who had, until
Maria's arrival, been Girey's favorite, is neglected, unhappy,
jealous, and bitter. It is night. Zarema steals past the sleeping
eunuch, enters Maria's room, wakes her, and pleads with Maria
to restore to her Girey's love. After telling Maria of her former
happiness, Zarema goes on:

> And then, Maria, you appeared,
> Since then, alas, his soul's obsessed;
> Only one vile desire is his. . . .
> I know that you are not to blame.
> Then listen: I have beauty too;
> In the whole harem you alone
> Can bring misfortune on my bliss;
> But I for passion's joys was born,
> You cannot love as I can love;
> Why then should beauty cold as yours
> Mislead his weak and errant heart?
> Give me Girey, for he is mine. . . .

> By scorn, entreaties, sorrow, tears—
> I care not how—dismiss Girey. . . .
> But listen and beware: if I
> Must use my dagger, then beware!
> The Caucasus was once my home!

Some time has elapsed. Maria is dead. We are not told exactly how she met her end. But it was undoubtedly at Zarema's hand. For Zarema was drowned by the guards on the same night that Maria died. Girey, neglecting his harem (as did Hassan in *The Giaour*), once again departs to fight wars; but his heart is broken. Returning home, he erects a fountain in Maria's honor. The narrator concludes by relating that he has himself visited Bakhchisaray. It made him think of the khans, their warlike exploits, their feasts, their voluptuous pleasures, their harems. It seemed to him that the shadow of a maid flitted through the palace. Was it Maria? or Zarema?

> Another's charms, as great as theirs,
> Still grace this Earth; her I recall,
> And toward her my heart takes flight,
> I grieve in exile, long for her. . . .

The Gypsies was begun in January 1824, in Odessa, and completed (apart from one passage) in Mikhaylovskoe in October 1824. Thus, strictly speaking, it straddles the two periods, Pushkin's "Southern" exile and his "Northern" exile. However, it was conceived in the South, the bulk of the work was done in the South, and in genre it clearly belongs with *The Prisoner of the Caucasus* and *The Fountain of Bakhchisaray*. Like its predecessors, it is written mainly in freely rhymed iambic tetrameters. It consists of a number of paragraphs or sections and an epilogue (569 lines in all). It can at once be seen to differ from its predecessors in one important respect. While *The Prisoner of the Caucasus* and *The Fountain of Bakhchisaray* contained a certain amount of dialogue inserted in the narrative, in *The Gypsies* the proportions are reversed: there is, rather, a certain amount of narrative inserted in the dialogues. The paragraphs or sections referred to above can in many cases be likened to short dramatic scenes; in *The Gypsies* Pushkin can, in fact, be seen feeling his way toward the dramatic genre, in which he was shortly to try his hand full-scale.

As may be inferred from the title, the exotic background is here provided by gypsies—specifically, a band of gypsies roaming the plains of Bessarabia. Zemfira, a young gypsy girl who lives with her elderly father, brings home a Russian, Aleko, who wishes to join the gypsy band. He is, it seems, wanted by the law, and he suffers the spiritual torments associated with the Byronic hero. He nevertheless settles down fairly well among the wandering gypsies, forgetting the past. His task is to lead a bear on a chain and sing, while Zemfira collects money from the audience. He loves Zemfira, and lives with her and her father. Here is part of a dialogue revealing Aleko's negative attitude to civilization:

> *Zemfira.* Tell me, my friend: don't you regret
> All you have left behind for good?
> *Aleko.* What did I leave hehind?
> *Zemfira.*   You know:
> Your country's people, city life.
> *Aleko.* I've no regrets. Could you but know,
> Could you but feel how city life
> Imprisons, stifles, warps the soul! . . .
> What did I leave behind? Deceit,
> Bertrayal, prejudice's voice,
> The persecution of the mob—
> Or glory, triumph, crowned with shame.
> *Zemfira.* But there are mighty mansions there,
> And many-colored carpets too.
> And games and merriments and feasts,
> And maidens clad in rich attire.
> *Aleko.* Such noisy pleasures have no worth,
> Empty is pleasure without love.
> You are far better than those maids
> Without their costly rich attire. . . .

This harmonious life lasts about two years, after which Zemfira grows tired of Aleko and finds a lover. Aleko, aware of Zemfira's growing indifference, turns moody and morose. The following exchange between Aleko and Zemfira's father reveals the total difference between the gypsy approach and "civilized" man's approach to the problems of love and infidelity:

> *Old Man.* Tell me, crazed youth, why all the time
> You sigh and sorrow as you do.
> Free are our people, clear the sky,
> Our women's beauty is well known.
> Weep not: such grief will bring your ruin.
>   *Aleko.* Father, Zemfira loves me not.
>   *Old Man.* Take courage, friend: she is a child.
> 'Tis foolish thus to rend your heart:
> Your love is heavy with your grief,
> But women's love is mirth and play. . . .

And the old man goes on to tell Aleko how years before he had been left by Zemfira's mother who had gone off with a gypsy from another band:

>   *Aleko.* Why did you not pursue in haste
> The cunning and ungrateful wench?
> And thrust a dagger in her heart?
> Bring death to those who helped her flee?

And this is in effect what happens. Aleko surprises Zemfira and her lover in the night and stabs them to death. Dawn finds him still sitting, dagger in hand, at the scene. The old man banishes him from the gypsy band with the following words:

> Leave us, proud man. Away, be gone.
> We are wild people without laws.
> We punish not with pain or death.
> Your blood, your groans we do not need;
> But we can't brook a killer here . . .
> You were not born for freedom's ways. . . .
> Begone, and peace be with your soul.

And the gypsy band moves out over the steppe, leaving Aleko behind.

It is not difficult to point out the marks of Byron's influence in the "Southern" poems. Pushkin is clearly indebted for certain features of situation and plot. The characters of Pushkin's and Byron's heroes also have much in common: a certain emotional impotence: disillusionment caused by some past mishap; the feeling of having been betrayed; and the feeling of estrangement from society. The violent, passionate natures of the Circassian maid and of Zarema also owe something to Gulnare. Finally, in narrative technique the two poets reveal definite similarities: notably, a tendency to break off the narrative abruptly and without explanation (more in evidence in Byron), and the tendency to concentrate on the highlights of the story which are given in the form of dramatic scenes or confrontations between characters.

There are, at the same time, some clearly marked differences between the two writers. Pushkin's heroes, notwithstanding the traits they share with Byron's, lean more toward apathy and passivity, while Byron's appear to have to a greater extent translated their disillusionment into energetic and destructive action. It is true that Aleko consummates a double killing and that his delight in the thought of revenge is reminiscent of the Giaour; nevertheless, throughout most of the poem, it is his passivity which is emphasized, and leading a bear on a chain is not really a fitting occupation for one of Byron's heroes. In their general lack of dynamism Pushkin's heroes come closer to the nebulous and passive figure of Childe Harold than to either the Giaour or Conrad. This difference in character is reinforced by a difference in descriptive techniques. While Pushkin gives almost no physical descriptions of his heroes, Byron does, and he frequently portrays them in action.

Another vital distinction between Pushkin and Byron concerns the important "technical" matter of writing good poetry. Byron was notoriously slipshod as a craftsman; Pushkin was the reverse. His Byronism did not cause him to unlearn the lessons in lucidity, concision, and restraint which came to him from the French Classical tradition and which were also an essential part of his poetic nature. A comparison between poets writing in different languages is inevitably hard to substantiate. Nevertheless, to anyone reading the "Eastern" tales and the "Southern" poems in the original, it must be clear that the latter are on the whole greatly superior as verse.[2]

Pushkin's attitude to Byronism and the Byronic hero did not remain constant during his Southern period. His initial infatuation is reflected in the subjectivity of *The Prisoner of the Caucasus.* By the time he came to write *The Gypsies,* Pushkin had learned to stand back and view the Byronic hero with objectivity. The view has frequently been put forward that in *The Gypsies* Pushkin "dethroned the Byronic hero" and "overcame Byronism."[3]

The passage normally cited in support of this view is the speech in which the old man condemns Aleko and banishes him from the gypsy band. But this is to interpret Pushkin's poem too narrowly. *The Gypsies* is, it is true, a poem of ideas. It is a demonstration (which Chateaubriand had already offered in his *René*) of "civilized" man's inability to return to some primitive golden-age society. But it is also more than that. There is in *The Gypsies* the feeling—which was to become very much a part of Pushkin's mature outlook—of man's inability to escape his fate, of a certain tragic inevitability in man's destiny. Pushkin exposes, if you will, Aleko's egotism and violence. But is he then applauding Zemfira's promiscuity? And was her father, simply because he was a primitive gypsy, any the happier when he was betrayed by Zemfira's mother? On the contrary. *The Gypsies* is *not* a demonstration of the superiority of the primitive to the "civilized." It is, rather, the reflection of Pushkin's awareness of the fragility of human happiness and destiny—an awareness which he expressed in the epilogue:

> But even you, nature's poor sons,
> Cannot lay claim to happiness!
> And in your tattered tents you dream,
> Like other men, tormented dreams.
> Wandering through the steppes, you feel,
> Like other men, misfortune's blows.
> Everywhere passions wreak their ills,
> And against Fate there's no defense.

In *The Gypsies* Pushkin did not "overcome" Byronism; he broadened its theme by giving to the rather narrow and specific problem of the Byronic hero a wider application, a more universal dimension.

One further widely held misconception arising from the change between 1820 and 1824 in Pushkin's attitude to Byronism is deserving of comment. To talk of "overcoming" Byronism is by implication to assume that Pushkin was in 1820 completely overwhelmed by the philosophy of Byronism from which he gradually succeeded in emancipating himself. But this would be at best no more than a partial truth, and a misleading truth. Pushkin was affected by Byronism, not engulfed by it. It represented only one side of his outlook on life. And the Byronic poem was never a full and complete reflection of his poetic personality—any more than it was of Byron's poetic personality. The Byronic poem was for Pushkin a new genre, and like other genres it imposed a number of conventions and restrictions. One of these, for example, was the deliberate elimination of humor, which is completely absent from the "Southern" poems. Yet it is clear from other works written by Pushkin during the same period that his sense of humor had not abandoned him: *Gavriiliada* was written in 1821, the same year in which *The Prisoner of the Caucasus* was completed; and *Evgeny Onegin,* influenced by Byron's very different later works, *Beppo* and *Don Juan,* was started in 1823 while Pushkin was still working on *The Fountain of Bakhchisaray.*

Notwithstanding the breakdown of the rigid Classical distinctions between genres, Pushkin remained all his life aware of the concept of genre, that is, of what facets of his poetic personality could appropriately be exposed in a given type of writing. Consequently, the reader should be wary of any attempt to equate too closely the poet's outlook with his individual works. The undoubted superiority of *The Gypsies* to *The Prisoner of the Caucasus* and *The Fountain of Bakhchisaray* is to be ascribed not so much to any decisive change in the author's philosophy, though his more objective view of Byronism may justifiably be held to have made possible the broadening of the Byronic theme noted above. The superiority of *The Gypsies* is to be ascribed, first and foremost, to the simple fact that it is a better structured and better written work than its predecessors in the Byronic genre.

It is not easy for today's critic to assess the merits of the "Southern" poems. We live in an anti-Romantic age which is nevertheless in many ways indebted to Romanticism, and we tend to resent any suspicion that we may still be enmeshed in Romanticism's toils. Certainly, the somewhat naïve exhibitionism of the Byronic hero is alien to our taste. The temptation to smile at some of Byron's utterances has already been mentioned. It is well to remember, however, that on occasion, in the hands of a master like Pushkin, such sweeping lyrical outpourings have about them a certain clarity, simplicity, and even grandeur. What is really wrong with them is simply the context in which they are placed—the Byronic poem designed to magnify the image of the Byronic hero. Separated from this rather juvenile background and treated on their own merits, many lines and many passages reveal themselves as poetry of a high order. In this respect Pushkin's restraint and craftsmanship prove more durable than the loosely constructed and often verbose hyperbole of Byron's "Eastern" tales.

And yet, contradictory though this may seem, Pushkin's very craftsmanship seems at times to render him a disservice. One cannot escape the impression, though impressions cannot be proven, that it is in fact the precision and perfection of his verses that make them on occasion an imperfect vehicle for the expression of profound emotions. For this the choice of meter or Pushkin's use of the meter should, perhaps, bear the responsibility. The relative shortness of the lines; their unvarying length; the high degree of regularity in their stress patterns; the fact that the syntactic units and syntagmas normally coincide with the unit of the line; and the strongly felt, exact end rhymes: these factors tend at times to make of the iambic tetrameters of the "Southern" poems an adroit tour de force; their very neatness seems to argue against depth of feeling. The iambic tetrameter was, of course, entirely appropriate for the light irony of *Ruslan and Lyudmila.* This is not to say that its function should be limited to irony and humor. Pushkin himself had already put it to an entirely different use in, for example, his "Ode to Freedom," and the versatility of this meter is clearly demonstrated in such Pushkin masterpieces as *Evgeny Onegin* and *The Bronze Horseman.* But against this it should be borne in mind that Pushkin's iambic tetrameter was to develop a syntactic freedom and general flexibility which are only beginning to be in evidence in the "Southern" poems. While, then, Pushkin's sense of form, artistic judgment, and dexterity as a writer enabled him to produce some excellent verse where in roughly analogous situations much of Byron is, alas, beyond salvaging, these same redeeming qualities—given Pushkin's use of the iambic tetrameter—are responsible, on occasion, for lines and passages which seem somehow too facile, too pat to carry the weight of emotion they were intended to carry.

It must be clear from the foregoing that in my opinion, the "Southern" poems judged in their entirety as works of art, should not be ranked too high among Pushkin's achievements. In this

Pushkin himself would most probably have concurred—at least as far as the first two are concerned. Of *The Prisoner of the Caucasus* he wrote jestingly: "The character of the Prisoner is a failure, that proves that I do not qualify as the hero of a romantic poem." And elsewhere, again dubbing the Prisoner's character a failure, he relates how Nikolay and Alexander Raevsky and he had enjoyed many good laughs at the expense of the Prisoner. *The Fountain of Bakhchisaray* he regarded as "weaker" than *The Prisoner,* though he remained satisfied with the dramatic quality of the scene in which Zarema confronts and threatens Maria; but here again amusement—provoked by a melodramatic description of Girey in battle—is mentioned. The most generally accepted view of the "Southern" poems is that the first two are weak; whereas *The Gypsies,* marking the "overcoming" of Byronism, is one of Pushkin's masterpieces. I would not rate *The Gypsies* that high. If certain features of the first two "Southern" poems provoked laughter, there are passages in *The Gypsies* which appear naïve: for instance, Aleko's "exposure" of the evils of city life or his extolling of the joys of vengeance. The latter passage (given above in part) continues:

> Oh no! If o'er the sea's abyss
> I found my enemy asleep,
> Why even there, I swear it, I
> Would have no mercy on the villain;
> Unblenching, with my foot I'd thrust him
> Defenseless down into the waves;
> His sudden horror as he woke
> My savage laughter would deride,
> And long I'd hear in mirth and jest
> The sweet sound of his rumbling fall.

Pushkin himself has pointed the way to a critical evaluation of the "Southern" poems. In labeling *The Prisoner* a failure, he attributed its success to "a number of elegiac and descriptive verses."[5] It is this sort of selective approach which seems most meaningful. While none of the three "Southern" poems can, I believe, be judged an unqualified success, none of them can be ignored or forgotten; they continue to be read and reread with pleasure. The reason for this lies not so much in the conception of the works themselves, but in a number of felicitous verses which, better than the poems in which they appear, preserve a lasting appeal.

II Gavriiliada

Written in 1821 in Kishinev, *Gavriiliada* has nothing in common with the "Southern" poems or with Pushkin's Byronism. It is a reversion to the eighteenth-century anti-clerical tradition of Voltaire and Parny, and, as will be seen, is extremely blasphemous in its handling of the sensitive topic of the Annunciation of the Virgin Mary. The poem was provoked, allegedly, by Pushkin's mild pique at being obliged—as a civil servant under General Inzov—to observe the fasts and participate in the services prescribed by the Orthodox Church for the period of Lent and Easter. It reflects also Pushkin's negative attitude to the often hypocritical pietism which had come to prevail in administration circles during the later years of Alexander I's reign. It should not, however, be regarded as a serious declaration of principle. It was not inspired by the militant sentiments and propagandistic aims characteristic of Pushkin's French predecessors. It was, rather, in the words of Vyazemsky, a "delightful prank."[6]

Given the close ties that united Church and regime and the official distrust of anything smacking of atheism, there could be no question of publication; *Gavriiliada* circulated in manuscript form among Pushkin's friends and acquaintances. And later, in 1828, when one of the copies came to the attention of the authorities, Pushkin was obliged, notwithstanding his initial denials, to admit to authorship. The 1828 *Gavriiliada* investigation culminating in Pushkin's confession, which was transmitted in a personal sealed letter to Nicholas I, was to be one of several unpleasant incidents in the story of Pushkin's troubled relationship with the government.

It goes without saying that the reader's reaction to *Gavriiliada* will be affected by his individual sensibilities with regard to Christian doctrine. To many the poem may appear to be in poor taste. Pushkin himself was in later years reluctant to be reminded of his authorship, though in what measure this was due to a changed and less irreverent attitude or to the embarrassment he suffered in 1828 is not easy to determine.

Gavriiliada is written in freely rhymed iambic pentameters with a caesura after the fourth syllable, a choice of meter which reflects the tradition on which Pushkin was drawing. Though only 552 lines long, it is written in the mock-epic style, as indicated by the title, and sub-title ("A Poem in One Canto"), and by its possession of various typically epic accoutrements.

The poem opens with a description of the quiet life led by Joseph and Mary. Joseph is an elderly "inefficient carpenter," who works day and night, and completely neglects the charms of his still virginal wife. He "Lived like a father with the innocent maid,/Provided her with food—and nothing else." Meanwhile, God has "in his profound wisdom" decided to bless and reward Mary. Surrounded by the heavenly throng, He appears to Mary in a vision and addresses her:

> Most beautiful of our dear, earthly daughters,
> Of Israel the youthful hope and joy!
> I summon thee, aflame with burning love,
> To share my glory. Harken to the call.
> Make ready for a fate not yet revealed,
> The bridegroom comes, draws near unto his slave.

The vision fades, but not before Mary's attention has been caught by the imposing figure of the Archangel Gabriel standing among the heavenly throng, his blue eyes fixed on her. Mary awakes:

> But from her memory the wondrous vision
> And Gabriel's charming figure did not fade.
> She wished indeed to love the king of heaven,
> The words he spoke were pleasing to her ear,
> And filled her with humility and awe—
> But somehow Gabriel took her fancy more.
> Thus the slim figure of some adjutant
> Finds favor, maybe, with the general's wife.
> So fate decrees; there's nothing we can do,
> As all men, wise or foolish, are agreed.

Back up in heaven, meanwhile, God is experiencing the pangs and frustrations of love:

> No joy the Creator found in his Creation,
> And heavenly prayer delighted not his ear;
> He busily composed his psalms of love

> And loudly sang: "Mary I love, I love,
> My immortality means nothing now . . .
> Where are my wings? To Mary I will fly
> And on her beauteous breast I will repose!"
> And so on . . . phrase on phrase on phrase; the Lord
> Leaned to a colorful and Eastern style.
> He summoned then his favorite Gabriel and
> To Gabriel explained his love in prose. . . .

And Gabriel

> Reluctantly became the faithful servant
> Of heaven's king—in earthly terms his pimp.

However, Satan is aware of God's intentions:

> He goes to work. The Almighty sate meanwhile
> Up there in heaven in sweet despondency;
> Forgot the world that He was wont to rule—
> Without his rule it went on just the same. . . .

Mary, meanwhile, is in her garden, sad and lonely, afflicted by her thoughts of Gabriel. Satan appears before her in the guise of a beautiful serpent. He is so submissive that Mary, though aware of his true identity, is induced to listen, and Satan proceeds at some length to give his version of the Adam and Eve story. He had not ruined Eve; he had saved her, he had introduced Adam and Eve to the voluptuous joys of passion. Mary's imagination is fired by his erotic descriptions. Suddenly the serpent disappears and is replaced by a handsome young man:

> Prone at her feet, not uttering a word,
> Fixing on her his wondrous shining gaze,
> With eloquence he supplicates, entreats,
> And with one hand he proffers her a flower,
> The other hand rumples her simple blouse
> And hastily beneath her vestment steals
> And the light fingers playfully caress
> Her hidden charms . . . The marvel of it all!
> For Mary this is, oh, so subtly new.
> But lo, her virgin cheeks light with a flush,
> A crimson that is not the blush of shame.
> A languid warmth and an impatient sob
> Cause her young breasts to rise and fall—and rise.
> No word she speaks; but she can stand no more;

> Scarce breathing now, her languid eyes half-closed,
> She bows her head toward the expectant Satan,
> Screams: "ah! ..." and falls full length upon the grass ...

At this point—or shortly after—Gabriel arrives, drives Satan away after a hard-fought battle, won by a deft blow aimed at the most vulnerable of all places. The victorious Gabriel then addresses to Mary a parody of the "Ave Maria," in which the punch thought is that more blessed than the fruit of her womb will be the father of the fruit. He presses her hand, kisses her, touches her breast, and again Mary succumbs:

> What shall she do? What of her jealous God?
> Be troubled not, my beauteous maidens fair.
> O women, you who know love's ins and outs,
> You know full well the wiles that can deceive
> The vigilant observance of the groom,
> The expert vigilance of the well-wishers,
> That cover up a pleasant little lapse
> With all the trappings of sweet innocence.
> The errant daughter from her mother learns
> The lesson of submissive modesty.
> And on the first and all-decisive night
> She feigns false fears and pains that do not pain;
> And on the morrow, feeling better slowly,
> Gets up, can hardly walk, is languid, pale.
> Elated the proud spouse, relieved her mother,
> And soon once more the old flame's back again.

Gabriel flies back to God and reports that all is ready. God prepares. Mary lies dreaming about Gabriel. Then suddenly:

> A sweet, enchanting dove flies in her window,
> Above her flips and flaps its wings and flutters,
> And sings its little winsome birdlike songs,
> Then suddenly between her legs flies in,
> Alights upon the rose and trembles there,
> Claws, turns around, and claws again, again,
> Works with its feet and with its little beak.
> Oh, this is God! Mary has understood
> That this the dove is an Almighty guest;
> Her knees drawn tight, the Hebrew maid cried out,
> Began to sigh, to tremble, and to plead,
> To weep. But no, triumphant is the dove,

> In love's hot heat he quivers and he chirrups,
> Then falls into light sleep, by love undone,
> Resting an idle wing across the rose.

> He's flown away. All-weary, Mary thinks:
> "What furious pranks and happenings are these!
> One, two and three—how eager they all seem.
> This has been quite a day, I must admit:
> In one and the same day I fell a prey
> To Satan and to Gabriel and to God."

God recognized the result of this affair as his own. Gabriel continued to pay visits to Mary. The author concludes with a prayer, initially addressed to Gabriel, to give him aid in his love suit with a certain Elena; otherwise he will turn for help to Satan:

> But time still passes by, and slowly time
> Will ring my head with silver, by and by,
> And then before the altar I will stand:
> A fitting marriage and a fitting wife.
> Oh, Joseph, be my consolation then.
> I pray you, yes, I pray you on my knees,
> Preserver, guardian-saint of cuckolds all,
> I pray you then to cast on me your blessing.
> Grant unto me the blessed gift of patience,
> Grant unto me, again and yet again,
> Sweet sleep at night, and in my spouse full trust,
> A family at peace, love of my brother.

Readers of *Ruslan and Lyudmila* will recognize in *Gavriiliada* the same use of bathos, achieved mainly through stylistic switches from the biblical to the erotic, and of the author's digressions which here again serve as a focal point around which the entire poem operates and which lend to the narrative a contemporary and sometimes personal dimension. Peculiarly effective, in terms of Pushkin's artistic intent, is the fact that Mary's seduction by Gabriel is relatively shorter and easier than her seduction by Satan, while her reluctant submission to the dove's clawing endeavors approaches shoulder-shrugging resignation. Those who seek in *Gavriiliada* for depth of feeling or thought will naturally be disappointed. But its scintillating wit and flawless artistry make this poem—in its own way—a perfect minor masterpiece.

CHAPTER 3

Exile and Return:
Boris Godunov, Count Nulin *and* Poltava

PUSHKIN'S dismissal from the service meant the end of the fiction, maintained up to then, that he was being transferred from one post to another. He was now officially an exile. On July 30, 1824, he left Odessa. He was under orders to travel by a prescribed route to his mother's estate of Mikhaylovskoe, in the neighborhood of Pskov. He found there his mother, father, older sister and younger brother. But reunion with the family was not to bring happiness. Relations with his father had never been good. The latter's stinginess had been a constant source of complaint for the poet. Worse, however, was the fact that his father had agreed to act as a semi-official supervisor of his son's activities. For the father, the son was a disgrace to the family, and something of a threat to the family's security; for the son, the father appeared in the role of spy and jailer. Relations deteriorated rapidly, and there were violent scenes between the two. On one occasion the father accused Pushkin of having struck him, or having gestured to strike him—a very serious offense in the Russia of those days. Pushkin was sufficiently alarmed at this accusation to write to Zhukovsky, claiming his innocence and asking for the latter's protection if that should become necessary. The intolerable situation came to an end when the father relinquished his supervisory duties and moved away from the estate, taking the rest of the family with him.

For the next two years Pushkin was to live in virtual isolation at Mikhaylovskoe. He suffered greatly from loneliness. The presence in the house of the family nurse, Arina Rodionovna, for whom Pushkin felt genuine affection, helped to mitigate his ordeal, and it was from her that Pushkin heard many of the folk and fairy tales which he came to love and which were to find a place in his work. He was fortunate too in having as neighbors on the nearby estate of Trigorskoe a large family with whose female members Pushkin enjoyed varying degrees of intimacy and where he was always a lionized and welcome guest. There were also visitors to Mikhaylovskoe, but these were few and far between. Pushkin attempted to escape from this isolation by requesting permission to go abroad for treatment for his allegedly varicose veins, but permission was not granted. Meanwhile, he rode, read, and wrote. He also fathered a child by one of the serf girls on the estate. But he missed the social life and activities of the city.

However, the two years spent at Mikhaylovskoe were among the most fruitful of his life. His enforced isolation gave more time for reading, thus expanding his intellectual horizons, and more time for writing. His productivity as a lyric poet continued high, and in his work on *Evgeny Onegin* he made considerable progress. The two major works, completed during this period and discussed in this chapter, were his drama, *Boris Godunov*, and the less serious but brilliantly witty short poem, *Count Nulin*.

A change in Pushkin's life was to come from an unexpected quarter—the death in November 1825, of Alexander I at Taganrog. The Tsar's death produced a temporary state of confusion with regard to the succession to the throne. Konstantin, the next oldest brother and therefore presumably next in line to succeed, had previously renounced his claim to the throne, and the younger brother, Nicholas, was in fact the legitimate heir. However, Konstantin's renunciation was not generally known, and some time elapsed during which attempts were made to have Konstantin, who was in Warsaw, make some statement which would clearly establish Nicholas' legitimate right.

Meanwhile the secret societies, which had been forming from 1816 on, had become increasingly impatient with the government's reactionary policy, and their activities had by this time assumed a definitely conspiratorial character. At the time of Alexander's death there were two main groups of conspirators, the so-called Northern Group and the Southern Group, composed largely of Army officers. The decision was taken to make use of the confusion which had arisen with regard to the succession in order to launch an uprising.

The uprising occured on December 14, 1825 in Petersburg and was speedily repressed. Pushkin, aware of the troubled atmosphere which prevailed, had even contemplated leaving his place of exile and traveling surreptitiously to Petersburg. The story has it that the poet actually set out on his way, but—deterred by bad omens, for Pushkin was extremely superstitious—decided to turn back to Mikhaylovskoe. If this is so, it was a piece of extremely good fortune, for the poet would apparently have arrived in Petersburg on the eve of the uprising and would inevitably have been implicated in the catastrophe, which led to the hanging of five of the conspirators and the exiling of more than one hundred to Siberia. Pushkin's own exile, therefore, and his decision to remain at Mikhayloskoe undoubtedly saved him from sharing the fate of the conspirators, among whom he numbered many of his friends.

With the Decembrist uprising crushed and Nicholas I clearly in control, Pushkin again decided to use the state of his health as a pretext for petitioning for clemency. Some time between May 11 and the middle of June, 1826, he sent the following letter to Nicholas I:

MOST GRACIOUS SOVEREIGN!

In 1824 I had the misfortune to incur the wrath of the late Emperor by an ill-considered judgment regarding atheism set down in a letter, and I was expelled from the service, and exiled to the village where I still am under the surveillance of the provincial authorities.

Now, with reliance upon Your Majesty's magnanimity, with sincere remorse, and with the firm intention for my opinions not to be at variance with the generally accepted order (in which matter I am ready to obligate myself by my signature and by my word of honor), I have decided to have recourse to Your Imperial Majesty with my most humble request.

My health, which was shattered in my early youth, and a kind of aneurysm, have now for a long time been needing constant treatment in support of which I present the testimony of physicians: I make bold to request most humbly the permission to go for this purpose to Moscow, to Petersburg, or to foreign lands.

Most gracious Sovereign,
Your Imperial Majesty's
Loyal subject,

ALEXANDER PUSHKIN.

(On a separate sheet)

I, the undersigned, obligate myself henceforth not to belong to any secret societies, under whatever name they may exist; I hereby certify that I have not belonged and do not belong to any secret society, and that I never had knowledge of them.

Civil servant of the Tenth Class Alexander Pushkin.

11 May
1826

Nicholas I's reign can scarcely be said to have had an auspicious beginning. And it was natural that the Tsar now felt strongly the need to balance his stern treatment of the Decembrists with measures of mercy and compassion. One example of this desire was the granting of a pension to the widow of the poet, Ryleev, who was one of the five conspirators hanged. So Pushkin's case also offered the Tsar the possibility of demonstrating to the Russian people his capacity for generous and human feeling. Pushkin had, as was pointed out earlier, never been a member of any of the secret societies. His main sins in the eyes of the authorities were the liberal verses which had in 1820 led to his removal from Petersburg and the charge that he was an atheist; it had in fact been this latter charge which had enabled Count Vorontsov to secure his dismissal from the service. It was true that Pushkin's liberal verses had been a powerful influence for many of those involved in the Decembrist uprising. Nevertheless, Pushkin's letter to the Tsar was, in effect, a pledge that he would not only not become a member of any secret society but that his writings would not be in opposition to the established regime. For Nicholas I other considerations were undoubtedly the hope that Pushkin could be induced to lend his influential writings to the support of the regime, and that at the least he would in any case be less dangerous if shown mercy than if he were left in the bitterness of his exile. This time, then, Pushkin's plea for clemency met with a positive response. The decision was taken to summon Pushkin to Moscow.

"Not as a prisoner and under the escort of the courier only," as the order stipulated, Pushkin set out for Moscow and arrived, travel-weary and rather unwell, on September 8, 1826. He was ordered to present himself to the Tsar that same afternoon, and at four o'clock was received in private audience by Nicholas.

The exact details of this man-to-man confrontation will probably never be known. However, accounts of the meeting, emanating from both sides, differ very little on essentials.[1] It would seem that Nicholas I sought to persuade Pushkin that he was not merely a tyrannical despot but that his love of Russia was no less than that of the poet. The crucial question between the two was clearly that of the recent Decembrist uprising. Pushkin was asked what role he would have played if he had been in Petersburg on December 14. To this the poet replied: "I should have been in the ranks of the rebels." Pushkin acknowledged too his friendship with many of the conspirators and his sympathy for their plight. However, he agreed, as indeed his letter had pledged, that he would no longer form a part of any opposition to the regime. Another question, from the poet's point of view, was that of his sufferings at the hands of a bureaucratic censorship. The Tsar appears to have expressed sympathy with the poet's predicament and to have reassured him: "You will send me everything you write; from now on I will be your censor." Pushkin was told that he was now free. The meeting appears to have lasted between one and two hours.

The meeting itself was from the points of view of both men an unqualified success. Nicholas was pleased with Pushkin's showing and the fact that he had apparently persuaded the poet to abandon his past attitudes. The Tsar allegedly remarked that evening that he had talked earlier in the day to "the most intelligent man in Russia." Pushkin was no less pleased. He had found himself powerfully drawn to Nicholas I, whose personality for some years to come seems to have exerted an almost magnetic charm on the poet. There *were* limitations on his freedom: for example, he would not be allowed to visit the capital city of Petersburg without permission. Meanwhile, the returned poet was the most popular hero in Moscow. The social pleasures, of which he had been so long deprived, were his again, and he had the satisfaction of knowing that he had held his head high in conversation with his Tsar, had spoken frankly, and had kept his honor intact. It was not long, though, before the poet came to realize that his problems with the regime, and with himself, were far from being solved. The tribulations which awaited him in the next few years will be discussed in the following chapter. Meanwhile, we will proceed to examine *Boris Godunov, Count*

Nulin, and *Poltava,* the last written after his return from exile, in 1828.

I Boris Godunov

Boris Godunov is an historical drama or tragedy in twenty-three scenes.[2] It was started in November or December 1824, and finished in November 1825. In *Boris Godunov* we are confronted by a new and important influence—that of Shakespeare. Some critics have maintained that it was Shakespeare's influence which emancipated Pushkin from Byronism. This is inexact. The mere fact that *Evgeny Onegin* was begun, as already noted, in May 1823 in Kishinev indicates clearly that Pushkin had been for some time in the process of discarding his earlier Byronism.[3] In this process, furthermore, the influence of the later Byron of *Beppo* and *Don Juan* had played its part.[4] Shakespeare's influence was no less significant and beneficial for that: it opened up hitherto unexplored avenues of creative work; it facilitated Pushkin's emergence as a fully fledged dramatist; it helped Pushkin formulate his ideas on the techniques of characterization; it stimulated his theories on the development of the Russian theater; and it marked the serious beginning of his life long interest in the evolutionary processes of Russian history—and of history in general. Not that Shakespeare should be credited with all these developments. The prime movers here—as in the earlier case of the influence of Byronism—were Pushkin's own expanding intellectual horizons and inner needs. The direction and form these took owe, however, much to Shakespeare.

Pushkin's interest in Shakespeare was, of course, no fortuitous predilection on the part of the Russian writer. Shakespeare's influence had been on the rise in Germany before Goethe's *Götz von Berlichingen* (1773) and had grown into a European phenomenon. For the pre-Romantic *Sturm und Drang* followers and for the Romantics his appeal was inevitably strong: many of his plays dealt with the historical past of his own country, and his dramatic techniques offered a refreshing example to writers and theorists who had come to feel that the established principles of French Classicism were overly rigid and restrictive.

In writing *Boris Godunov* Pushkin was making a conscious effort to give a new direction to the development of the Russian theater. As he later expressed it, "I am firmly convinced that the *popular* rules of Shakespearean drama are better suited to our theater than the courtly customs of Racine's tragedy."[5] The principles of French Classical drama had been imported into Russian literature in the eighteenth century—notably in the tragedies of Sumarokov—and although this influence had not remained entirely unmodified, in the 1820's it was still a sufficiently dominant force for Pushkin to feel the need of attacking its constraints. *Boris Godunov* dispenses with two of the three Classical unities (time and place), preserving only the unity of action. It follows Shakespeare in introducing crowd scenes, thus no longer observing the Classical limitation whereby only characters of princely or noble origin appear on stage. As in Shakespeare's plays, and contrary to the tradition of Classical tragedy, moments of high drama are interspersed with comic scenes— though not, in my opinion, always with success. The language of *Boris Godunov* displays the wide stylistic range—from high to low—of Shakespeare's writing, as distinct from the unbrokenly highflown quality of the language of French tragedy. Also, Pushkin alternates, as did Shakespeare, between verse and prose passages. And his verse, like Shakespeare's, is in mainly unrhymed iambic pentameters, interspersed with occasional rhymes, the main difference being that Pushkin's pentameters follow the French syllabic tradition in placing a caesura after the fourth syllable.

Of considerable significance is the influence on Pushkin of Shakespeare's characterization techniques. On two occasions the Russian expressed himself so clearly on this score that his words can best be left to speak for themselves. "How amazing Shakespeare is!" he wrote in 1825, while still at work on his tragedy; "I can't get over it. How petty by comparison with him is Byron as a tragedian! Byron who created only one character . . . Byron distributed among his heroes various traits of his own character; to one he gave his pride, to another his hatred, to a third his melancholy etc., and thus from one integrated character, gloomy and energetic, he created a number of insignificant characters; that's not tragedy at all."[6] While Byron was found lacking as a result of his egocentricity, Molière was later compared unfavorably with Shakespeare for the limitedness and unrealistic consistency of his characters: "The characters created by Shake-

speare are not, as with Molière, personifications of a specific passion or vice. They are living beings, full of many passions and
many vices; changing circumstances bring out before the spectator the diversity and manysidedness of their characters. With
Molière Harpagon is miserly—and only miserly; Shakespeare's
Shylock is miserly, enterprising, vindictive, fond of children,
witty."[7] Pushkin saw, then, in Shakespeare's characterizations
objectivity, breadth, diversity, psychological verisimilitude.

The action of *Boris Godunov* is based on historical events
which took place between 1598 and 1605. At issue in the play is
the question of who shall sit upon the throne of Russia. The
problem of succession arose in 1598 when the death of Fyodor
Ivanovich brought to an end the long-established Ryurik dynasty. But the origins of the problem go back a few years, earlier,
and a brief summary is relevant to an understanding of the play.
Ivan the Terrible died in 1584. Though married eight times in
all, Ivan had had only three sons. Of the two sons by his first
marriage the older, favorite son and heir apparent, Ivan, had
been killed by his father in a fit of temper provoked by a dis-
pute about the seemliness of the clothing worn by the son's
pregnant wife in the presence of Ivan, her father-in-law. The
throne thus passed in 1584 to the second son, Fyodor, who was
sickly, devout, and ill-suited to temporal rule. The third son,
Dimitry, was by Ivan's fifth marriage. Should Fyodor die childless—and he appeared to have no procreative aptitudes—the
young Dimitry would have had a claim to the throne. This was
the position when in 1591 Dimitry died under mysterious circumstances. Some said that the nine-year-old boy had killed
himself with his own knife during an epileptic fit. Others had
it that he had been murdered—on the orders of or at the instiga-
tion of Boris Godunov, a nobleman who had, as a result of
Fyodor's ineptitude for rule, succeeded in effectively taking into
his own hands the reins of government.

The question as to whether Boris was in fact guilty will probably never be finally resolved. His innocence has been defended
on the grounds that it would have been foolishness to risk murder when at any time Fyodor might be expected to beget an
heir. On the other hand, if—as was rumored—Fyodor was impo-
tent, the one person certain to know this would presumably have
been his wife, who was the sister of Boris. Thus Boris, it is ar-

gued, had certain inside information that no heir would be forthcoming. Karamzin, whose *History of the Russian State* was Pushkin's main source, took the view that Boris Godunov *was* responsible for the murder, and Boris is treated as guilty by Pushkin.

Fyodor did die childless in 1598 and Boris, already the effective ruler of Russia, became the logical candidate to the throne. This he accepted—with seemly reluctance and after some delay, occasioned by a sort of tacit power struggle between the boyars (noblemen) who wished to limit the powers of the monarchy and Boris who wished to continue the Ryurik tradition of absolute rule and to found his own hereditary dynasty in the Ryurik manner. From this struggle Boris emerged triumphant. But, though an able ruler, he was not destined to reign in peace. There arose a succession of pretenders, each one claiming to be the dead Dimitry. The first of these was a fugitive monk, Grigory Otrepev, who secured the backing of the Poles and marched on Moscow, aided and abetted by many dissident Russian nobles. As the false Dimitry advanced, defections from the Russian side increased. At this point Boris Godunov died and, unimpeded by any further opposition, Dimitry entered Moscow at the head of a basically Polish army and was crowned (1605). However, Dimitry's Western ideas and Polophile tendencies aroused the antagonism of the Russian boyars, and one year later he was murdered. The country was now plunged into complete chaos (this period is known as "the Time of Troubles"), and it was not till 1613 that the various pretenders were finally eliminated, order restored, Polish intervention turned back, and a new dynasty established—that of the Romanovs who survived to 1917.

The play opens in Moscow in 1598. Boris agrees, with the apparent hesitation and seemly reluctance already mentioned, to become Tsar. He addresses the Patriarch and assembled boyars:

> Most reverent Patriarch, you boyars all,
> My Soul is bared before you: you have seen
> How I now undertake this so great power
> With, in my heart, humility and awe,
> How heavy are these bonds I lay upon me! . . .
> Boyars, I look to you for aid and succor.
> Serve me as you once faithfully served him [Fyodor]
> When I still shared your labors, one of you,
> Not yet elected by the people's will.

The boyars assure him of their loyalty. The next incident takes
place five years later, in 1603, and lays the groundwork for the
emergence of the Pretender who is destined to threaten Boris'
rule. The scene takes place in a cell in the Chudovo Monastery.
A young monk, Grigory, is asleep. His aged colleague, Father
Pimen, is writing by the light of a lamp. He is putting the finish-
ing touches to a historical chronicle. Grigory awakes. He tells
Pimen his dream:

> I dreamed I saw steep stairs up-spiraling,
> Led to a tower; and from this height I looked,
> Below lay Moscow like some ant-heap spread;
> Upon the square below the people surged,
> Pointed their fingers up at me and laughed,
> And I felt overcome by shame and fear—
> And, falling headling, wakened from my dream . . .
> And three times now I've dreamed the selfsame dream.
> Is this not strange?

Grigory envies Pimen for the adventuresome youth the latter
spent as warrior and courtier, fighting and feasting. He himself
has from adolescence known only the monastic life. Pimen com-
forts him. He had indeed experienced many of this world's joys,
but true bliss has been his only since the Lord brought him
within the walls of a monastery. Now, however, Russia has fallen
on evil days and, in response to Grigory's question, Pimen relates
how the murderers of the boy Dimitry repented before their
execution and pronounced Boris guilty of their crime. If he had
lived, Dimitry would have been the same age as Grigory—nine-
teen. The murder of Dimitry on Boris' orders will be the final
episode in Pimen's chronicle. Left alone by his elder, Grigory
reflects:

> Boris! Boris! Before you all things tremble,
> And no one dares to even call to mind
> The cruel fate of that poor hapless infant.
> Yet meanwhile in this dim, secluded cell
> A hermit monk writes down the loathsome truth:
> Just as God's judgment you shall not escape,
> Nor shall you scape your judgment here below.

Grigory, declaring himself to be Dimitry, flees to Poland, enlists the support of the Poles and of Russian dissidents, and starts

his march on Moscow. Boris' reign has been darkened by famine,
Boris himself is saddened by the death of his daughter's betrothed (for which some people blame him), plagued by his
conscience (for thirteen years he has dreamt of the murdered
child), and weary with the burdens of rule; he is seen consoling
his daughter and talking to his son, Fyodor. The boyars are uneasy and insecure—and alert for news from Poland. The false
Dimitry emerges as enterprising, bold, intelligent, educated,
diplomatic in his handling of people—and susceptible to feminine beauty. After leaving Cracow, he has halted his forces at
Sambor, and is staying in the house of a certain Mnishek, whose
beautiful and extremely ambitious daughter, Marina, has captivated his heart. Dimitry has a nighttime rendezvous with
Marina. He declares his love. But Marina wants to hear only of
his plans for capturing Moscow. This upsets the Pretender, who
desperately wants to be loved for himself:

> Do not torment me, beautiful Marina,
> Don't tell me that it was my rank that won you,
> Not I myself. . . .
> Enough! Enough!
> I will not share with the departed dead
> A mistress that belongs to him by right.
> Be gone deceit and falsehood! I shall tell
> You the whole truth; know then that your Dimitry's
> Long dead and buried—nor shall quit his grave. . . .

And he proceeds to tell Marina who he is. Marina treats him
with scorn. After several exchanges the Pretender retorts with
pride:

> The shade of dread Ivan has called me son,
> Spoke from the grave and named me his Dimitry,
> Roused to revolt the nations round about me,
> And marked Boris my victim. Shame on me
> That I, who shall be Tsar, should bow my head,
> Humble myself before your Polish pride. . . .

He bids her farewell, saying that she will perhaps regret her
unwillingness to share his destiny.

> *Marina.* Tsarevich, wait. At last your words   ..
> Are those not of a stripling, but a man. . . .
> Win Moscow, in the Kremlin mount the throne,

Then send your envoy who shall speak your suit.
But God's my witness, till your feet have trod
Those steps ascending to proud Moscow's throne,
Until Boris is routed and cast down,
I shall not heed nor hear your words of love.

Dimitry moves his forces on into Russia, and Boris prepares
to counter the threat. We witness part of a battle scene in which
Dimitry is victorious. We see Dimitry, after defeat, bemoaning
his dead horse, but still confident. In Moscow there prevails an
atmosphere of terror, repression, and intrigue. We see Boris in
conversation with his ablest lieutenant, Basmanov. Boris is not
misled by the recent victory. He knows that Dimitry has reas-
sembled his scattered forces and that his own army is half-
hearted and ineffective. He proposes to put Basmanov in command. Summoned to receive some foreign visitors, Boris leaves,
telling Basmanov to wait for his return. But a minute later Boris
is carried back on stage, stricken with a mortal sickness and
dying:

Go all from hence—I wish to talk alone
With the Tsarevich. (*All leave.*) Death approaches me;
Embrace, farewell, my son: for shortly now
You shall begin to reign . . . O God, my God!
Soon must I stand before Thee—with no time
To do my penance, purify my soul.
And yet, my son, to me you are more dear
Than is salvation; let God's will be done!
A subject I was born, and should have died
In deep obscurity, a subject still;
But I attained the highest power of all . . .
Don't ask me how. You, are without guilt,
And you shall rule by right, while I alone
Will answer to my Maker for my deeds. . . .

The dying Tsar then warns Fyodor of the extent of the threat
posed by the Pretender and advises him—among more general
counsels on how to handle the situation—to put Basmanov in
charge of the armed forces. The Patriarch, Boris' wife and
daughter ,and the boyars enter. Boris makes them swear loyalty
to his son. The last rites begin.

In the following scene Basmanov, now in charge at the front.
decides to betray Fyodor, Boris' son; although Dimitry's troops

are little better than a rabble, Basmanov fears the treachery of his own men, for defections have been numerous and many cities have welcomed Dimitry without resistance. In the penultimate scene Pushkin (an ancestor of the poet) pleads successfully with the Moscow crowd to transfer their loyalty. In the final scene, outside the Kremlin, several boyars thrust through the crowd, enter the Kremlin, there is a commotion within and cries, after which one of the boyars appears on the threshold and announces:

> Men and Women! Maria Godunova [Boris' wife] and her son
> Fyodor have taken poison. We saw their dead bodies.
> (*The crowd is horrified and silent.*) Why say you nothing?
> Shout: long live Tsar Dimitry Ivanovich! (*The crowd is
> silent.*) END.

Boris Godunov rated high in its author's affection and esteem, and it rightfully occupies a permanent and distinguished place in Russian letters. Those unacquainted with the original will have to take on faith that it contains poetry of a very high order. There is, however, something about it which does not entirely satisfy. As Belinsky expressed it, "in none of his earlier works did Pushkin attain such artistic heights and in none of them did he reveal such vast defects as in *Boris Godunov*. This drama was for him a genuine Waterloo, in which he deployed the full breadth and depth of his genius, and nevertheless suffered a decisive defeat."[8] Needless to say, there are many who do not share Belinsky's view. Many critics tend in general to exaggerate the merits of *Boris Godunov*. For example: "As Pushkin scholarship has demonstrated, Pushkin's social-historical and social-philosophical realist tragedy was a new phenomenon in Russian and world dramaturgy at that time.... However, the criticism of Pushkin's day was incapable of rising to a serious understanding of the innovative character of the dramaturgic system created by Pushkin."[9] Indeed, opinions vary widely as to the merits of the play. A critical examination of *Boris Godunov* may help to explain these divergencies and to arrive at an understanding of what Pushkin achieved and failed to achieve.

First, the reader of recent Soviet evaluations cannot fail to be struck by the fact that much of the praise lavished on *Boris Godunov* is elicited by the role allegedly played in this work

by the *people* (*narod*). For example, "in *Boris Godunov* we find
demonstrated for the first time—not only in Russian literature
but in Russian historiography—the decisive role of the *people* in
the historical process and the potentiality of a victory by the
people over the autocracy."[10] The same critic informs us that
the central problem of this tragedy is the role of the *people* in
the historical process.[11] Pushkin's handling of the *people* is, in
Soviet criticism, held to be fundamentally different to that of
Shakespeare. This may be so. It is, however, noteworthy that in
his numerous surviving comments on *Boris Godunov* Pushkin
nowhere gives an inkling of any intended radical change in his
approach to this problem. And on the evidence of the play itself
the *people*, formidable force though it undoubtedly is, appears
in a somewhat passive role, as something to be manipulated by
boyars and Tsars. Sometimes quoted as evidence of the *people's*
"decisive role" are the following lines used by Pushkin, the Pretender's intermediary, to convince Basmanov that the cause of
Boris' son is a losing one:

> I will be frank: our army is a rabble. . . .
> But listen then, Basmanov, our strength lies
> Not in our army, nor the Poles' support,
> But in the minds and feelings of the *people*.

These lines convey, however, no more than what can be found
in Shakespeare's plays and what has been proved many times
since the beginnings of recorded history, namely that no ruler or
military commander can survive if a sufficient number of his
followers defects to the enemy. But the main quarrel here with
the Soviet approach is not with the interpretation of the historical process; it rests rather on the fact that Pushkin's view of
the *people's* role, whatever it was, and whatever understanding
it may reveal of the process of history, is largely irrelevant in any
consideration of the artistic merits of *Boris Godunov*.

Pushkin's own expressed views on the *people*, or rather on
the "popular" or "folk" quality (*narodnost'*) in literature, are
instructive. *Narodnost'*, for Pushkin, meant in part the Shakespearean opposite of French Classicism with its courtly tradition
and polished conventions. As noted above, "the *popular* rules of
Shakespearean drama" were held to be better suited to the
Russian theater than were "the courtly customs of Racine's

tragedy."[12] But this remark is made specifically in terms of what would be desirable for the Russian theater. It is significant that on other occasions Pushkin accords to Racine as well as to Shakespeare the quality of *narodnost'*. Racine, whose stage is peopled exclusively by "upper-class" characters, is even cited in the following definition of tragedy which includes, be it noted, a mention of the people: "What is it that tragedy develops? What is tragedy's goal? Man and the *people*. Man's fate and the fate of the *people*. That is why Racine is great, notwithstanding the narrow form of his tragedy. That is why Shakespeare is great, notwithstanding the unevenness, carelessness, ugliness of his execution."[13] When it comes to *narodnost'*, Pushkin's definition is remarkably broad: "For some time past people have been talking about *narodnost'*, demanding *narodnost'*, complaining of its absence in works of literature; but it has not occurred to anyone to define what is meant by the word *narodnost'*. One of our critics, it seems, assumes that *narodnost'* consists in selecting themes from our nation's history, others discern *narodnost'* in the choice of words, i.e., they take pleasure in the use of Russian expressions in Russian. But it would be difficult to deny Shakespeare's *narodnost'* in *Othello, Hamlet, Measure for Measure* and other plays. Vega and Calderon transport us all over the world, taking the subjects for their tragedies from Italian *novelle* and French lays. Ariosto sings the praises of Charlemagne, French knights and a Chinese princess. Racine's tragedies are taken from ancient history. But it would be difficult to deny to any of these writers the quality of *narodnost'*.... Climate, the form of government, religious beliefs give to each people its own particular physiognomy, which to a greater or lesser degree is reflected in the mirror of its poetry. There exists a way of thinking and feeling, a thousand and one customs, beliefs and habits which belong exclusively to any given people."[14] Pushkin's focus in thinking of *narod* and *narodnost'* is, as we see, a consistently literary one. Further, it lacks the democratic and class overtones which in the latter half of the nineteenth century and in the twentieth century came to be associated with the concept of *narod*. Pimen, whose origins are noble, is as representative of the spirit of *narodnost'* as is the poorest and most ignorant member of the masses.[15] Within the thoroughly reasonable terms of the literary definition laid down by its author, *Boris Godunov* may be said to possess in full measure the quality of *narodnost'*.

However, *narodnost'* as a quality, while it may permeate a work, cannot be regarded as esthetically an end in itself. Pushkin most often referred to *Boris Godunov* as a "tragedy," also as a "genuinely romantic tragedy;"[16] and, "romantic" or not, it is as a tragedy that it is most often treated today and can be most profitably considered. The term *tragedy* immediately brings to mind such concepts as "inexorable necessity," "inevitability," "conflict," "fate," and "character" (or the tragic flaw in a person's character which brings about his undoing). It is right that such concepts should lurk at the back of the mind, for taken together they are not simply arbitrary rules, but the essentials of the tragic mood. However, from Aristotle on, there have—naturally enough—been many varied theories on tragedy, and it would be a mistake to measure *Boris Godunov* by any preconceived, rigid set of principles. Nevertheless, it is within the general framework of the tragic mood that the organizing principle of this work must be sought.

In 1831 I. V. Kireevsky wrote: "The shadow of the murdered Dimitry dominates the tragedy from beginning to end, controls the entire course of events, serves as a link between all the characters and scenes. . . ."[17] Much has subsequently been written on *Boris Godunov*, but no one has pinpointed more accurately than Kireevsky the dominant theme. This is, first and foremost, a play about power, about the evil and futility of ambition, about a man wracked by his guilty conscience. The tragic mood is centered on Boris. Here is a hero of truly tragic stature. He has committed murder and thereby achieved the power he craved. Power has not brought him the anticipated satisfactions. He is weary and troubled.[18] Yet ambition is an essential part of his make-up, and his ambitions have not died—only now they are transferred to his children. In order to see his children established, to found a dynasty, Boris, plagued by ill-luck and ill-repute, and rendered skeptical by his experience of rule, still continues to exert all his intelligence and skill in government, and is even ready to go unshriven to his Maker so long as he can ensure his son's successful take-over of the reins. The play's tragedy and irony lie not so much in Boris' death, but in the fact that the great crime with which he has burdened himself is all for nothing: his daughter's fiancé dies and his son is overthrown and killed (though the latter event takes place after Boris' death, it may fairly be maintained that Boris in dying is aware that his son's survival is problematic, i.e., that all his efforts have very probably been in vain). The play's dominant poetic mood—recognition of the vanity of power and the evil of ambition—is built up, over and above the focal tragedy of Boris, in many ways: the intriguing of the survival-minded boyars; the incomprehension of the common people; Pimen's praise of the contemplative life and, in particular, his recollection of how both Boris' predecessors wished to lay down the burdens of power; the Pretender's impetuous willingness to abandon his ambitions for love (Dimitry is adventuresome rather than ambitious); Marina's coldbloodedness and the unabashed nakedness of her ambition; Dimitry's reluctance to spill Russian blood in war, to say nothing of his sorrow over his dying horse; the sorrow of Boris' daughter over her dead fiancé; the feeling of her and her brother's vulnerability; and the murders which mark Dimitry's successful seizure of power and conclude the play. At the end of *Richard III* (the Shakespeare play with which *Boris Godunov* is most often compared) there is the feeling of a new start, of England's having been liberated from a tyrant and malefactor. *Boris Godunov* offers no such emotional release; the play ends without triumph, on a note of gloom.[19] Such is, I believe, the conceptual framework in which this tragedy can most fruitfully be viewed.

Why then this talk of Pushkin's Waterloo? The reason lies, in my opinion, in the play's structuring. Boris is of tragic stature, but he is simply not on stage enough nor active enough to hold down his central role as tragic hero (he appears in six scenes out of twenty-three and his crime was committed before the play opens) and create a focus for the entire plot. Second, there is the matter of Boris' death. This simply occurs. We know that Boris is aweary. But one moment he is giving perfectly sensible orders to Basmanov; the next he is a dying man. Not only does the lack of all apparent causal relationship between Boris' death and his problems deprive us of that feeling of inevitability which so heightens awareness of the tragic in literature; its very abruptness makes it seem like some irrelevant, alien element, introduced out of nowhere, and destructive of the prevailing mood at that stage in the play. That mood is one of suspense. For whatever the true facts of history may have been, the artistic development of this drama calls for some more serious confrontation—not necessarily face to face—between Dimitry and Boris; whereas Boris' sudden death not only permits him to escape vengeance in this world, but—by depriving Moscow of a skilled and experienced ruler—hands Dimitry an easy triumph, so easy that it is disappointing and anticlimactic.[20]

If Pushkin failed in some respects in *Boris Godunov* as a dramatist, he nevertheless succeeded as a poet, and the work will continue to have a very strong appeal.

II   Count Nulin

Count Nulin is a short comic poem (370 lines) in freely rhymed iambic tetrameters. It was written, according to Pushkin, in two mornings—December 13 and 14, 1825.[21] The setting of the poem is the remote Russian countryside, with its atmosphere of tedium and isolation which Pushkin got to know so well in Mikhaylovskoe. The poem is in the nature of a parody of Shakespeare's *The Rape of Lucrece*. "The thought occurred to me," Pushkin relates, "of parodying both history and Shakespeare, and I could not resist this double temptation."[22] But though *Count Nulin* does indeed modernize and rework—with a difference—the story of Lucrece's rape by the infamous Tarquin, it has artistically little in common with what Pushkin called "Shakespeare's rather weak poem."[23] The true affinities of *Count Nulin* are with the comic verse tale (*conte*) of the Italian Renaissance, of La Fontaine, and—more immediately—with Byron's *Beppo*. In common with these literary predecessors Pushkin's poem is characterized by its racy style and sophisticated, amused view of sex.

The poem opens with a lively description of horns, huntsmen, and hounds in front of a country home. The landowner emerges, equipped with such essentials as a knife, a horn, and a flask of rum, and inspects the scene with satisfaction. Meanwhile, his wife, in nightcap and shawl, looks through the window, sleepy-eyed and irritated. The husband mounts his horse, shouts to his wife not to wait for him, and rides out.

What does a wife left alone do in her husband's absence? The wife, Natalia Pavlovna, takes no interest in such household chores as pickling mushrooms, feeding the geese, ordering meals, checking on the barn and the cellar; for she was not brought up according to the old patriarchal traditions, but in a foreign type boarding school for girls of noble families. She is bored. Suddenly a passing carriage overturns. Enter Count Nulin, limping slightly from his mishap, accompanied by his French servant, Picard. He is returning from abroad where he has dissipated his future income but acquired all the accessories of alien fashions—clothing of all sorts, the "right" books, opinions on the theater, the opera, the actresses, the latest *bons-mots* from Paris, and a contempt for all things Russian. He is on his way to Petersburg to display himself and his newfound talents. Meanwhile, it is time for dinner; Nulin joins the hostess

> And launches into conversation:
> Russia is frightful, he's amazed
> That folks can tolerate this place,
> He misses Paris, yes egad.
> "How's the theater?" "In poor shape.
> *C'est bien mauvais, ça fait pitié.*
> Talma has really gone downhill,
> Mad'moiselle Mars is getting old.
> There's really only Poitier left. . . ."
> "What writer is in fashion now?"
> "Still d'Arlincourt and Lamartine."
> "They're imitated here as well."
> "By Jove! You mean that here as well
> The mind is starting to develop!
> God grant enlightenment to Russia!"
> "How are the waistlines?" "Very low,
> Down almost to . . . well, down to here.
> If I may see your dress, Madame;
> Oh yes . . . the trim, the bows, the pattern;
> Almost exactly like the fashion."
> "You see, we get the *Telegraph.*"
> "Aha! Perhaps you'd like to hear
> A most delightful little song?"
> The count begins to sing, "But, count,
> Your food." "I've really had enough."

Enchanted by each other and by their scintillating conversation, the two spend a delightful evening together. But it is past

midnight and Natalia Pavlovna says that it is time they went
to bed:

> Reluctantly the Count,
> All tenderness and half in love,
> Rises to kiss her hand. Oh no!
> Oh what will coquetry not do?
> The flirt—and may she be forgiven—
> Just barely squeezes Nulin's hand!

They part company. Natalia Pvlovna is undressed by her maid,
Count Nulin by the French servant who provides him in bed
with a cigar, a cigar-clipper, a bedlamp, a carafe, a silver glass,
an alarm clock and a Walter Scott novel with uncut pages. The
count glances idly through his novel, but he is distracted by
thoughts of Natalia Pavlovna; he should have pressed his suit,
but it is still not too late:

> He straightway resolute threw on
> His gaudy, silken dressing gown,
> Knocked over in the dark a chair
> And, with soft expectations filled,
> This modern Tarquin 'gainst Lucrece
> Stole forth prepared to do or die. . . .

> Along the hall the amorous count
> Gropes in the dark and feels his way
> Aflame with ardor and desire. . . .
> Tries the brass door handle—and lo
> Quietly it yields; the Count goes in,
> Looks round: the lamp now burning low
> Casts through the room its feeble light;
> The lady's lying sound asleep—
> Or is her sleeping only feigned?
> The Count draws near, retreats, draws near
> Then flings himself down by her bed.
> And she . . . With great respect I ask
> The ladies of Saint Petersburg
> To picture to themselves the horror
> With which my heroine awakes
> And to decide what she should do.

> She, her large eyes wide open now,
> Looks at the Count—and he meanwhile
> Mouths amorous Gallic platitudes

> And stretches an audacious hand
> Toward the covers. Paralyzed,
> Confused, she lies unmoving . . . then
> Comes to her senses with a start,
> And—filled with anger and proud scorn,
> And, to be frank, maybe with fear—
> She swings with all her might, and on
> Our Tarquin's face implants a slap—
> And no mean blow it was at that!

At this point her small dog begins to bark, and Count Nulin retreats hastily. Next morning he is somewhat embarrassed at the prospect of having to confront his hostess. But she appears to be secretly amused and is as animated and charming as on the previous evening. Within a short space of time the Count is again at ease—and half in love again. There is a noise in the hall. It is Natalia Pavlovna's husband returning from the hunt. He greets Count Nulin cordially and invites him to stay. But the carriage has now been repaired, and Count Nulin leaves. After Nulin's departure Natalia Pavlovna tells her husband and the neighbors of his nocturnal exploit. The husband is furious. The one who is most amused over the incident and who most fully shares Natalia Pavlovna's merriment is a certain Lidin, a neighboring landowner, twenty-three years old.

This delightful little verse tale depends largely for its effect on the variations which Pushkin has worked on the Shakespeare theme: in place of Ancient Rome contemporary Russia and its benighted countryside; in place of a husband absent in the noble cause of war a husband absent hunting hares; in place of an event which allegedly changed the course of history a trivial incident which amused the neighbors; in place of a sinister Tarquin a foppish Nulin; and in place of a faithful wife who succumbed, an unfaithful wife who repulsed the onslaught—with the help of a hefty slap and a barking Pomeranian. The three main characters are sketched briefly, but with a sure hand: the husband noisy, hard-riding, hard-drinking, and imperceptive; Natalia Pavlovna useless, robust, and flirtatious; and, of course, the pivotal character of Count Nulin, in whom fatuousness, foppery, gallomania, and a sophisticated veneer go hand in hand with a so human weakness which is here voided of its darker implications—if only by the failure of his attempt.

With *Count Nulin* Pushkin proved again, as he had proved with *Ruslan and Lyudmila,* that when he turned his hand to the lighter genres of poetry and the lighter sides of human experience, his sense of humor and proportion and his over-all artistry almost invariably stood him in good stead. *Count Nulin* is a slender little poem, and its subject matter is trivial and frivolous indeed. It is also an unqualified success and deserves to be accorded its rightful place—among the best of Pushkin's masterpieces.

III   Poltava

Poltava was written in the short space of about three weeks in October 1828. It consists of a sixteen-line dedication, presumed to be addressed to one of the Raevsky daughters, Maria,[24] and three cantos (1487 lines in all). While the meter is familiar —iambic tetrameters freely rhymed—*Poltava* differs from anything Pushkin had written before. It is an interesting experiment in the fusing of different genres and linguistic styles: in structure and in certain passages *Poltava,* to some extent, calls to mind Pushkin's "Southern" romantic poems; but the narrator is no longer close as a person to his heroes, and the poem's involvement with history imparts a new epic quality. Stylistically and thematically parts of the poem are reminiscent of the eighteenth-century ode;[25] development of the action by means of dialogues (a technique already noted in *The Gypsies*) introduces the dramatic genre as a further element; one passage suggests the ballad form;[26] and stylistically and lexically the poem runs the full scale from the eighteenth-century "high style" (drawing on Old Slavonic elements in the language) to the oral tradition.[27] All in all, *Poltava*—whether thus consciously designed by Pushkin or not—was an ambitious literary effort.

For readers of English literature the plot will, as far as general orientation goes, call to mind Walter Scott's *Marmion;* both *Marmion* and *Poltava* are poems in which Romantic-type heroes and Romantic-type events are described on a known historical background. The main historical event described in Pushkin's poem is the Battle of Poltava (1709) in which the Russians under Peter the Great decisively defeated the Swedes under Charles XII. This Russian victory was the main turning point in the Russo-Swedish War. The main protagonists in Pushkin's poem were historical persons, though the heroine's real name,

Matryona, was changed in the poem to the more poetic Maria.

The first canto opens with a description of the wealth of Kochubey, a Ukranian noble. Kochubey's greatest pride is his daughter, Maria. She is both beautiful and modest, and has rejected many suitors. Her elderly godfather, Mazepa, who as hetman (military commander) is the leading power in the Ukraine, asks her parents for her hand; the parents refuse with indignation. The mother tells Maria:

> "No shame! No honor! At his age!
> How dare he? No, while we're alive,
> He shall not perpetrate this sin.
> Supposed to be a friend and father!
> And you, sweet innocent, his godchild!
> What madness! Bent with years, how dare
> He even think to be your spouse?"
> Maria trembled, and her face
> Grew mortal pale, and all her limbs
> Were seized with chill as from the grave,
> And down she fell into a faint.

It is indeed Mazepa whom Maria loves. For two days, weeping and groaning, she will not touch food or drink. On the third night she elopes. Kochubey, dishonored, plots vengeance. And at this point the personal fates of Maria, Kochubey, and Mazepa are affected by historical events:

> It was that troubled time in which—
> With Peter's genius at the helm—
> Embattled, straining nerve and will,
> Young Russia grew from youth to man.
> And in the arts of war and glory
> Stern master Peter proved; and harsh
> Were the lessons, swift and bloody,
> Dealt by the Swedish champion, Charles.
> But, after long and bloody trails,
> Weath'ring the heavy blows of fate,
> Russia grew strong. Thus is steel forged
> By blows which shatter glass to bits.

The Swedish forces under Charles are threatening Moscow, and the Ukraine is stirring with revolt. Though he feigns inactivity, Mazepa has secretly been making plans to betray Peter and

Russia by bringing the Ukraine over to the side of Charles XII.
Kochubey, knowing this, informs Peter. But his revenge mis-
carries because Peter believes Mazepa rather than Kochubey.
Kochubey is arrested by Mazepa. Maria does not know that her
father is being held in the dungeon of the castle in which she is
living with Mazepa.

The second canto consists mainly of dialogues. In the first of
these Maria complains to Mazepa that he is neglecting her.
Mazepa explains to her that he is preoccupied with his plans to
raise the Ukraine against Peter. He then asks her who is dearer
to her—her father or her husband:

> Now, answer me: if one of us,
> If either he or I must perish,
> And you were judge and had to choose,
> Whom would you name as victim? And
> Whom would your judgment spare from death?
> *Maria.* Oh, say no more! Do not torment
> My heart, nor tempt me so.
> *Mazepa.*   Reply.
> *Maria.* You're pale; the words you speak are harsh.
> Do not be angry. I am willing
> For you to sacrifice all things,
> Believe me. But say no more, your words
> Make me afraid.
> *Mazepa.*   Remember well
> What you have said just now, Maria.

The scene shifts to the dungeon. Kochubey is to be executed the
next day. He has already been tortured, and now he is tortured
again in an effort to pry from him where his treasures are hid-
den. His groans carry up to the ears of Mazepa who is unable to
sleep, wracked by his conscience and fearful of Maria's reaction
when she finds out about her father. Next morning Maria is
awakened by her mother who has come to her, unknown to
Mazepa, in the hope that Maria will persuade Mazepa to stay
her father's execution. Maria is appalled by what she learns.
The two women rush off. The canto concludes with a description
of the execution of Kochubey and his friend Iskra; two women,
tired and dusty, arrive at the scene—too late. Maria does not
return home. Mazepa sends out riders to search for her—without
result.

Sorrow does not prevent Mazepa from continuing his intrigues which he camouflages by pretending to be ill, at death's door. Suddenly Charles swings south into the Ukraine and, throwing off all subterfuge, Mazepa rises in revolt against Peter. Peter, taking energetic measures to minimize the spread of revolt in the Ukraine, hurries to meet Charles, and the opposing forces converge on Poltava. It is the night before the battle. In both camps all is quiet. In one tent, however, a whispered conversation is in progress. Mazepa confides to his friend, Orlik, that he has, he believes, made a great mistake in joining forces with Charles:

> .... No, I was wrong about this Charles.
> He is a brave and ready youth;
> Of course, he boldly leads the way,
> And twice or thrice can win the day. . . .
> But he is not the man to match
> And best the autocratic giant:
> The drums that wheel his regiments,
> He thinks, can change the course of fate;
> Impatient, stubborn, blind is he,
> And thoughtless and conceited too,
> And foolishly he trusts his luck,
> Measures the enemy's new strength
> With memories of past success.
> The hour of his defeat has come. . . .

Orlik suggests that Mazepa can still make his peace with Peter if the battle goes badly. But Mazepa tells him that it is too late; once during a feast, after Mazepa had said something that offended the Tsar, the latter had pulled him by his mustaches and threatened him; Mazepa had never forgiven the insult; let the dawn decide who shall flee.

The dawn comes and the battle begins; the Swedes begin to give ground:

> 'Twas then that Peter's ringing voice
> As though from heav'n inspired called forth:
> "On in God's name!"—and from his tent,
> A throng of favorites flanking him,
> Strides forth great Peter, eyes ablaze,
> His visage striking fear and awe,
> His movements swift, a prodigy
> Of nature, like the wrath of God.

The Russians are victorious. Charles and Mazepa flee. That night, while the fugitives sleep, Mazepa is awakened by Maria. She is thin, pale, tattered, with sunken flashing eyes and disheveled hair; she is mad, and her mind wanders through her fearful memories; she believes herself mistaken, this man is surely not her lover who was so handsome; she runs away, laughing wildly. In the morning the sleepless Mazepa, torn by sorrow and remorse, follows Charles, leaving behind him his native land. The poem concludes with a sort of epilogue, in which the author reflects, in effect, that only Peter the Great— of all those strong, willful people participating in the events described—truly left his mark on history.

Poltava has always been one of Pushkin's most controversial works. The reaction to its publication in 1829 was mixed, and on the whole hostile. Much of the criticism was of an historical rather than esthetic nature, concerning itself with Pushkin's interpretation of historical events, in particular his portrayal of the character of Mazepa, who was considered by some to have been in real life motivated by Ukrainian patriotism. The problem of historical accuracy was also raised in connection with the character of Charles, who was held to have fared badly at Pushkin's hands, being completely dwarfed by the formidable figure of Peter. To this Pushkin objected that the opinion of Charles as a madcap and irresponsible boy is expressed by Mazepa, not by the narrator. It must be conceded, however, that the whole tenor of the narrative describing the battle confirms Mazepa's low opinion.[28]

It is, in any case, on esthetic grounds that *Poltava* must be judged. Here, too, opinions have been divided—and continue to be so. Pushkin himself was sensitive to criticisms of this work which he regarded as "mature" and "almost completely original." He was at pains to understand how *Poltava* could be harshly treated, while *The Prisoner of the Caucasus*, which he rated far lower, had been accorded so enthusiastic a reception. *Poltava* must by all standards be reckoned a considerable achievement. There are, however, valid reasons for finding fault with it. First, Mazepa, however unpalatable his personality in real life may have been, is something of a literary cliché, portrayed in the melodramatic tones reminiscent of a Gothic novel villain. Then too, the childish business in the second canto of Mazepa's tricking Maria into choosing him over her father is a blemish. The battle scene in the third canto is described in intentionally hyperbolic language, and the larger-than-life portrait of Peter is acceptable in terms of the laudatory tradition of the eighteenth century, but one cannot help wondering why both Charles and Mazepa—in contrast with Peter—should at various moments in the battle be "plunged in thought." In this and other details *Poltava* gives evidence of overly hasty workmanship. But the main quarrel—and this has been expressed in different ways by various critics from Belinsky on—is with Pushkin's failure to fuse successfully the personal and the historical, or, one might say, his failure to fuse the "Romantic" poem and those elements in plot and style which reflect the genres of the heroic ode and the epic. At the beginning of the poem—in the excellent first canto—it is the individual fates of Maria, Mazepa, and Kochubey which hold the attention, while historical events provide the background; but in the third and final canto, notwithstanding Maria's nocturnal confrontation with Mazepa, the individual fortunes of the protagonists are completely overshadowed by the civic, patriotic theme of the Russian victory at Poltava. This shift of emphasis is—esthetically—disappointing. The attempted fusion between the civic theme and the personal in *Poltava*, is, in fact, imperfect. That such a fusion is possible was to be proved with remarkable success by Pushkin some five years later in the writing of *The Bronze Horseman*.

CHAPTER 4

Thoughts of Marriage: The "Little Tragedies"

I Restless Years (1826–1831)

PUSHKIN's return from exile in 1826 had been a personal triumph. It was not long, however, before his life again began to run into trouble. He found himself under police supervision. It was not enough that he, as a member of the Russian aristocracy, had given his word of honor to his Tsar. He found himself constantly obliged to account for his actions to Count Benkendorf, chief of the Third Section of the Tsar's private chancery, and in effect chief of security police. Upon requesting permission to visit Petersburg, Pushkin was obliged to suffer the latter's admonishments that he be on his best behavior while in the capital. Furthermore, the Tsar's promise that he would become Pushkin's personal censor was not kept. Either through indifference or lack of time, Nicholas delegated these duties to Benkendorf and his staff. One pinprick after another produced in Pushkin the feeling of being constantly surveyed and harassed. A genuine crisis arose in his life when in 1828 a copy of the blasphemous *Gavriiliada* came to light, and Pushkin was accused of having written it. A special investigating commission was set up by Nicholas I, and Pushkin, required to appear before the commission, denied authorship. His denial was not accepted. In all probability the authorities had in their possession reliable evidence to the effect that Pushkin was indeed the author. The Tsar ordered the commission to summon Pushkin once more and to "tell him in my name that, knowing Pushkin personally, I believe his word. But I desire that he help the government in discovering who could have composed such an abomination, and who could offend Pushkin by placing it under his name." Driven to the wall, Pushkin asked permission to send a sealed letter to the Tsar. Permission was granted and the letter written. Pushkin admitted to writing *Gavriiliada* and begged forgiveness. The Tsar ordered that the investigation be dropped.

Partly as a result of the government's harassments, Pushkin developed a growing sense of restlessness. We find him requesting permission to take part in missions to Paris and even to China. But his participation was not required. In 1829 his restlessness, aggravated by lack of success in the courtship of his future wife, drove Pushkin to make an unauthorized journey south to the Army of the Caucasus, in which his brother was serving and where he found many of his friends. The journey was not made in secret, and Pushkin's moves were followed faithfully by the authorities who warned the commanding officer of his impending arrival and told him to allow Pushkin to visit. However, on Pushkin's return, he was assailed by one of Benkendorf's letters and required to explain his unheralded and unauthorized journey.

The trouble did not lie entirely with Nicholas I or with Benkendorf. The trouble lay also in Pushkin himself. The social pleasures, of which Pushkin had been deprived during his exile in Mikhaylovskoe, did not entirely suit the poet and tended to produce in him a sense of aimlessness. While on the one hand he professed to despise social life, on the other hand he found difficulty in abstaining from it when it was available. Also, he was a near compulsive gambler and frequent loser. And as a result of these varied activities, the work he was able to produce diminished in volume. He was also becoming convinced that his youth was past and that so far he had failed to achieve a satisfying way of life. All in all, Pushkin was becoming increasingly afflicted with moods of despair, and particularly in 1829 we find in his poetry what amounts to almost an obsession with the thought of death.

The way out of this impasse which seemed most feasible to Pushkin was that of marriage. As early as 1826 he proposed and was turned down. It was not, perhaps, that marriage would lead to ecstatic happiness; rather, marriage seemed to be the conventional thing at Pushkin's age, and Pushkin felt that the conventional paths—which he had hitherto neglected—might offer the possibility of a more peaceful and more stable existence. The woman whom he finally chose to court was Natalia Nikolaevna Goncharova, a young and beautiful girl who was just coming out in Moscow society. The choice can scarcely be considered a felicitous one if stability was to be his goal. Natalia Nikolaevna had almost no interest in literature, considerable social aspirations, and her family had no money. For Pushkin, who himself had no money, to take upon himself the burden of promoting Natalia Nikolaevna's social career was in itself an act of pure folly. But, thoughts of the stable life apart, Pushkin was strongly attracted to Natalia Nikolaevna, and his ego was flattered by the thought of winning this beautiful prize.

From the standpoint of the Goncharov family, Pushkin himself was by no means a desirable match. He lacked money, had a record of dissipated bachelor living, and had been in trouble with the authorities. Here again, ironically enough, Benkendorf was to play a role in Pushkin's life. In order to satisfy the Goncharov family as to the fact that he was *persona grata* with the authorities, Pushkin was obliged to request a letter of recommendation from Benkendorf. It should be added that the fiancée was not in love with Pushkin and was simply obeying her mother's orders.

After Pushkin eventually gained the mother's consent, the engagement was constantly marred and threatened by quarrels over money. The impoverished Pushkin was obliged to provide his bride's trousseau and help financially in other ways. More than once the engagement appeared on the verge of being broken. And when the marriage eventually took place, on February 18, 1831, there was almost no one—friend of the bride or the groom—who has willing to predict a happy future.

Pushkin hoped desperately that marriage would bring him new happiness and give a new meaning to life. But he, too, was a prey to misgivings. It is remarkable that the period of his engagement is marked in his writings by a constant nostalgic looking backward to the past—to past loves, past experiences, past freedoms. Not surprisingly, this was one of the most productive periods of his life. During the autumn of 1830, in particular, when, owing to a cholera epidemic, the engaged Pushkin was reluctantly confined to his father's estate of Boldino, Pushkin wrote more than ever before or later. Confrontation with marriage caused Pushkin to weigh very deeply some of life's most basic problems. This found expression in many of his lyrics (discussed in Chapter 7). It also found expression in the so-called "little tragedies" which form the subject of the present chapter.

II   *The "Little Tragedies"*

The "little tragedies" are four in number: *The Covetous Knight, Mozart and Salieri, The Stone Guest* and *The Feast During the Plague*.[1] They were written in an incredibly short space of time during Pushkin's highly productive autumn of 1830 at Boldino; but (with the exception of the fourth, which is basically a translation of part of an English play) their conception dates back several years, to the Mikhaylovskoe days when Pushkin wrote his *Boris Godunov*. Like *Boris Godunov* the "little tragedies" are written in unrhymed iambic pentameters, but—unlike *Boris Godunov*—they dispense with the regular caesura after the fourth syllable; intonationally, therefore, their lines represent a complete break with the French *décasyllabe* tradition (already under way in *Boris Godunov* notwithstanding the caesura). We recall from our earlier discussion of *Boris Godunov* that part of Pushkin's admiration for Shakespeare rested on the breadth and manysidedness of Shakepeare's characters. In the "little tragedies" there is a deliberate striving for the psychological complexity which Pushkin admired in Shakespeare.

The format for the "little tragedies" came to Pushkin from the now little-known English writer, Barry Cornwall (1781–1814), whose "dramatic scenes," while they had little impact on the essence of Pushkin's works, did serve as a model from the standpoint of genre. The "little tragedies" are indeed "little," ranging in length from about 550 to 231 lines. The successful staging of the "little tragedies," if only because of their brevity, will always present a difficult challenge to the producer. But this is not in itself important. Their merit, as I shall attempt to show, lies elsewhere.

In the "little tragedies" the highlights are not really of a dramatic nature—if by *dramatic* one means decisive action, by word or deed. The most impressive passages in these plays have about them a decidedly lyric quality.[2] This is not to say that they do not fit in perfectly with their dramatic setting. But their impact has definite affinities with that of the lyric in that—over and above the action—they hold us with what they have to say about life, about a specific problem, or an emotional attitude.

Another quality, which is characteristic of so much of Pushkin's writing, and certainly of the lyric poems of his mature age, is the concision and terseness of his style, the compression of thought. As has been noted by others, every line is made to count.[3] This compression should be borne in mind lest our expectation of "theater" in the normally accepted sense lead to frustration and blind us to the true qualities of these outstanding works. Whether "tragedies" or "little," the works now under discussion are best thought of, in effect, as belonging to a genre other than the conventional, accepted, and familiar genres of the literary tradition.

Pushkin toyed with the idea of calling them "dramatic investigations."[4] This would have been by no means inappropriate, for each of the four pieces holds up for examination—through the medium of the characters involved—a specific problem, dilemma, or conflict of life. This concentration on a single dilemma is at first sight more reminiscent of Molière—with his "personifications of a specific passion or vice"—than of Shakespeare. It is in his depiction of the dilemma's complexities that Pushkin comes closer to Shakespeare. Nevertheless, a basic difference between the methods of the Russian and the Englishman should be noted. We know already Pushkin's view that Shakespeare's characters are "living beings, full of many passions and vices; changing circumstances bring out before the spectator the diversity and manysidedness of their characters." Shakespeare, of course, had five acts in which to present the "changing circumstances." The poetic medium chosen by Pushkin—by its brevity—is clearly more restrictive when it comes to characterization. Pushkin's "little tragedies," with the exception of The Stone Guest, present very few "changing circumstances"; instead they present conflict-laden situations. Thus the breadth of character sought by Pushkin is achieved by depicting the many complex facets of the problem as seen through the eyes of the character or as inferred from the character's words and reactions.

The Covetous Knight centers on a conflict between father and son over money. The son desperately needs money in order to participate in tournaments and, in general, further his knightly career; the rich but miserly father, the Baron, regards the son as a spendthrift, hoards his wealth, and deprives his son. It is generally believed that there was a link between The Covetous Knight and the differences over money between Pushkin and his own miserly father. It was probably to conceal the suspicion of any such link that Pushkin added the misleading subtitle: "Scenes from Shenstone's Tragicomedy *The Covetous Knight*," for neither William Shenstone (1714–1763), the English poet, nor any other English author, is known to have written anything comparable.

In the first of the three scenes which make up *The Covetous Knight* the son, Albert, is found lamenting over his predicament to his servant, Ivan. His helmet was broken in his most recent tournament, his horse is limping, he wishes to buy another one—but the Jewish moneylender, with whom he has had dealings, refuses to lend him any more, Ivan tells him, unless he can provide security. The Jew enters and Albert both pleads with him and browbeats him in an attempt to get the money. Is not his knightly word of honor sufficient? His father is rich; surely his father will not outlive him? The Jew replies:

> Who knows? Our days are numbered—not by us;
> The youth who thrives today, tomorrow's dead,
> Laid out, and lo, is to the graveyard borne
> On the stooped shoulders of four aged men.

The baron is in good health, the Jew says, and may live even thirty years more. The Jew then suggests that through an acquaintance he might obtain some poison so that the son could poison his father. Albert becomes furiously indignant and threatening, and the Jew beats a hasty retreat. Shaken, Albert calls for a glass of wine. Ivan reminds him that there is no wine; he has given away his last bottle to a sick blacksmith. Albert asks for water and decides that he will go to the Duke and demand that his father be forced to treat him justly.

The second scene takes place in the Baron's cellar and consists entirely of a 118-line monologue, in which the miserly Baron lovingly examines his treasures and expounds on their significance for him. In this scene, which is undoubtedly the highlight of this short drama, Pushkin's characterization techniques are at their best. It is, as indicated above, not "changing circumstances" that are involved, nor even really breadth of character. It is, rather, as we shall see, Pushkin's ability to play devil's advocate. After a first scene in which miserliness is viewed in the simplest terms—from the standpoint of the victimized son—as a thor-

oughly uncongenial vice, Pushkin now about-faces and permits
us to see—from the inside—all the complicated motives and attitudes which underlie the father's behavior:

> Like a young rake who waits his evening tryst
> With some lewd, profligate deceiving wench
> Or foolish woman tricked by him, so I
> Have all day waited till I might descend
> In secret to my trusty treasure chests.
> O happy day! Today one handful more. . . .
> 'Tis but a pittance, true; but in small ways
> Do treasures grow. Somewhere I chanced to read
> Of how some King once bade his warriors fetch
> Handfuls of earth and pile them in a mound,
> And a proud hill rose up—and thence the king
> Could from the summit happily survey
> The vale below, where tent on tent gleamed white,
> And the blue sea alive with scudding sails.
> So to my cellar here I too have borne
> My daily tribute, piece by little piece,
> And built my hill—and from its summit I
> Can look upon what lies in my domain.
> What lies not there? Like some divinity,
> I can from here hold sway o'er all the world;
> If such my wish, then palaces shall rise;
> And in my sumptuous gardens, if I wish,
> Will gather sprightly nymphs in loveliness;
> To me the Muses will their tribute pay,
> Genius' free spirit shall obey my whim,
> And virtue shall, sleepless endeavor too,
> Stand meekly by, begging of me reward.
> One finger lifted, and obediently
> Shall bloodied malefactors timid wait
> To lick my hand and look into my eyes
> To read my will and take their orders thence.
> All things obey me, I no thing obey;
> I am above desire; I am content;
> I know my power; and 'tis enough for me
> That I should know it. . . .

His treasure is for the Baron not merely gold. He knows what it
represents in terms of human suffering, crime, deception, tears,
entreaties, and curses. And then the agonizing thought of his heir:

I rule ... but who will follow in my steps
To rule this realm when I am gone? My heir!
A young and giddy-headed squanderer,
The bosom friend of fellow debauchees!
Scarce I'll be dead, and he will hither come,
Hither beneath these peaceful, silent vaults,
He and his fawning, greedy courtiers.
Stealing these keys from my dead body, he
Will open up these treasure chests—and laugh. ...
He'll squander all ... But by what right? What right?
Was it at such small cost I made this mine?
Like some lighthearted gambler who in jest
Shakes out the dice and gathers in his gains?
Who knows the bitter sacrifices made,
The passions held in check, the heavy thoughts,
The daily cares, the long and sleepless nights
That this has cost me? Or will my son say
That I knew no desires? Will he say too
That conscience never gnawed into my heart ...?
Let him first suffer that hard road to wealth;
Then let us see if the unhappy wretch
Will squander what was won by sweat and blood.
Could I but from unworthy eyes conceal
This treasure vault! Could I but from the grave
Come hither as a ghostly sentinel,
Stand watch upon my chests, and from the living
Preserve my treasures as I can today ...!

The concluding scene opens with Albert's complaint to the Duke. The Duke is sympathetic and has already summoned the Baron. As the Baron enters, the Duke orders Albert into the next room. After some moments of courteous converstion, the Duke asks the Baron why his son is never at court. After giving various excuses, the father charges that his son has wanted to kill him and has tried to steal from him. The latter accusation provokes the son, who has been listening from the next room, to burst in and accuse his father of lying. The father throws down his glove and the son picks it up, accepting the challenge, and exclaiming: "I thank you. My father's first gift to me." The Duke intervenes and hounds the son from the room, but the father collapses and dies, uttering his final words: "Where are my keys? My keys, my keys!"

Where lies, we may ask, the esthetic appeal of this three-scene drama? The drama ends with the father's death, but this end is no climax of the type to be found, for example, in the last act of *Hamlet*. Some commentators have seen a climax in the father's challenge accepted by the son with the remark that this is the first gift he has received from his father, and the allusion here to a somewhat similar episode in Molière's *L'Avare* has been studied. A certain amount of psychological interest—from the point of view of characterization—is to be derived from the son's underlying desire for his father's death, a desire which he has never formulated or faced up to until he is provoked by the Jew's suggestion of poisoning the Baron and becomes vehemently indignant precisely because this suggestion echoes his own subconscious wish.[5] But these happenings and psychological insights are sketched in very summary fashion. They do not in themselves justify the high acclaim accorded to this drama. In effect, scenes 1 and 3 really do little more than provide a framework and a justification for the second scene, the truly moving and effective monologue of the Baron. The father's death in the last scene is, it is true, no real climax, but it is significant that his dying words—"My keys! My keys!"—re-evoke the entire second scene and, in particular, its closing thoughts. It is then the second scene that is esthetically the focal point of *The Covetous Knight*, and the fact that this scene is a monologue recalls to mind what was said above with regard to the lyric quality of the "little tragedies." To feel the appeal of the second-scene monologue, it is not necessary to be a miser or imagine oneself a miser; one has only to know—what many know—that success is sometimes obtained at the expense of others and leaves in its wake a troubled conscience, and that worthwhile achievement is usually the fruit of painful endeavor and deliberate self-denial.

The "problem" of *Mozart and Salieri* is envy (Pushkin appears to have contemplated calling it *Envy*)—the envy of industrious and conscientious talent for effortless and unmerited genius. Here again, in this shortest of the "little tragedies," we are struck not so much by the breadth of character of the protagonists as by the complicated nature of the problem. Just as in *The Covetous Knight* miserliness was not dismissed as a mere vice, so here Salieri's envy of Mozart is not a simple emotion; it is based on Salieri's outraged feeling for justice and purpose in the scheme of life; it raises a metaphysical question as to the ordering of the universe.

Mozart and Salieri consists of only two scenes. It is based on a rumor that on his deathbed Salieri confessed to having murdered Mozart out of envy. The first scene opens with Salieri ruminating alone:

> They say that there's no justice here on earth.
> But there's no justice—this I clearly see—
> No justice either in the heavens above.

He was born with a love of art. He sacrificed pleasure and other pursuits to devote himself entirely to music. First, he had sought perseveringly to acquire knowledge and technique. Only when these had been mastered, had he started—diffidently and in secret—to compose. When the great Gluck appeared and opened up new horizons, Salieri had abandoned all that he had learned and loved and, modestly, uncomplainingly, followed in Gluck's footsteps. At long last his perseverance had brought him renown: he had found a tranquil pleasure in his labor and in his success, and in the labors and successes of his friends, co-workers in the service of glorious art. Never had he known envy. Until now. He admits:

> . . . . I feel envy—deep,
> Tormenting envy. O ye heavens above,
> Is this your justice when the sacred gift
> Of deathless genius is bestowed upon—
> Not upon ardent love, self-sacrifice,
> Not upon labor, diligence and prayer—
> But sent to crown with light a madcap's head?
> Idle reveller, Mozart, that you are!

Enter Mozart. He had been on his way to visit Salieri with a piece he has recently composed, but—passing a tavern—he had heard a blind old violinist mutilating one of his arias. He brings the old man in and has him play an aria from *Don Juan*. The excruciating performance amuses Mozart, but Salieri is disgusted and deeply shocked at Mozart's amusement. Mozart gives the old man some money and sends him on his way. Mozart then plays for Salieri his latest composition—a sad, haunting, and beautiful piece. Salieri exclaims:

> . . . .'Twas this that you were bringing;
> Yet on your way you at some tavern stopped
> To listen to this blind violinist! God!
> You, Mozart, are not worthy of yourself.
>   *Mozart.* You think it's good?
>   *Salieri.* What depth that music has!
> What bold invention, perfect harmony!
> You, Mozart, are a god, and know it not;
> But I—I know.

Mozart leaves after agreeing to dine with Salieri at the Golden Lion. Salieri decides to poison him. For years Salieri has had poison in his possession. Perhaps it would be used on someone who insulted him. Often life has seemed liked some "unendurable wound," and often has he sat at one table with some "carefree enemy." But no—though no coward, Salieri has held his hand; there would come, perhaps, a worse enemy, a more grievous insult. Perhaps he would use the poison on himself, for "life I love but little"; but then, too, he has been deterred by the thought that new gifts may suddenly be bestowed on him:

> And ecstasy, perchance, would be my guest,
> Nights of discovery and inspiration;
> Perhaps some great new Haydn would create
> New marvels in which I could take delight. . . .

But now the hour has struck. The poison will be for Mozart— Mozart who never had to acquire his skills by labor, Mozart whose genius was given him by the gods, Mozart who—sin of sins—seems even unaware of his own gifts, Mozart who is discrepancy and contradiction in the established order of effort and just reward which Salieri seeks to defend.

The second scene takes place in the Golden Lion. Mozart is low in spirits. He has written a Requiem, ordered by an unknown visitor in black. The visitor has not returned, but Mozart feels haunted by his unseen presence. Salieri recalls how Beaumarchais once told him that, when besieged by dark thoughts, a person should either open up a bottle of champagne or read through *The Marriage of Figaro*. Mozart asks Salieri if there is any truth in the rumor that Beaumarchais once poisoned someone.

> *Salieri.* I doubt it: he was too much of a jester
> To ply a trade like that.
> 　*Mozart.* He was a genius.
> As you and I are. Genius and evil,
> Like oil and water, do not mix. Agreed?
> 　*Salieri.* You think so? (*He pours the poison into Mozart's glass.*)
> Well, drink up then.
> 　*Mozart.* To your health,
> My friend, I drink, and to that loyal bond
> Which joins together Mozart and Salieri,
> Two of sweet music's sons.

Mozart then plays his Requiem for Salieri who is in tears. Mozart ponders:

> If only one and all could feel the power
> Of music! No! It could not be, for then
> The world would cease to turn; none would there be
> To take in hand life's lowly, trivial tasks;
> And all would know that freedom which is art. . . .

Mozart feels unwell and leaves, bidding Salieri farewell.

> 　*Salieri.* Good-bye.
> (*Alone.*) You'll sleep a long, long sleep,
> Friend Mozart! But could it be that he's right,
> And I'm no genius. Genius and evil,
> Like oil and water, do not mix? Not true.
> Great Michelangelo—did he not kill?
> Or was that but a fairy tale put out
> By idle tongues, by the dull-witted crowd?

And so Salieri is left with his tormenting doubts.

Here again Pushkin has played devil's advocate with telling effect. While one can harbor no doubts as to the author's sympathy for Mozart, while Salieri's indignation at the blind violinist's faulty playing and at Mozart's jesting emphasizes his pedestrian pedantry as contrasted with the ironical playfulness of genius,[6] Pushkin has made a strong case for Salieri, whose sense of injustice also clearly commands the author's sympathy. It is not, surely, pure chance that *The Covetous Knight* was dated by Pushkin October 23 and that *Mozart and Salieri* was completed on October 26—only three days later. For the problems posed in these two "little tragedies" are by no means dissimilar. While the settings are very different, the two dramas have this in common: they both depict characters who have acquired something by painful effort and who resent the thought of someone else acquiring the same thing—or more—with no effort at all, and—worse still—without even being aware of the painful effort involved. And this sense of injustice is pleaded—convincingly—in one case through the mouth of a miser, in the other through the mouth of a poisoner![7]

The Stone Guest is the longest of the "Little Tragedies" and the most "dramatic" in the sense that it contains more events, more "changing circumstances" than the other three. At the same time, the "problem" that preoccupied Pushkin in *The Stone Guest* was one that greatly preoccupied him in his personal life at the time of writing; consequently, there is in this short drama a strong *lyrical* and *subjective* element.

The first of the four scenes comprising *The Stone Guest* opens outside the gates of Madrid. Don Juan is returning secretly from exile, accompanied by his servant, Leporello. The place recalls to his mind a past affair—with Ineza, poor Ineza, who has perished, presumably as a result of Don Juan's attentions. Ineza was not really beautiful, the Don concedes, but her eyes . . . ! He had wooed her for three months. Her husband was a scoundrel and a harsh man, Don Juan had discovered—too late. Poor Ineza! But, as Leporello points out to his master, Ineza was followed by other women and there will be others in the future too. The Don agrees and, shaking off his remorse, announces that his first visit in Madrid will be to Laura. Enter a monk who, not recognizing Don Juan and Leporello, tells them that Doña Anna will arrive shortly, as she does every day, to weep and pray in front of the monument she has erected to her late husband, the Commander, killed by Don Juan in a duel. She will talk to no man except a monk, and she is beautiful. Don Juan's amorous curiosity is aroused. Enter Doña Anna to pray, but she is so shrouded in her cloak that Don Juan's curiosity remains for the moment unsatisfied. Meanwhile, dusk has fallen, and it is safe to enter Madrid.

The second scene opens with Laura entertaining guests. She is an actress and has just finished an absolutely inspired performance. Her guests beg her to sing for them while she is still in this aroused state. She obliges, to their delight, and on being asked who composed the words of the song, she informs them that the words are by Don Juan, "my faithful friend, my fickle-hearted lover." This admission provokes a jealous outburst from one of the guests, the taciturn Don Carlos, who is in love with Laura, and whose brother has been killed by Don Juan in a duel. Incensed at Don Carlos' outburst, Laura threatens to have Don Carlos killed by her servants. Swayed not by fear but by love, Don Carlos begs forgiveness, and the quarrel ends. As the guests leave, Laura bids Don Carlos to stay: his passionate fury reminds her of Don Juan. Suddenly there is a knocking. Enter Don Juan. Laura throws herself into his arms. Don Carlos and Don Juan fight, and the former is killed. Don Juan, indifferent to the presence of the corpse, proceeds to make love to Laura.

The third scene takes place, like the first, in the vicinity of the Commander's statue. Some time has elapsed, during which Don Juan, disguised as a monk, has been coming to this spot every day in order to see Doña Anna. He is resolved that today he will speak to her. Enter Doña Anna. Don Juan addresses her. Doña Anna is surprised to hear such flattering and ingratiating words from a monk. Don Juan reveals to her that he is no monk. He is, he tells her, Don Diego, and he loves her without hope of reward; but his love for Doña Anna has for the first time revealed to him life's value and the meaning of happiness. Doña Anna is alarmed that someone will come, and agrees to receive him on the evening of the following day, provided he will respect her virtue. Doña Anna leaves, greatly agitated. Enter Leporello, who is informed by the triumphant Don that he has obtained a rendezvous. Leporello wonders what the Commander will think of that; the statue, he thinks, looks angry. But there is no stopping Don Juan. Carried away by his success, like a triumphant rival, he issues his invitation: "I, Commander, bid you come tomorrow/To your widow's home, where I shall also be,/And stand at the door on guard. Well? Will you come?" To Don Juan's surprise and horror, the statue nods agreement.

The final scene takes place on the following evening. Don Juan tells Doña Anna how happy he is to be alone with her in some place other than at her husband's graveside. Doña Anna is surprised that he can be jealous of the dead. She had not, she reveals, chosen her husband; she had been ordered to marry by her mother; but she cannot listen to words of love, a widow must be faithful even to the dead. Don Juan skillfully lets slip that he feels guilty toward Doña Anna. The latter's curiosity is aroused and, having been induced, in return for his frankness, to forgive him in advance, whatever his crime, she insists that he explain. Don Juan then reveals his true identity. Doña Anna almost faints from shock. Don Juan then admits that his reputation as an evil profligate is not altogether undeserved, but he has never loved before. Only now, through his love of Doña Anna, has he been reborn; only now for the first time, loving Doña Anna, has he learned what it is to love virtue. Doña Anna becomes concerned for Don Juan's safety; discovery would mean death. Don Juan is quick to retort that he will gladly lay down his life for one moment with her. He also points out that her concern for him surely means that, in spite of all, she does not hate him. Preparing to leave, he begs for another meeting, and Doña Anna agrees to receive him again the next day. He also begs for and receives one kiss—as a token of her forgiveness! Suddenly there is a knocking. Don Juan leaves, but immediately runs back in, followed by the Commander's statue. The statue asks for Don Juan's hand. They vanish together. Don Juan is killed. His last words: "Oh Doña Anna!"

The Stone Guest constitutes in many ways a radical departure from its predecessors in the Don Juan tradition. Both the character of the hero and the plot differ significantly from the earlier versions not only of Tirso de Molina (which Pushkin probably did not know), but also of Molière and Mozart—da Ponte, with both of which Pushkin was familiar. The changes which Don Juan underwent at Pushkin's hands are to be explained, partly, by the very brevity of his play which made change inevitable; partly, by the spirit of Pushkin's age; but largely, also by the relationship of the author to his hero and the nature of the problem which Pushkin took it upon himself to investigate.

The traditional Don Juan of de Molina, Molière, and Mozart was dedicated almost to the point of obsession to the act of seduction, completely promiscuous, recklessly brave, ruthless, and untroubled by remorse. Some of these characteristics reappear in Pushkin's Don Juan. But it is the manner in which Pushkin's hero differs from his predecessors that is revealing. For the differences in character and situation clearly indicate a close relationship between hero and author.

Like his predecessors, Pushkin's Don Juan is cavalierly gay, carefree, and reckless—a type which, however, let us note, appears in several Pushkin works and which corresponds to one of Pushkin's favorite images of himself. Pushkin's Don Juan is, of course, in the approved tradition, physically brave—and that Pushkin undoubtedly was. But, in contrast with his predecessors, Pushkin's hero is a poet. In contrast with his predecessors, Pushkin's hero is no mere lecher, with an unflagging and impartial zest for seduction. He is, rather, a connoisseur of women, capable of savoring their individual characteristics and taking delight in their difference rather than their sameness. His easy-come-easy-go relationship with Laura is the relationship of a man with a tolerant mistress—far removed from the catastrophe-laden affair with Ineza. His reminiscences of Ineza reveal, further, another aspect of his nature which sets him off from his predecessors: there is something of the poet in his approach to Ineza, in his ability to see what other men missed—the beauty of her eyes—which for him compensate for the mediocre appeal of her other physical attributes. The Ineza affair shows, too, that, contrary to tradition, he is capable—at certain moments—of remorse. Again contrary to tradition, he is willing to devote considerable time to the business of wooing and seducing: three months in the case of Ineza, and an unspecified period during which he masquerades as a monk in order to gain acquaintance with Doña Anna. Incidentally, masquerading and lying are basically alien to his nature. While the traditional Don Juan is willing to make use of the dark in order to impersonate another man, to promise marriage, to resort in fact to any device that will enable him to *gain his end,* Pushkin's Don Juan rejects all such deceits—not so much, one is tempted to feel, on moral grounds, but because his attitude to women and to himself impels him to demand that he be loved as himself and for himself. Pushkin's Don Juan is—at least until he encounters Doña Anna—a sophisticated hedonist with a touch of the poet and a touch of the lonely introspective in his nature. All of which, to a greater or lesser degree, brings him closer to his creator.[8]

If Pushkin's own personality influenced the character of his hero, so too, his personal life had a hand in shaping the plot. One minor detail is the transfer of the action from Seville to Madrid. In *The Stone Guest* Don Juan returns secretly and illegally from exile. In 1825 Pushkin himself had contemplated a similar unauthorized return from exile—to Petersburg, the capital of Russia. Since Pushkin *nearly* returned to the Russian capital, his hero must return to the Spanish capital; Madrid, therefore, is substituted for Don Juan's traditional Seville. Seville does appear, we may note, in a draft of Pushkin's work. The switch to Madrid in the final version must, therefore, be regarded as deliberate—and a further indication of the poet's tendency to identify with the hero.

A far more important break with tradition concerns the person of the Commander. The Commander is, traditionally, Doña Anna's father, killed by Don Juan defending his daughter's honor. Pushkin made him the ex-husband. This change may have been dictated by purely artistic considerations. But it is difficult to escape the conclusion that it was also tied in with Pushkin's subjective thoughts and feelings. In the fall of 1830 the poet was still only engaged to his future wife. Yet, without having possessed her, he was already morbidly obsessed by the thought of one day being replaced by another man. As early as April 5, 1830, he wrote to his future mother-in-law: "God is my witness that I am ready to die for her, but to have to die leaving her a beautiful widow, free to choose a new husband on the day after: this thought is hell." It should also be noted that Doña Anna did not marry the Commander for love, but in obedience to her mother—which was precisely the case with Pushkin's wife. Thus, Pushkin not only infiltrated some of his own personality into that of Don Juan; he was able to put himself in the situation of the Commander.[9] Returning to the work, it has been pointed out that in switching the Commander's role from ex-father to ex-husband, Pushkin was left without a motive for the duel that caused the Commander's death. But this is an insignificant loss indeed. And it is more than offset by the added meaning that Pushkin was able to give to Don Juan's invitation.

But by far the most important manner in which Pushkin's own preoccupations influenced *The Stone Guest* has to do with the central emotional problem of the work. Pushkin's bachelor existence had not been particularly happy; yet at the same time the prospect of marriage caused him considerable misgivings. Now, in the fall of 1830, as he prepared himself for this decisive change in life, the question of love and happiness was constantly on his mind. Could love bring true happiness? Could love give a value to life that it had never had before? Could a man through love of a woman be redeemed, born anew? These questions are basic to the whole conception of *The Stone Guest.*

It is legitimate to harbor doubts as to whether Don Juan's protestations of newfound love, newfound happiness, and newfound redemption are sincere. Could not all these lofty statements be simply ploys to ensnare Doña Anna? She herself is very much aware of this possibility: "Don Juan is most eloquent—I know./I've heard; he is a skilled and cunning tempter. . . .", and again: "Should I believe/That for the first time Don Juan's now in love!/Or does he seek in me his latest prey?" The thesis that Don Juan was in his dealings with Doña Anna seeking only to add to his list of victims has been maintained—most persuasively by C. Corbet.[10] Corbet sees Don Juan as a satanic seducer, intent—to the point of sadism—on Doña Anna's total humiliation, total undoing. He derives, according to Corbet, a diabolic pleasure from revealing to her his true identity as the man who killed her husband. Human motives are indeed mixed, and Corbet's insight on this last point may have a certain validity. However, there is another stronger motive—the need to be loved for oneself, for what one really is, without the aid of disguise or false pretenses. H. Kucera has astutely pointed to a parallel situation in *Boris Godunov,* where the Pretender, like Don Juan, is jealous of the dead, and where he insists on revealing to Marina what he really is—a poor monk. "In both the Pretender and Don Juan," Kucera observes, "one detects the same striving for completeness of love, manifested in their desire to be loved for themselves, in their own identity."[11] This seems to me to give the truer picture of Don Juan's psychology. Yet the doubt remains, a doubt which on the evidence of *The Stone Guest* alone cannot be finally resolved. Each one of Don Juan's fine phrases does indeed gain a point for him in the wooing of Doña Anna. Nor was Pushkin naive enough not to know that *today's sincerity can become tomorrow's falsehood.* Yet believe in Don Juan's sincerity of the moment we must, not merely because of the extrinsic evidence offered by Pushkin's biography, but because, without this belief, *The Stone Guest* loses much of its point.

Pushkin loved concision. In this case, however, his concision and the consequent ambiguity have rendered him a disservice. The one weakness of *The Stone Guest* lies in a certain degree of failure to make absolutely clear to the reader that Don Juan is experiencing feelings that are for him totally new. If the reader were completely convinced of this, if there were less room for ambiguity, then the reader's sympathy for Don Juan at the end would be increased and the feeling of tragedy would be heightened. For the tragedy of *The Stone Guest* is to be found, ambiguity notwithstanding, in the irony that Don Juan, who has never truly loved before, never known true happiness before, never before set much store by life, and never before believed in virtue, is snatched away from life at precisely the moment when life has acquired meaning and value for him, when love, happiness, and redemption seem within his grasp.

According to one interpretation, "Don Juan is really saved— saved by a woman."[12] But this is to impose on Pushkin's work the Christian ethic of the original Don Juan legend. Equally absent from *The Stone Guest* are both the Christian belief in damnation and salvation, and the romantic notion of salvation through love of a woman. If Juan had come to believe in redemption, it was redemption here on earth; the love and happiness he thought to have found were to be lived in this life —not in the hereafter. What *The Stone Guest* offers in place of the Christian ethos is the idea of poetic justice, retribution, the nemesis of Greek tragedy. Don Juan is, at the very start, revisiting the scene of a crime—involving Ineza. He goes on not merely to kill Don Carlos, which was unavoidable, but to make love to Laura with the dead Don Carlos in the room. There is, in effect, a macabre parallel between the second and the fourth scenes. In the former he consummates his love in the presence of the victim; the latter scene, following his callous and sadistic invitation to the statue to play the role of voyeur, could, if things had worked out that way, have produced a sort of repetition of the second scene; instead, at the most poignant moment in Juan's life, the tables are turned, retribution catches up with him, the dead man—his former victim and now apparently defeated rival —returns to exact his vengeance and destroy the Don. Juan does not really suffer the just punishment meted out by a Christian God; he is, rather, the victim of a pagan Nemesis. And when he dies, it is not fear of Hell or hope of Salvation that agitate him; it is the agony of being deprived of life—just when life had taken on a new meaning.

The Feast During the Plague is a fairly accurate line-by-line translation of Act I, scene 4, of John Wilson's *The City of the Plague* (1816), the setting for which was the London plague of 1665. The topic was obviously suggested to Pushkin by the cholera epidemic which was keeping him a prisoner at Boldino. The scene translated by Pushkin depicts a group of young revellers who are carousing and wantoning, although preserving a certain ritualistic dignity—as an act of defiance in the face of Death. The threat of nearby death goads them on, heightens the need for intense emotions, emancipating them from their normal habits and moral standards. They are driven by fear and by a sort of frenzied ecstasy induced by the consciousness of living on the brink of the grave.

A young man makes a speech in honor of the late departed Jackson [in Wilson's original Harry Wentworth] who but two days past was regaling them all with his keen jests and merry anecdotes. Let Jackson's death not bring sadness to the feast. He proposes a toast to Jackson. They drink. The Master of Revels then proposes that Mary sing them a sad, slow song, from her own part of the country—deliberately sad, so that afterwards they may readdress themselves to merriment with even greater zest. Mary sings a song (Pushkin here departs from the original) describing a village in its flourishing and prosperous days. Now church and school are empty, the fields unattended, only the churchyard is full as the victims of the plague are brought in. If (the song continues) an early grave is to be my fate, you whom I loved so much, do not come near the body of your Jenny. Leave the village and, when the plague is past, visit my poor dust, but even in heaven Jenny will not abandon her Edmond. The Master of Revels thanks Mary for the song. Mary wishes that she had never sung it outside her parents' cottage and bemoans her lost innocence. Louisa upbraids Mary for so playing on people's sympathy. At this point the hearse passes; Louisa faints, and is revived by Mary. The Master of Revels is then asked to sing a song—a hymn in honor of the Plague. Here again Pushkin departs from the original, with one of his most famous lyrics which, in part, translates roughly as follows:

> There is an ecstasy in battle,
> And on the edge of the abyss,

And in the raging ocean's might,
Mid threat'ning waves and darkling storm,
In the hurricanes of Araby,
And in the foul breathing of the Plague.

All, all that threatens us with death
Brings to the heart of mortal man
Some unexplained, delight—the pledge,
Perchance, of immortality.
And happy he who in the storm
Can find and feel these awesome joys.

And so to You, O Plague, our praise!
We shall not fear the tomb's deep dark,
We shall not tremble if You call!
Our sparkling goblets one and all
We raise, and quaff the fragrant wine,
Perchance, the fragrance of the Plague!

Enter a priest who remonstrates with the revellers. They bid
him leave. He reminds the Master of Revels:

Art thou that groaning pale-faced man of tears
Who three weeks since knelt by thy mother's corpse,
And kiss'd the solder'd coffin, and leapt down
With ragelike grief into the burial vault . . . ?
. . . . Would she not weep,
Weep even in heaven, could she behold her son
Presiding o'er unholy revellers. . . .

The Master of Revels refuses to leave; he is held here by self-
contempt and

by the new
And frantic love of loud-tongued revelry—
By the blest poison mantling in this bowl—
And, help me Heaven! by the soft balmy kisses
Of this lost creature, lost, but beautiful
Even in her sin. . . .

Let the old priest go in peace, he says, but cursed be he who
follows him. The priest reminds him of his dead wife. The
Master forbids him to mention the name of one who had "Once
thought my spirit lofty, pure, and free/And on my bosom felt
herself in Heaven."[13] The priest leaves, the feast continues, and
the Master of Revels remains brooding.

The connection between death and the excessively felt need for intense emotion that reasserts the awareness of living and seeks to cram a maximum of experience into a short span that may at any time be abruptly ended: this has been observed before—in war, in times of plague and disaster. It is not new in literature either with Pushkin or John Wilson. And the format in which this phenomenon was here worked out was, with the exception of the two songs, of Wilson's choosing rather than Pushkin's. Not too much, then, should be made of the underlying dilemma exposed in this short scene. But nor should the fact that *The Feast During the Plague* was basically a translation obscure the poignancy of the situation or the beauty of Pushkin's verse.

CHAPTER 5

Evgeny Onegin: *A Novel in Verse*

I Evgeny Onegin: *A Novel in Verse*

PUSHKIN started work on *Evgeny Onegin* in May 1823, while still in Kishinev. The poem was virtually completed in the fall of 1830, though it still lacked one short but essential passage which the author did not supply until October 1831.[1] Thus *Evgeny Onegin* was more than eight years in the writing. And even after 1831 Pushkin considered the possibility of returning to his poem. It goes without saying that Pushkin did not work uninterruptedly on *Evgeny Onegin:* it was often laid aside in favor of new endeavors, and there were frequent periods of idleness. But to no other work did Pushkin devote a comparable amount of his life nor, it is safe to assume, a comparable amount of thought. And this in itself makes *Evgeny Onegin* particularly deserving of attention.

In its final form the poem consists of eight cantos. Pushkin also wrote parts of two further cantos. One of these, now generally known as "Onegin's Journey," describes the hero's travels through different parts of Russia and gives the author's impressions of life in Odessa. The other, only fragments of which have so far come to light, appears to be the beginning of a sequel to *Evgeny Onegin* proper. The hero, existing evidence suggests, was in this canto to have become involved in the Decembrist movement. Pushkin burned one copy of this canto (1830), and the surviving fragments had to be deciphered from his notebooks where they were found in crudely coded form. On the basis of these fragments alone it can be confidently stated that the politically sensitive subject matter would have made this canto totally unacceptable to the censors and would have had most unpleasant consequences for the author.[2] Apart from these two omitted cantos, a number of passages which Pushkin eventually ruled out have survived, and his notebooks contain a great many textual variants showing his uncertainties as to the way

102

in which he would develop the story and, in general, providing interesting insights into the creative process. Worth mentioning also, in connection with the creative process, is the fact that Pushkin originally published the sixth canto as the "End of Part I," a certain indication that he at one time contemplated writing twelve cantos; indeed, doubt exists among scholars as to whether *Evgeny Onegin* was completed—or abandoned.[3] But with all these variants and vacillations, most of them normal enough in the work of any writer, it is the final version, as approved by the poet, that is here our concern.[4]

Each canto, or chapter as Pushkin preferred to call them, contains between forty and fifty-four stanzas, each stanza (excepting those few that are incomplete) consisting of fourteen lines which follow a regular rhyme scheme. (There are only four passages which do not conform to this pattern: the dedication; a song sung by peasant girls; and two letters, one from the heroine to the hero, one from the hero to the heroine.)

A detailed analysis of the characteristics of the "Onegin" stanza lies beyond the scope of this discussion. But the following points, briefly noted, may be of interest: (1) The "Onegin" stanza is written in four-foot iambics, still Pushkin's preferred meter at the time of writing, and alternates between masculine and feminine rhyme, that is, eight- and nine-syllable lines. (2) The rhyme scheme is as follows (small letters for masculine and capital letters for feminine rhymes): *AbAbCCddEffEgg*. (3) *Evgeny Onegin* was one of the first and one of the few occasions on which Pushkin used a regular stanzaic arrangement for anything beyond a lyric or short poem—the idea being most probably suggested to him by Byron's use of the Italian *ottava rima* in *Beppo* and *Don Juan*. (4) Although fourteen lines naturally call to mind the sonnet, the "Onegin" stanza is basically new— the final rhymed couplet, which lends itself so well to the epigrammatic or bathetic ending, being probably also suggested by Byron and, in general, the *ottava rima* with its similar "home-striking final couplet."[5]

It has already been noted that Pushkin preferred, in publishing *Evgeny Onegin*, to use the term *chapter* rather than *canto* (though in his letters he casually speaks of *cantos* quite often), and this preference is consistent with the subtitle: *A Novel in Verse*. That Pushkin chose to refer to his work as a *novel* is important for the literary historian. Unfortunately, it has generated a great deal of misplaced emphasis in critical works on *Evgeny Onegin*. It has been hailed as the first genuine Russian novel and the first great work of Russian Realism.[6] Such pointless claims are encouraged by the well-known fact that at that time the novel was the up-and-coming literary form; it was destined to dominate the nineteenth century; furthermore, the novel was (to cite only Balzac as an example) to prove itself an admirable vehicle for social analysis. Thus, to treat *Evgeny Onegin* as a novel (in the normally accepted sense) enables the critic to thrust it forward in time and to seek in this masterpiece virtues of a sociological order which have nothing to do with its esthetic merits. Pushkin's perfectly justifiable decision to call his work a *novel* is best seen in the light of the conscious efforts of contemporaries to break down the rigid Classical distinctions between genres and, specifically, of the tendency to speak of narrative poems as *tales* or *stories* (witness Byron's "Eastern Tales"). Furthermore, *Evgeny Onegin* does have very definite affinities with the novel: in particular, where subject matter is concerned, with such Sentimental-Romantic novels as Rousseau's *La Nouvelle Héloïse* and Benjamin Constant's *Adolphe*.[7] But in noting as an interesting fact of literary history the subtitle of Pushkin's work, let a plea be entered against exaggeration and against the misplaced emphasis to which this has given rise; and let us, finally, bear in mind that *Evgeny Onegin* is inconceivable outside the framework of the stanzas and verses in which it was written and which are of its very essence.

Actually, the stimulus to the writing of *Evgeny Onegin* came from another *novel in verse*: Byron's *Don Juan*, or rather from the first two cantos, which started Pushkin on his way. On November 4, 1823, Pushkin wrote to his friend and fellow poet, P. A. Vyazemsky, "I am writing, not a novel but a novel in verse —a devil of a difference. It's in the genre of *Don Juan*." The "novelty" of the *Don Juan* "genre" consisted precisely in its unification of prose and verse genres which had most often existed in separation. "The real model of *Don Juan*," Elizabeth Boyd notes, "is the picaresque novel, the great catchall of narrative and reflection, subject to no law but the author's desires." She goes on to list among *Don Juan*'s literary predecessors Lucian, Rabelais, *Don Quixote*, *Gil Blas*, *Gulliver's Travels*, *Candide*,

Tom Jones, Peregrine Pickle, and *Tristram Shandy.*[8] At the same time, *Don Juan* is also linked with an English verse tradition going back to Chaucer, and with the French and Italian tradition of the *conte* and the comic epic going back through Voltaire and La Fontaine to Berni, Ariosto, and Pulci. The "genre" of *Don Juan* is thus a hybrid which weaves together a goodly number of strands from the literary tradition, and of these strands the two most immediately evident are the comic epic and the novel—two genres which had themselves expanded to embrace most of the others.[9] Almost exactly the same can be said of *Evgeny Onegin.* Deriving to a great extent from the same literary tradition as *Don Juan,* and no less a hybrid than *Don Juan, Evgeny Onegin* is a combination of several genres, of which the two most obvious are the novel and the comic epic.[10]

The events described in *Evgeny Onegin* are supposed to be contemporary. The first chapter opens with the young hero, Evgeny Onegin, posting through the dust of the Russian countryside on his way to his uncle's sick bed. He reflects: "But, my God, how boring to sit day and night with a sick man, never leaving his bedside! What base deceit to keep a living corpse amused, to rearrange his pillows, sadly bring his medicine, sigh and think to oneself: Oh, when will the devil take you?" At this point the narrator interrupts his story to introduce the hero of the "novel" to his readers whom he addresses as "friends of Lyudmila and Ruslan"—thus establishing the link between *Evgeny Onegin* and Pushkin's earlier comic epic. Onegin, "my good friend," was born in Petersburg, on the banks of the Neva. His father had served nobly, now lived in debt, gave three balls a year, and finally went bankrupt. Onegin received a superficial education from his governess and tutor, and then came out in society, his hair done in the latest fashion, dressed like a London dandy. He could speak and write French perfectly, dance the mazurka, and bow with graceful ease: "What more can you expect? Society decided that he was clever and perfectly charming." His Latin—and Latin is not in fashion these days—was sufficient to decipher an epigraph, say a few words about Juvenal, put *vale* at the end of a letter or misquote a couple of lines from the *Aeneid.* He had no great urge to become a poet. He disliked Homer and Theocrites; however, he read Adam Smith and rated himself a profound economist. But his real *forte* and most con-

stant preoccupation was the art of tender passion glorified by
Ovid. In this he could play a part to perfection; appear gloomy
and depressed—or proud—or obedient—or attentive—or indifferent. He could be languidly silent—or passionately eloquent. He
could be casual and offhand—or could seem to forget himself
entirely in love. His gaze could be swift and tender—or shy—
or insolent, and at times his eyes would glisten with an obedient
tear. He could suit his techniques to either the innocent maiden
or the experienced coquette. He was diabolically clever in elim-
inating rivals. And, with all this, he still managed to remain on
good terms with the husbands.

Following is a description of a typical day in Onegin's Petersburg life. He rises late, goes for a drive, enjoys a gourmet dinner
with a bachelor friend, arrives late for the ballet which he finds
boring, and leaves before the end to dress in leisurely and
dandyish fashion for the ball. And the narrator, who has already
discoursed on the ballet, again breaks off to recall how he, too,
"in his days of gaiety and desire" had loved the ball: there is
no better place for a rendezvous or a billet doux, and he warns
the wives to be prudent and the mothers to watch their daughters more carefully; but "I am writing this now because it's a
long time since I myself was a sinner." Yes, but the narrator
would still love balls, were it not that they are bad for morals:
the crush, the glitter, the carefully planned attire of the women,
and especially their little legs and feet—but, alas, in all of Russia
you could find scarcely three shapely pairs. And for four stanzas
the narrator reminisces on feet: one pair of feet still torments
him in his dreams and he wonders where those feet are now;
for him the feet have more charm than the breasts or the cheeks;
he remembers envying the waves as they lapped lovingly over
those feet; and another time he held the fortunate stirrup in his
hand and felt in his hand that little foot. But he must cease to
sing the praises of haughty women; they are not worth the passions or the songs they inspire; their words and looks are as
deceiving as their little feet. Meanwhile, as Petersburg awakes,
Onegin returns sleepily to his bed; his day is ended. After mid-
day he will awake, and the same round will begin again.

But neither the social whirl nor his conquests bring happiness
to Onegin. These pleasures have palled, his feelings have con-
gealed; he is suffering, like Childe Harold, from spleen and

melancholy, from the *mal du siècle:* "neither society gossip, nor the game of boston, nor a tender glance, nor an immodest sigh, nothing moved him, he remained oblivious to all of these things." He tries to improve himself by reading, but books have no more appeal than women.

It was at this low ebb in Onegin's life that the author-narrator, suffering himself from a similar disenchantment with life, had become Onegin's friend: "He who has lived and pondered cannot help but despise people in his heart; he who has known emotion, is disturbed by the phantom of days gone past forever: for him enchantment is no more. . . ." On summer nights Onegin and the narrator would stand together above the Neva, reminiscing about the past and listening to the night sounds from the river. But the two had been separated by fate. Onegin learned that his uncle lay dying [here the narrator picks up at the point where he had started in the opening stanzas], hurried off to the estate, and arrived to find the old man already dead. He now finds himself the owner of the estate and for two days is charmed by the novelty of country living; but he soon sees that boredom and melancholy await him in the country no less than in the capital.

Installed in his old-fashioned home, Onegin—partly to pass the time—improves the lot of the serfs by putting the estate on a quit-rent basis. This change pleases the serfs, but is regarded by neighboring owners as a dangerous precedent, and they decide that Onegin is a crank and leave him to his own devices —to Onegin's relief. His one friend is Vladimir Lensky, a good-looking youth who has just returned to his estate from the university at Göttingen. As yet too young to have become disillusioned by the world's depravity, Lensky has brought back from Germany a "Göttingen soul," a love of Kant and Schiller, and, in general, an idealistic, romantic, impassioned view of life. He writes poetry about his lofty and sublime feelings, about parting and sorrow, about life's mystery, and about love. He believes in the unshakable loyalty of friends, and he believes that he will be joined in marriage to his predestined *âme soeur*. Lensky is rich and the neighbors consider him an excellent match for their daughters; but Lensky prefers the company of Onegin who, notwithstanding his own entirely different view of life, is alone capable of understanding the young poet.

Lensky confides to Onegin his love for Olga: "Ah, he loved as in our time people no longer love; he loved as only the poet's crazed soul is still condemned to love." Olga is the younger of two sisters from a neighboring estate. Lensky has loved her since she was scarcely more than a child; Olga is his *âme soeur,* his every thought, his young life's great love.

Olga is modest, obedient, cheerful, simple, and charming. Blue eyes, a sweet smile, flaxen hair, graceful movements, a pleasant voice, a slender figure, everything: but, the narrator says, "take any novel and you will surely find her portrait. It is very charming. I myself once found it most appealing, but I have grown immensely tired of it. Allow me, reader, to tell you about her older sister."

The older sister, Tatiana, is, unlike Olga, not really beautiful. She is pale, retiring, sorrowful, silent, and shy. She seems a stranger. Even to her own family. As a child, she did not know how to show her affection to her parents. She did not play with the other children, but would sit all day dreaming at the window, and she did not sew or play with dolls. Rather, her heart was captivated by the fairy tales told by the nurse. She loved to sit on the balcony watching the dawn come up, and at an early age she had become an avid reader of the sentimental novels of Richardson and Rousseau which had become more real to her than the life going on around her.

The third chapter opens with Onegin asking Lensky where he is off to and where he spend his evenings. On learning that he spends them with the Larin family [Olga, Tatiana, and their widowed mother]. Onegin expresses the opinion that this must be very boring; he nevertheless asks to be presented to Olga; Lensky is happy to comply that very day, and the two gallop off to the Larin home, where they are made welcome and subjected to the somewhat oppressive hospitality of oldtime rural Russia. Later, as they ride back together, they discuss the Larins. Onegin is yawning, but he assures Lensky that this is only "habit." "Which one," he wants to know, "was Tatiana?" "The sorrowful, silent one who came in and sat by the window." "Surely you're not in love with the younger one then?" "Why not?" "I would choose the other one if I were a poet as you are. Olga has no life in her features, just like a Van Dyck Madonna, round and red like that stupid moon on the horizon." Lensky replies curtly, and remains silent for the rest of the way back.

Onegin's visit to the Larin home gives rise to much gossip among the neighbors who link him with Tatiana and even talk about a date for the betrothal. Tatiana is vexed by the gossip, but in her heart she thinks with joy of a possible betrothal: her hour has come and she has fallen in love. For a long time now, her longings inflamed by her romantic imaginings, she has been waiting—for someone—and now her eyes are opened and she thinks: "this is the man!" Now all her thoughts, day and night, are of Onegin. She wanders in the woods, reading her "dangerous" novels, casting herself in the role of heroine.

"Tatiana, sweet Tatiana:" the narrator commiserates with his heroine, "I shed my tears with yours; you have surrendered your fate into the hands of a fashion-conscious tyrant. You will perish, dear one." Tatiana is afflicted with the pains of love. She tries, without success, to gain the understanding of her elderly nanny. "In my time," the nanny says, "we never heard of love." Tatiana calls for pen and paper, and, by the light of the moon, sits down to write to Onegin. Here the narrator feels it necessary to defend Tatiana against criticism of her imprudence; she is neither cold-hearted nor is she an experienced coquette adept at manipulating men; she is straightforward, knows no deceit, loves with all her heart, and is naïvely trusting. But another difficulty arises from the fact that Tatiana, who writes Russian imperfectly (like so many other delightful women whom the author has known), has used French in her letter; the narrator is obliged, "saving the honor of my native land," to offer "an incomplete and weak translation."

"I am writing to you," Tatiana's letter begins, "what more can I say? I know that it is now in your power to punish me with your contempt." She would never have written, if only he had continued to visit them—even once a week; but Onegin, people say, is unsociable. If he had never come, she would never have know him and she might have found someone else and become a faithful wife and virtuous mother. But no! She could never have given her heart to another! She belongs to Onegin; that was predestined, the will of heaven; all her life has been a preordained prelude to her meeting with him. She had dreamed of him before she saw him; when she met him, she recognized him at once. Perhaps all this is the self-deception of her inexperi-

enced heart; perhaps destiny has decreed otherwise. But so let
it be! She entrusts her fate to him; she begs for his protection;
here she is alone, no one understands her, she must perish in
silence. She waits for him. Let him give her hope with one
glance or shatter her painful dream with a rebuff, alas, deserved:
"I end my letter. I'm afraid to read it through. I am dying of
shame and fear. But I am protected by your sense of honor, to
which I boldly entrust myself."

The letter is sent. Anxiously Tatiana waits for a reply. But
the days pass—and nothing. Then one day suddenly the sound
of galloping hoofs: it is Onegin. In panic Tatiana rushes out by
a side door into the garden and beyond. She collapses breathless
on a bench, and waits for the pounding of her heart to subside.
Finally she gets to her feet and starts to walk. But as she turns
the corner into the garden walk, there—with flashing eyes, like
some menacing shadow—Onegin stands before her. But the narrator lacks the strength today to relate what happened; he must
relax and rest; he will finish off later—somehow or other.

The fourth chapter opens with the narrator reflecting on love
and the art of seduction. The less we love a woman, the more
attractive we are to her, and the easier it becomes to work her
destruction. At one time the art of coldhearted seduction was
highly esteemed; but the hypocrisy, the deceit, and the repetition are in reality boring and nauseating. And this is precisely
how Onegin now felt: for some years a victim of passion, he
had engaged in the pursuit of love, but now he no longer falls
in love. If his advances are rebuffed, he does not care; if a
woman leaves him for a new lover, he is quite happy to rest; he
pursues without rapture and abandons without regret, like some
apathetic whist player who arrives, sits down, plays, goes home
calmly to sleep, and does not know next morning where he will
be that evening. But Onegin had been genuinely moved by
Tatiana's letter and for a moment he had felt something of his
former ardor; but no, he did not wish to deceive Tatiana.

And now to the garden where the two stand face to face. For
a moment neither speaks. Then Onegin goes up to Tatiana:
"You wrote to me, don't deny it. I have read the confessions of
your trustful soul, the outpourings of your innocent love, and I
was moved by your sincerity." Her letter, he tells her, reawakened feelings long silent, and he will repay her by being as

frank and straightforward as she. If he had wanted to settle down to married life, he would certainly have chosen Tatiana as his wife, and been happy—as far as possible. But he is not made for happiness; he is unworthy of her; however much he loved her before, once married he would cease to love her; her tears would not soften his heart; there are few things worse than a family in which a lonely wife grieves over her unworthy husband; surely this was not the lot decreed for her by destiny; the years cannot be rolled back, he cannot change or renew himself; he loves her with the love of a brother, and perhaps more tenderly than that; she will fall in love again: but she must learn to restrain herself, not everyone would understand her as he has done, and inexperience can be a woman's undoing.

Thus Onegin concludes his lecture. Tatiana does not argue. Half-blinded by tears, she takes Onegin's arm, and sadly the two make their way back to the house.

The pangs of her unrequited love cause Tatiana to grow pale and sickly. After describing her wretched condition, the sympathetic narrator declares himself relieved to be able to turn his attention to a happier love affair. Every day sees Lensky more and more deeply in love with Olga. He spends most of his time with her, sitting in her room, walking arm in arm with her in the garden, reading to her, playing chess with her (though he can hardly concentrate on the game). His love is chaste and timid: he only dares occasionally to play with a lock of her hair or kiss the hem of her dress. When he goes home, he still thinks incessantly of Olga and writes poetry in her album. This leads the narrator off onto a lengthy digression on odes, elegies, and, in general, literary trends. Returning to Lensky, he thinks of the good fortune of the poets who can read their verses to some beloved woman—although her thoughts may be altogether elsewhere. He himself has had to read his verses to his old nurse, or to some neighbor he has trapped into listening, or to the ducks who fly away from him in fear.

Onegin's desultory life in the country is described. He lives like a true Childe Harold—bored and idle. In the evening Lensky often arrives to dine with him and drink a bottle of champagne. The narrator recalls his own former fondness for champagne; at one time he had been ready to spend his last money for a bottle; and how many follies, he reminds his friends, the champagne had produced, and jokes, and verses, and arguments, and happy dreams! But champagne no longer suits his stomach; now he prefers Bordeaux, a more sagacious wine; champagne is like a glittering, fickle, self-willed, and hollow mistress; "but thou, Bordeaux, art like a friend, a companion ready to help us in misfortune or to share our quiet leisure...."

Now, with the fire burning low and the bottle still on the table, Onegin and Lensky start talking. Onegin asks after the Larins. Lensky tells him they are well and reproaches him for not visiting them. How Olga's shoulders have improved, and her bosom is magnificent! But he had forgotten: next Saturday is Tatiana's name day, and Onegin is invited. Onegin objects that there will be a crowd of people, but Lensky assures him that there will be just the family, and Onegin agrees to go. "How kind you are!" Lensky says and drains his glass, a libation to his betrothed, and starts off again on his favorite subject—Olga: such are the ways of love! Lensky is happy: the wedding is only two weeks away and, unlike the author, Lensky is untroubled by the prospect of the cares, the sorrows, and the boredom of marriage. Olga loves him—so, at least, he believes. Blessed is the man who believes and does not heed the promptings of cold intellect; pitiful is he who can foresee everything, whose head is never awhirl, whose heart has been chilled by experience!

The fifth chapter opens with a description of winter—a season of the year that Tatiana loves. Tatiana is "Russian in soul" and believes in the omens and fortune-tellings of Russian folklore: dreams, cards, the moon, a cat washing its face, a monk clothed in black, a shooting star, a hare crossing her path—all these things have meaning for Tatiana. On Twelfth Night an unmarried girl may see her future husband in the mirror, and Tatiana, going to bed, places her mirror under the pillow.

She dreams a strange dream: she is walking across a snow-covered clearing, when her way is barred by a dark, menacing stream. The only way across is on two poles which are frozen together with ice, and Tatiana hestitates. Suddenly a large, bristling bear emerges from a snowdrift and offers her his sharp-clawed paw. Trembling, Tatiana leans on the paw and crosses the stream. She starts off again walking, but the bear follows her. Not daring to look behind her, she quickens her pace, but the bear is still there, and she plunges on through the deep snow into the forest in panic. A long branch clutches at her throat, she loses her earrings, one of her shoes, her handkerchief. As she plunges on she is even afraid to lift the edge of her skirt—and still the bear is behind her. She falls exhausted in the snow. The bear picks her up and carries her off, unresisting and scarcely conscious. Suddenly they come to a hut: there is light in the window, and the noise of shouting comes from inside. The bear tells Tatiana: "Here is my relative [*kum*], warm up in his place for a while," and sets her down near the door. Coming to her senses, Tatinana sees that the bear has disappeared. Inside there are the sounds of shouting and of clinking glasses. She looks through a chink in the door and, to her amazement, sees a company of weird monsters around the table: one with horns and a dog's head; another with the head of a cock; a witch with a goat's beard; a stiff, proud-looking skeleton; a dwarf with a tail; a beast that is half crane and half cat; a lobster mounted on a spider; a skull on a goose's neck; a windmill dancing and waving its wings. But still more amazing: there seated at the table is Onegin, who is the leader of the company. Onegin rises, pushes wide the door, and Tatiana, who wishes to run but cannot move, is revealed to the gaze of the monsters. The monsters laugh wildly and, pointing at Tatiana, all shout: "Mine! Mine!" But Onegin says menacingly: "Mine!"—and the monsters disappear. Onegin gently draws Tatiana into a corner and, laying her on a rickety bench, puts his head on her shoulder. Enter suddenly Olga and Lensky; Onegin, eyes flashing, curses the unbidden guests. The argument grows more heated, and suddenly Onegin seizes a long knife and plunges it into Lensky. There is a chilling scream—and Tatiana awakes in horror to find that it is now daylight. The dream's ominous nature fills her with dark foreboding.

But now it is her name day, and the guests arrive for the party, many of them to spend the night; they are described satirically by the narrator, with allegorical names. Lensky and Onegin arrive late, and the guests, who are already at table, move up to make room for the two friends—right opposite Tatiana. Onegin is in a vile mood: he had had doubts about coming. Lensky had assured him that there would be only the family, and now it turns out that there are all these uninteresting guests. Worse still, Tatiana seems on the point of fainting from embarrassment and emotion, and he cannot abide fainting fits, tears, or other such displays. He swears he will get back at Lensky for all this. Meanwhile, the wine is opened, a Monsieur Triquet sings to Tatiana a French couplet he has simply copied out of an almanac. There is applause, and the "modest but great poet" is first to drink her health. When Onegin's turn comes, he bows silently, and—moved, perhaps, by pity or an involuntary flirtatiousness—gazes at her with a tenderness which revives Tatiana's spirits. With the meal at an end, some guests play cards, and others prepare to dance. Petushkov, the local dandy, dances with Olga, Lensky with Tatiana. And here the narrator reflects that at the beginning of his novel he had intended to describe a Petersburg ball, but he had been sidetracked by foolish memories of ladies' feet; but enough, with the passing of his youth it is time he became more sensible in word and deed, he must keep his fifth chapter free from digressions.

Meanwhile, Onegin is now ready to avenge himself on Lensky. He waltzes with Olga, seats her, talks to her, then waltzes again. People are amazed and Lensky can scarcely believe his eyes. Now it is time for the mazurka, and once more Onegin dances with Olga, his tender whisper and the pressure of his hand on hers bringing a blush to her face. Lensky waits for the mazurka to end, then invites Olga for the cotillion, but she can't!—she has already promised Onegin! Lensky, inveighing against feminine deceits and wiles, calls for his horse and gallops off in anger: only a pair of pistols and two bullets, he thinks, can settle his fate.

Next morning Onegin is visited by a neighbor, Zaretsky, who hands him a challenge from Lensky. Onegin declares himself "always at your disposal," but left to his own thoughts, he feels guilty: he should not have upset Lensky as he had. Also, even though Lensky's challenge was foolish, such an act was excusable at eighteen, and Onegin, who was really fond of the young poet, should act as a man of sense and honor—not allow himself to be helplessly swayed by public opinion and a false concept of honor. But Zaretsky, who has a malicious tongue, has become involved. It is, Onegin feels, too late.

Lensky, who had feared that Onegin would laugh off the challenge, is delighted at his acceptance. He swears he won't see Olga before the duel, which is set for dawn the following day, but time drags, and he gives up and goes anyway, persuading himself that his visit will embarrass her. But she runs to meet him, carefree and gay as ever, wanting to know why he left so early the night before. Now Lensky sees that she still loves him; he does not have the heart to reproach her, he is contrite, almost tempted to beg her forgiveness; but no, he rationalizes, he must be her savior against the seducer's wiles; he will fight. All evening he is preoccupied, silent at times, then suddenly lighthearted; but poets were ever thus. As he takes his leave, his heart is constricted with emotion, and Olga asks him what the matter is; "nothing," he replies. Returning home, he cocks his pistols and opens a volume of Schiller; but he can think only of Olga, and he spends the night composing verses about fate and love and about how, if he is killed, Olga will come to weep over his early grave. Just before dawn he falls asleep, but is awakened by Zaretsky, and they hurry off to keep the appointment.

Onegin, meanwhile, is still fast asleep. When he wakes, he orders his French servant, Monsieur Guillot, to accompany him as his second. Zaretsky, a perfectionist in the etiquette of dueling, is about to object to Monsieur Guillot as a second, but Lensky is ready to begin. Surely, the author reflects, these two friends, who so recently shared their leisure hours and their thoughts, might laugh and become reconciled; but no, false pride and the fear of what other people might say are against them, and they stand like "hereditary foes," as though in some "irrational nightmare."

"Advance." The two men advance five paces. Lensky takes aim, but at that moment Onegin fires, and Lensky falls. Onegin rushes forward and calls him by name, but he is dead. One instant before his heart had been alive with inspiration, with enmity, hope, and love; now all is silent and no trace remains. Onegin stands conscious-stricken, pistol in hand, then walks away. The corpse is loaded onto a sled and driven home.

My friends, the narrator addresses his readers, you feel sorry for the poet, struck down in the springtime of his happy, eager hopes. Where are his noble aspirations, his passionate desire for love, his longing for knowledge, his hatred of evil, his poetic dreams? Perhaps he was born to better the lot of mankind or, at least, to win glory. His now silent lyre might have sounded through the ages. Or, perhaps, the poet's lot would have been an ordinary one: the ardor of his soul would have passed away with his youth; he would have abandoned the muses; lived in the country, married, happy, and a cuckold; had gout at forty; have drunk, eaten, suffered from boredom, grown fat, grown sick; and finally died in his bed, surrounded by children, wailing womenfolk, and doctors.

The narrator reflects on his own fate. The years are turning his mind to prose; the years are driving away the frolicsome rhymes which his pen no longer pursues with the eagerness of past days. His springtime has passed, and there is no return, soon he will be thirty. Let him bid a friendly farewell to youth, give thanks for its sorrow and sweet torment, its excitement, storms, and feasts, for all its gifts. Farewell, he is starting on a new road; but he begs youth's inspiration not to abandon him, to visit him more often, not to allow his soul to grow cold, coarse, and unfeeling amid society's deadening round!

It is spring as the seventh chapter opens. But spring brings no joy to the narrator. His strength is not renewed as nature is renewed by the seasons. Nevertheless, spring is the time to go to the country, and he invites the reader to accompany his muse to where Onegin lived last winter and where, for a while, Olga and Tatiana wept over Lensky's grave. But things have changed: Onegin has gone; Olga, "inconstant to her sorrow," has fallen in love again, married, and departed with her husband to join his regiment; and Tatiana, bereft of her sister, mourning Lensky, still tormented by her love for Onegin, is left alone in her sorrow.

On an evening walk Tatiana, buried in her thoughts, comes unawares on Onegin's house. After some hesitation she asks if she may see the inside, and the housekeeper shows her the rooms. A cue lies forgotten on the billiard table, a riding whip on the couch. She sees the fireplace where "the master used to sit alone," and where "the late Lensky, our neighbor, used to dine with him in the wintertime." She sees his study with its books, a portrait of Lord Byron and a small cast-iron figure of Napoleon. Two days later she is back again at Onegin's house and is left alone in his study. She weeps for a long time and then begins to look over the books. She is struck by something strange in Onegin's taste and, as she reads, eagerly now, a new world opens before her. Onegin has little fondness for reading in general; but there are, Tatiana discovers, a few exceptions: works by Byron, and a few novels, which "depict fairly faithfully the modern age and contemporary man with his immoral, self-loving and cold soul, overly given to dreaming, his embittered intellect seething in futile activity." Tatiana pays particular attention to the passages which Onegin has marked, and slowly starts to understand better the man whom fate has condemned her to love. She wonders if he is not some sort of imitation, some parody of Byron or Childe Harold.

Some time later the reluctant Tatiana is taken to Moscow. A husband must be found for her. Tatiana and her mother arrive at the house of an elderly aunt. There are the inevitable greetings and reminiscences. Tatiana is touched by her aunt's warmhearted welcome, but she is unhappy, she longs for the countryside. Social life seems to her meaningless and superficial, the conversations dull and petty, and she herself makes no impression on the dandies, officers, and young Foreign Service men who look her over. But as she stands lost in nostalgic thought at a ball, she is watched by a fat, important general who cannot take his eyes off her. And at this point the narrator breaks off his story. He congratulates "my sweet Tatiana" on her conquest and closes his chapter with a classic introduction to the epic: "I sing of a young friend and his many vagaries. Bless my long labor, O thou, epic muse! And, handing me thy trusty staff, do not allow me to stray at random from the path." He has performed his duty, he remarks jestingly, in paying his respects to Classicism: now—though belatedly—his work *does* have an introduction.

The opening stanzas of the last chapter trace the progress of the narrator's muse on his journey through life. The muse first started to appear to him in his lycée days, when she sang of childish delights, the glories of Russia's past, and the tremulous dreams of his heart; and the first outpourings of his muse were kindly received by the world. Next, over a glass of wine his muse had sung of noisy feasting and loud argument, and among the young friends of past days he had felt pride in her singing. But he had left behind these friends, and his kindly muse had accompanied him, bringing him solace in his distant travels—in the mountains of the Caucasus, on the shores of the Crimea. Then in remote Moldavia his muse, forgetting the glitter and revelry of the capital, had visited with him the humble tents of the wandering gypsies. Suddenly all had changed, and the muse had appeared in his garden in the guise of a provincial maiden, with sad thoughts in her eyes and a French novel in her hands. Now for the first time he brings his muse into society and with jealous timidity gazes on her wild charms. She watches with quiet pleasure the serried ranks of aristocrats, officer dandies, diplomats, and proud ladies, the dresses glimpsed as they pass by, the snatches of conversation, the slow procession of guests moving forward to greet the young hostess, the dark clothes of the men framing the bright colors of the ladies, the well-ordered rhythm of distinguished conversation, the coldness of self-assured pride, and the blend of rank and years.

But who is this who stands silent, alien, and apathetic among this select group? It is Onegin, and the narrator speculates as to whether he has changed. What mask is he now wearing? Is he a Byronic hero, a "cosmopolitan," a Quaker, a bigot—or just an average decent person? The narrator warns the reader against forming a negative opinion of his hero: sometimes we condemn people because we really only feel at ease when dealing with mediocrity. Blessed the man who in youth is young; who matures in good time; who, with the years, gradually learns to endure life's coldness; who has not indulged in strange dreaming; who has not shunned the social crowd; who at twenty is a dandy or a blade; and at thirty has made a profitable marriage; who by fifty has freed himself from debt; who calmly acquires, one after the other, glory, money, and rank; the man of whom people have invariably said that he is a "fine fellow." But it is sad to think that youth was given us in vain; that we were false to youth and youth deceived us; that our finest aspirations and purest dreams turned rapidly to dust. It is unbearable to look ahead and see only innumerable dinners, to contemplate life as some empty ritual, and to follow the sedate crowd without sharing its opinions or ambitions. And this is the predicament of Onegin, whose strange ways have made him the target of general censure. Having killed his friend in a duel, he has now reached the age of twenty-six, and is still without position, without a wife, without occupation, and is incapable of serious activity. After the duel he could no longer stand living on his estate, and had started to travel aimlessly; but, like everything else, travel soon palled on him. So he has just returned to Petersburg and is attending a ball.

Suddenly there is a stir in the crowd. A lady, followed by an important general, approaches the hostess. The lady is calm, unpretentious, unassuming, unaffected, simple, perfectly *comme-il-faut;* men and women, old and young, approach her with affection and respect. Onegin is thunderstruck. The princess (for this is now Tatiana's title) greets him with absolute composure, makes a few conventional remarks, and leaves Onegin standing tongue-tied. He returns home astounded by the change in Tatiana—and hopelessly in love. Day after day he follows her in society, hoping in vain for some special sign of recognition, but Tatiana's poise is unshaken; she hardly notices him. He grows pale and sickly. The doctors advise him to take the waters, but he will not leave. He still hopes stubbornly; finally, he writes her a passionate letter.

He foresees, he writes, that his letter may offend her and make him an object of contempt and ridicule. He recalls his former indifference; how mistaken he was, how severely is he punished now. Now his only thought is to watch her with adoring eyes, to listen to her, to fathom in his heart her every perfection, to pine away in torment before her—that would be bliss! He fears that she will be angry, will see his plea as a contemptible stratagem. If she knew how terrible it is to ache and be consumed with love, to long to throw himself at her feet, embrace her knees and pour out his feelings—and all the time to be obliged to control himself, to feign casualness in word and deed! But he can no longer restrain himself; the die is cast: he is in her power and submits to his fate.

There is no answer. Onegin writes a second and a third letter. Still no answer—only, when he meets her, Tatiana's icy reserve, Once more Onegin withdraws from society. He reads voluminously, indiscriminately, and without concentration. In his distracted mind he sees again Lensky lying dead, he sees the forgotten enemies, unfaithful women, and despised friends of the past; and he sees again a country house where, in the window, *she* is sitting. He almost goes mad; he almost becomes a poet. The days pass by and spring arrives: Onegin is not a poet, not dead, not mad. Spring revives him. The recluse leaves the study where he has spent the winter and dashes to Tatiana's house. There is no one in the hall or in the drawing room; he opens a door; there sits the princess alone, weeping over a letter; Onegin falls at her feet and kisses her hand; she looks at him without anger or surprise; she is again the Tatiana he once knew. Finally, after a long silence, she begins to speak.

Enough, she says, bidding him stand up; she must talk to him frankly; she recalls how, in the garden walk, she had once listened meekly to Onegin, but today it is her turn; she had been younger and, perhaps, better then, and she had loved him, but he had answered her love with a stern lecture; a humble girl's love had been no novelty to him, but she will not blame him; he acted honorably, and she is grateful, but now he pursues her; she wonders if this is not because of her prominent position in high society, and because her surrender would flatter his vanity. She reproaches him for his letters and his tears, for being the slave of his feelings; she would gladly exchange all her social success for the humble countryside where she had first known him and where happiness had then been so possible, so close. But now she is married and he must leave her alone; she loves Onegin (why deny it?), but she belongs to someone else, and she will be faithful to that one forever.

She leaves the room. Onegin stands stricken. Just then Tatiana's husband enters, and so, the narrator suggests, let us leave the hero in this bad moment—leave him forever; for long enough we have followed him through the world; let us congratulate each other as we reach the shore; it was high time (isn't it true?) a long while ago! And in a light bantering tone the author-narrator takes leave of his readers. He bids farewell also to Onegin, "my strange companion," to Tatiana, "my true ideal," and to his work. Blessed is he who early left life's feast, without draining its wine-cup to the dregs, without reading life's novel to the end, able to part company in a trice, even as now the author parts company with his Onegin.

Clearly, an outline of this sort cannot come close to conveying the real merits of *Evgeny Onegin*. Meanwhile, it must here be pressed into service as the only means of offering some, at least, of the raw materials on which any critical discussion of the poem will inevitably be based. How then define the fundamental theme of *Evgeny Onegin?* Its unifying principle? Its own peculiar esthetic impact on the reader?

Evgeny Onegin has been characterized as "the story of a twice-rejected love"—Tatiana's love for Onegin, and Onegin's love for Tatiana.[11] Indeed, the symmetry between the two incidents is striking. First Tatiana writes a letter to Onegin, and Onegin rejects her love in a monologue which (since Tatiana neither interrupts nor objects) has itself something of the character of a letter.[12] Then in the last chapter the process is reversed: Onegin writes, and Tatiana delivers the rejection speech, again without interruptions or objections from the listener. The parallelism between the two situations is underlined by certain similarities in the letters: formally, both stand out from the remainder of the poem by virtue of their being written in freely rhymed paragraphs of varying length rather than in the "Onegin" stanza. Further, the subject matter of the two letters is developed along roughly the same lines: each writer fears the other's contempt; both claim to be writing with reluctance, *à contre-coeur*. While Tatiana complains of not being able to see Onegin, Onegin complains that his meetings with Tatiana in society do not allow him to vent his feelings, and both conclude by putting their fate in the hands of the other. The parallelism is further reinforced by the visible behavior of the two protagonists: in the first encounter Onegin is poised, while Tatiana is gauche and tongue-tied. Later the roles are reversed, and it is Tatiana who is poised, Onegin who is tongue-tied. This parallelism in reverse of the two Onegin-Tatiana confrontations does have a very real significance.[13] In one sense, it is possible to think of *Evgeny Onegin* as "the story of a twice-rejected love." It can be seen as a tragedy of mistiming; if only, we are tempted to speculate, Onegin had had the discernment to see in the early Tatiana what he came to love too late in the married Tatiana, then everything might have ended happily. But Pushkin's poem, clearly, is not simply a tragedy of blindness, of failure to recognize. Something more needs to be said—about the underlying motivations of the two principal characters.

First, Tatiana. Why did she choose—of all people—Onegin to fall in love with? Almost anyone else, it seems, would have been more suitable than the self-centered and aimless Onegin; and she fell in love without knowing anything of Onegin's character! But in the poetic world of *Evgeny Onegin* such reflections are unsubstantial. The point, surely, is that Tatiana did not have a choice—or had very little choice, and she did know about Onegin one very important thing, namely that he was "different." Tatiana's sensibilities and romantic expectations have been fostered by her reading of sentimental novels. Furthermore, she is exactly at the right age (for her) to fall in love. But she cannot fall in love with the average young man whom she meets in the countryside. The gap between the romantic daydream and the prosaic reality is too wide. The principles of romantic love demand of Tatiana, among others, not only that she love once-and-for-all-time a specific and predestined person, but also—the corollary—that this person be not average, be special, be unique. Into this pattern of expectation the unfamiliar Onegin fits admirably, and to these principles of love Tatiana submits—inevitably. It is significant that Tatiana's letter is not only a declaration of love but also a call of rescue from a milieu which, she feels instinctively, can never bring her happiness: "I am here alone, no one understands me, my mind cannot bear the strain, and I must perish in silence." That Tatiana's falling in love with Onegin is indeed a "mistake" is made very clear by the author's comments and by what follows in the story; but it is a "mistake" which could not have been avoided and which, once made, cannot be remedied. Tatiana's love for Onegin is not simply a case of faulty judgment, it is a tragic inevitability.

In the final chapter Tatiana rejects Onegin: she still loves him, but she will remain faithful to her husband. This denouement, which leaves Tatiana playing her part in society as a faithful wife, has been seen as a "realist" element in Pushkin's poem, in that it appears to constitute a break from the Romantic tradition exemplified by such novels as Rousseau's *La Nouvelle Héloïse* and Benjamin Constant's *Adolphe* where the heroines are destroyed.[14] However, this view, though it does indeed point up a valid distinction, must be treated with reserve. Tatiana neither dies of pneumonia (*Adolphe*) nor drowns (*La Nouvelle Héloïse*): she plays the role of a prominent and fashionable society hostess; she is the source of her fond husband's pride; but she never does "get over" her love for Onegin, this one great love remaining a permanent burden and blight on her life. To overemphasize the maturing of Tatiana's character, her strength, her sense of duty, and her "constructive" approach to life's problems (as much criticism tends to do) is, I believe, to misinterpret the author's artistic intent and to disregard Tatiana's own sad words as she dismisses Onegin: "But happiness was so possible, so close! But my fate is already decided." She has had her one small chance of happiness (not really a chance at all) and it is gone—forever.[15]

The main outlines of Onegin's character are clear enough and have been frequently noted. He is one of the first examples of a long series of Russian male heroes who, because of their inability to conform to the unambitiously philistine norms of Russian society or to carve out for themselves an independent and productive way of life, are often referred to as "superfluous people"—to be treated, depending on the critic's standpoint, as objects of pity or censure. Onegin is also undoubtedly an example of a certain type of person (common in European life and literature in the latter half of the eighteenth and first half of the nineteenth century) who suffered from romantic melancholy, *mal du siècle, Weltschmerz;* thus he has affinities with such literary figures as Werther, Adolphe, and Childe Harold.[16] But to define Onegin as a "superfluous man" or a Russian Childe Harold tells us little of the author's attitude toward him or of his function in this work. It is clear that Onegin does not cut a very admirable figure: his assumption of his own superiority is based on no achievement whatsoever; his rejection of Tatiana, though honorable enough in itself, does not particularly endear him to the reader; he kills Lensky in a duel which, he knows, he should have stopped; his choice of reading makes Tatiana wonder if he is not a "parody"; and then he pursues Tatiana when she is a married woman. Would it not therefore be true to say that in the character of Onegin the Childe Harold type, which had once appealed to Pushkin, is exposed and condemned? Certainly this view has been expressed—and not infrequently[17]—and there is a good deal to be said in its favor. It is true that Pushkin had come to recognize the sterility and negativism of the Childe Harold approach to life, and it is true that he was at pains to draw a clear distinguishing line between himself and his hero (as Byron, too, had sought to distinguish between himself and Childe Harold).[18] But a difference must be made between objectivity and antipathy—or, better, between objectivity and lack of understanding. For the more important truth is that Pushkin understood Onegin only too well: Pushkin was not immune to Onegin's sickness. Pushkin's very reluctance to have himself identified with Onegin is in itself an indication of their closeness, and a side glance at some of the works he wrote during the same period (e.g., his 1825 "A Scene from Faust") will serve to convince that the type whose spontaneous emotional reflexes are atrophied by intellectual self-analysis remained a preoccupying problem. It is, surely, one thing to be aware in mind of the inadequacies of an attitude to life; it is something very different to free oneself of its emotional commitments and penalties. To say that Onegin was Pushkin's disguised *alter ego* would be a gross oversimplification, would be inaccurate, but recognition of the fact that he represents one important facet of the poet's most intimate emotional experience is essential to any true understanding of the entire work. For Pushkin realized poetically—and we have to accept this—that Onegin's predicament was in fact insoluble. Indeed, his conduct was not very admirable, but his poetic function in *Evgeny Onegin* rests on the premise that his actions were in reality no freer than those of Tatiana and that Onegin, no less than Tatiana, was foredoomed.

The question is sometimes raised as to whether, in the final chapter, Onegin really is in love with Tatiana or whether it is simply that his ego is tempted by the thought of conquering this poised and socially prominent woman. Tatiana herself, in rejecting Onegin, speculates shrewdly on the latter possibility. But the whole point of the episode lies in the fact that both hypotheses are true: Onegin grows pale and sick and is certainly in love. At the same time, a surrender on the part of Tatiana would not have solved Onegin's problems. For his problems lie not in his ability or inability to love Tatiana, but in his whole negative approach to life. Not only in the field of love, but in all other fields, he is incapable of constructive effort. Deep down he prefers to be ironically condescending and detached rather than wholeheartedly committed to any undertaking and the efforts it would involve.

No discussion of *Evgeny Onegin* can be complete without mention of an important secondary character—Lensky. He is immature and inexperienced, and the author has no hesitation in making him a target for his irony. Yet Lensky, like Onegin represents a facet of the author's emotional experience of life:

Lensky's naïve idealism was something which Pushkin himself
had at times experienced and with which, in spite of his irony,
he could still sympathize.[19] Also, from the standpoint of plot,
Lensky has several significant functions: his enthusiastic idealism serves as a foil to Onegin's world-weariness; his death serves
to part still further Onegin and Tatiana (his death is mentioned
both in Onegin's letter to Tatiana and in her spoken reply—to
Onegin); and his death frees Olga to marry someone else—an
event which, notwithstanding the author's lack of interest in
Olga, plays an essential part in the conception of the work. For
Olga's remarriage and her easy forgetfulness (a completely non-
Romantic trait) set her apart from the other main characters,
who all display in one form or another that extreme vulnerability
to life's trials which is characteristic of the Romantic: Lensky is
happy for a while in his illusions, but he is cut down before he
has time to come to grips with reality; Tatiana believes for a
short while that she has a chance of happiness, but then realizes
she is doomed; and Onegin, who initially denies the possibility
of happiness, deludes himself later into believing that he failed
to recognize his chance of happiness. These people had no
chance of happiness, or what chance they seemed to have was
missed and, once missed, irretrievable. There is no question here
of trying again, mending, rebuilding; once gone is gone forever;
Olga, on the other hand, after losing her fiancé, remakes her life
with an almost callous imperviousness.

But no discussion confined to plot and characters can ade-
quately convey the feelings evoked by a reading of *Evgeny
Onegin*. For the events concerning the characters are not in
themselves the dominant force which determines the over-all
esthetic impact of the poem; rather they constitute *one* vitally
important, but not *the* decisive, factor. Any work of literature
is made up of various component elements, all of which, be their
significance greater or smaller in what may be termed the work's
"esthetic hierarchy," cannot help but have some function in
terms of the whole. While some of these component elements
may be so unobtrusive as to escape the analyst's eye, others will
inevitably attract attention. One such element in *Evgeny Onegin*
is, for example, the metaphor of the revolving seasons which is
used to emphasize the irrevocable passage of time.[20] And among
such component elements, clearly, of great significance in this

"hierarchy" is the plot, the entire composite linking events and characters. But over, above, and beyond the plot there is another, higher element: the author-narrator's poetic personality. The author-narrator's personality is not simply one of several component elements; rather it is a presence which binds together all the other component elements, which pervades the entire work and which gives it a whole new focus, a whole new dimension.

The author's poetic personality is expressed mainly through the digressions (of which we were able to show all too few in all too summary form in our outline of the story). Not only do the digressions provide, structurally, the connecting chain which links the various elements of the narrative together, they also enable the author to maintain an unbroken commentary on the plot: he can with his sympathy reinforce the feelings of his characters; he can by his detachment and irony dissociate himself from their feelings. Events and characters are thus seen not only directly but, more, through the prism of the author-narrator's emotions. Moreover, the author does not confine himself to commenting on the plot. On the contrary, he is himself provoked by the events of the plot to relate his personal experiences and to convey his subjective, lyric feelings toward life in general. Thus, there is in effect a two-way flow of causes and effects: while on the one hand the author's poetic personality helps to color the reader's perceptions of the characters and reactions to the plot, on the other hand plot and characters are themselves instrumental in forging the image of the author. The relationship between the author-narrator and the plot has been aptly expressed in the following comment: "The originality of *Evgeny Onegin's* structure consists therefore, in our view, in the fact that in this work not only do the digressions, which indicate the author's presence, perform a function in terms of the characters and events of the novel, but also the characters and events perform a function in terms of the digressions."[21] In effect, the characters, like all the other elements of the work, are subordinated to the author-narrator's poetic personality, and this constantly felt presence is, esthetically, the unifying and organizing principle of the work. In this sense, *Evgeny Onegin,* notwithstanding its affinities with the novel and the comic epic, may justifiably be labeled a lyric poem and be said to have a lyric author-hero.[22] For the reader's most basic emotional reactions are stirred not by the doings of Tatiana (or of Onegin or Lensky) but by something else—this something else being, in my view, the poetic personality of the author, the poetic personality of Pushkin.[23]

What, in conclusion, is the fundamental theme of *Evgeny Onegin? Evgeny Onegin* may indeed be described as "the story of a twice-rejected love." Yet this definition covers, we know, only one aspect of the work. Love was for both Onegin and Tatiana merely one facet of their problems. Furthermore, if our insistence above on the esthetically dominant role of the author-image was correct, then no explanation which takes into account solely the good or evil fortunes of the protagonists can be considered a complete answer. *Evgeny Onegin* cannot be treated simply as one more unhappy love story. Nevertheless, the theme of unrequited love is important and is to be borne in mind as a valid part of a larger answer.

Another valid partial answer is to regard *Evgeny Onegin* as a poetic analysis of that spiritual sickness which is loosely associated with Romanticism. The three main protagonists are, in their different ways, products of the Romantic age. And the putative author-hero is also, as he himself recognizes, afflicted in his way with the disease of Romanticism. But to label *Evgeny Onegin* as an analysis of Romantic ailments is to run at least two risks. It is, first, to run the risk—invariably incurred in mentioning a literary movement—of losing sight of the very specific qualities which make the work what it is. It is, second, to run the risk of unjustifiably dating a work, the significance of which cannot be limited to one country or one period. Thus, while the subject matter of *Evgeny Onegin* undoubtedly derives from Romanticism, the treatment is peculiarly Pushkin's own and one, furthermore, which transcends Romanticism in time and place. This explanation, then, is another partial truth—also to be borne in mind for the help it may afford in our attempt to arrive at a larger answer.

It may be fruitful—in this attempt—to begin by pointing out that the mood of *Evgeny Onegin* becomes increasingly somber as the work progresses. Of Byrons's *Don Juan* one critic has remarked: "*Don Juan* begins in fun, but it ends in bitterness and sadness."[24] The same, roughly speaking, can be said of *Evgeny Onegin*. The first chapter gives little indication of what is to follow or of the mood which comes to prevail at the poem's end. For the first chapter—notwithstanding talk of spleen and melancholy—is "fun," while the sum total of *Evgeny Onegin* is not. A shift in mood or several shifts in mood occur. And this is of primary significance in determining the fundamental theme.

The transition in *Evgeny Onegin* from "fun" to "sadness" is conveyed in several ways—not least in the comments of the author. But it is, naturally enough, most easily traced in the events of the narrative. In the first chapter the reader is informed in lighthearted vein of Onegin's upbringing, his superficial education, his social prowess, his dandyism, his cynical attitude to women, even of his "spleen." None of this weighs very heavily. It is amusing, not to be taken too seriously. But in the second chapter a definite change takes place with the introduction of Tatiana. The author whose attitude to Onegin and Lensky has been on the whole detached and ironical, adopts a more serious and respectful tone in speaking of Tatiana; even her naïveté and her penchant for sentimental novels are handled carefully and without irony. In the third chapter Tatiana falls in love and writes her letter—an imprudent act which the author takes pains to explain and defend. With Tatiana lovesick, the flippancy of the early stanzas is gone. But the reader is not unduly disturbed. Even Onegin's kindly rejection of Tatiana in the fourth chapter comes as no surprise. But in the fifth chapter a darkening of the poem's mood is produced by Tatiana's shockingly bad dream. The function of Tatiana's dream is to prepare the reader for the tragic turn of events to come.[25] Clearly a parallel is intended between the monsters seated round the table in the dream and the guests at Tatiana's name-day party, and in the dream Onegin kills Lensky just as he will shortly do in real life. With Lensky's death a further change takes place. It is not so much that the mood becomes more somber. Rather it is the feeling that something irrevocable has happened.

Up to this point the plot could still have been salvaged and brought to a reasonably happy conclusion. Now this is out of the question. Because of a foolish quarrel a man is dead. It is with a feeling of shock that we realize that death allows of no salvaging, no healing. And from this point of no return on, a great deal of *Evgeny Onegin* is devoted to backward glances, to speculation as to why things turned out the way they did and to what might have happened if things had been different. If Lensky had not been killed, what, the author wonders, would have become of him? Would he have become a great poet or would he have succumbed to mediocrity? Tatiana reads Onegin's books and tries to understand how he became what he is. And in the final chapter Onegin's courtship of the married Tatiana and Tatiana's rejection of him: this whole incident is not so much a defeat for Onegin or a victory for Tatiana; it involves rather the vain hope of a second chance, and the grim certainty that there are no second chances.

The lesson is reinforced by a certain symmetry between the first and the last chapters.[26] In both the scene is Petersburg. In both our main attention is focused on Onegin. In both he attempts in vain to become interested in reading and to become a poet. But that was before, and this is after. Now Lensky is dead, and there is the lost opportunity of Tatiana's love. So symmetry there may be, but nothing is really the same. For time has elapsed and is irretrievably and irrevocably lost. And this realization brings us close, I believe, to the poem's unifying sentiment which embraces all the component parts and other sentiments. It consists in a feeling of deep sorrow, unmitigated by redeeming hope, yet presented soberly, even at times ironically, always with restraint and balance, sorrow produced by this very thought of no return, this recognition that the years behind were wasted and that, alas, what lies ahead will be worse and not better than what lies behind.

CHAPTER 6

The Married Years: The Little House in Kolomna, Angelo, *Fairy Tales in Verse,* The Bronze Horseman, *and Prose Writings*

I *Marriage And the Last Years (1831–1837)*

PUSHKIN's choice of a marriage partner was an unwise one. But this certainly does not mean that the marriage was catastrophically unhappy. Natalia Nikolaevna bore him four children and was in many respects a dutiful wife. There was, of course, the wide physical disparity between the two; in fact, they were compared not very kindly to Vulcan and Venus. More important, perhaps, was the difference in interests. Natalia Nikolaevna had little or no interest in literature, little or no understanding of her husband's work, and was nevertheless jealous on occasions when Pushkin took his work to show to other intelligent and attractive women. On the other hand there was Natalia Nikolaevna's almost frenzied interest in social activities. As early as 1831, when the Pushkins moved from Moscow to Tsarskoe Selo, Pushkin's wife began to make an impression in court circles. She was fond of flirtation, which seemed to her to cast a sort of romantic aura over her life. Pushkin, although himself not averse to flirtation when he was the one involved, could not help but feel somewhat jealous as he felt himself forced to the sidelines and—even more—he felt impatient at the exaggerated importance his wife attached to her successes.

Nevertheless, the summer of 1831 in Tsarskoe Selo was not an unhappy one: Pushkin was pleased, at least at first, at his wife's social successes, and the establishment of improved relations between himself and Nicholas I. If we will recall, 1831 was the year of the Polish uprising, and Pushkin's pen was wielded in patriotic defense of Russia's position—a fact which, though it caused Pushkin to be highly criticized by his more liberal pro-

Polish friends and acquaintances, certainly met with the approval of Nicholas I. That same year Pushkin was restored to the service, with a small but helpful salary, and with the title of historiographer. His position, in effect, placed on him no obligations; it merely gave him access to the archives, something which was for Pushkin highly desirable in view of his growing interest in Russian history, in particular in the figures of Peter the Great and Pugachev. The only disadvantage, perhaps, in Pushkin's reappointment to the service was that it placed on him a debt of gratitude to Nicholas I. This growing dependence on the favor of the Tsar was, in effect, to mar the remaining years of Pushkin's life. His wife's social aspirations were far too ambitious for Pushkin's limited means. He found that he was obliged to ask the government, that is, Nicholas I, to subsidize first his history on the Pugachev uprising, and eventually his family life. By 1837 his indebtedness—both private and to the government—had reached disastrous proportions.

For a while, from 1826 on, Pushkin had been favorably inclined toward his new tsar. In fact, at one time, Nicholas' personality appears, as noted above, to have exerted an almost spellbinding charm on the poet. The Tsar's handling of the 1828 *Gavriiliada* episode may well have given cause for gratitude and surely cannot have diminished Nicholas in Pushkin's esteem. And the irksome tribulations the poet suffered from time to time seem to have been attributed by him to the overly zealous supervision of Benkendorf's Third Section, and to have aroused little or no rancor toward the Tsar. The summer of 1831 in Tsarskoe Selo was marked, as we have seen, by good relations between monarch and poet, but by 1834 Pushkin's attitude had altered radically. One of the unkindest blows of all was his appointment on December 30, 1833 as *Kammerjunker.* This position at court corresponded to Pushkin's service rank (he had lost several years' seniority), but this did not alter the fact that it was usually reserved for far younger men—aristocrats of about twenty years of age. Nor was Pushkin unaware that this court appointment was an administrative device to bring his lovely and admired wife closer into court circles. The appointment, then, was keenly resented by Pushkin, as is clear from the diary he kept in 1834, and into which he poured much of his bitterness. His letters to his wife during the summer of 1834—she was resting in the

country after a miscarriage following a ball—also reveal Pushkin's bitterness and unhappiness.

Another cause for bitterness was the opening of one of these
letters to his wife which was then passed on to Nicholas I, who
not only read it, but discussed with others its contents. Increasingly bitter, and with his wife away in the country, Pushkin
requested permission to retire. Permission, he was told, would
be granted, but at the Tsar's displeasure, and the archives would
be closed to the poet. Pushkin was also accused of "ingratitude."
Pushkin hastily withdrew his request for retirement, assuring all
concerned that his motives had been misunderstood; it had been,
after all, only his wish to repair his financial situation that had
caused him to request retirement. In the summer of 1835 Pushkin again requested permission to retire—this time for only three
or four years, and again to repair his finances. Permission was
again refused.

Natalia Nikolaevna's zest for society life would have been
somewhat more tolerable for Pushkin if he had not had the feeling that his own role in society was an insignificant one. That he
was Russia's greatest poet counted very little with many of the
philistine aristocrats surrounding the throne in Petersburg. Nor
would many of them give Pushkin what he felt was his due by
treating him as their equal. He felt himself to be in many cases
their superior, by virtue of his six-hundred-year-old aristocratic
lineage. But Pushkin was poor, and many of them were rich.
That in many cases their riches and titles had been acquired as
recently as the preceding century made no difference in their
attitude to the poet, whom they felt justified in treating with
condescension. He on his part thought of them as newcomers,
nouveaux riches. Their condescension and neglect wounded
deeply his pride and was felt as an insult to his honor, about
which Pushkin was always sensitive and was now becoming
increasingly, sometimes paranoiacally, sensitive. Adding to his
many discomforts was the fact that his later works were meeting
with far less acclaim than had been accorded his earlier efforts,
that he frequently found himself the target of unfriendly criticism from hostile and mediocre writers, and that he had become
embroiled in often trivial and heartwearing journalistic polemics.
All in all, the general circumstances of his social life and literary
career offered Pushkin little satisfaction. Marriage had held out

the hope for Pushkin of a more stable and meaningful life, but the way of life into which he found himself increasingly pushed as a result of his marriage was turning out to be a strait jacket. Meanwhile, Natalia Nikolaevna's star continued to rise.

His wife's flirtations had undoubtedly vexed Pushkin, but he had not felt his marriage to be seriously threatened until the arrival in Petersburg of a young Alsatian, George d'Anthès. D'Anthès was a royalist, and had therefore resigned from St. Cyr, the crack military academy, as a result of the 1830 French Revolution. He was now seeking his fortune in Russia, where through the influence of highly placed connections he was able to secure a commission in the cavalry guard. Georges d'Anthès was good-looking, good company, and there was no doubt that he was successful with women. His meeting with Natalia Nikolaevna took place some time late in 1834, after her return from the country, or possibly that spring, before her miscarriage. Unquestionably, a strong attraction developed between d'Anthès and Pushkin's wife. To begin with, his courtship remained within the bounds of propriety, but by 1836 d'Anthès' attentions had become so blatant as to become an object of gossip and scandal in Petersburg society. In at least one household d'Anthès was told to desist from his courtship of Natalia Nikolaevna or carry it on elsewhere. The situation came to a head on November 4, 1836, when Pushkin received the following anonymous letter or "diploma":

The Grand-Cross Commanders and Chevaliers of the Most Serene Order of Cuckolds, convened in plenary assembly under the presidency of the venerable Grand Master of the Order, His Excellency D. L. Naryshkin, have unanimously elected M. Alexander Pushkin coadjutor of the Grand Master of the Order of Cuckolds and historiographer of the Order.

> *Permanent Secretary*
> COUNT I. BORCH

The personalities in the letter were well known. Naryshkin's wife had been for years the mistress of the late Tsar Alexander I, and the wife of Count Borch led a notoriously promiscuous sexual life. The mention of Naryshkin's wife, mistress of Alexander I, has led recent commentators to argue that the anonymous letter was in reality aimed at Nicholas I, who had also not hesitated to pay court to Pushkin's wife. However, this theory seems very improbable. The fact is that Pushkin's contemporaries, including Pushkin, took the anonymous letter, of which seven or eight copies circulated, to be a reference to d'Anthès' courtship. Pushkin immediately challenged d'Anthès to a duel. After lengthy negotiations on the part of several mediators, all equally interested in avoiding a duel, Pushkin was eventually induced to withdraw his challenge. The pretext was that d'Anthès had actually been courting not Pushkin's wife, but his sister-in-law, Ekaterina Nikolaevna, who was living in the same house with the Pushkins; and that d'Anthès intended to propose marriage, but *only* provided the challenge be withdrawn *without* any reference being made to d'Anthès' intended proposal, so that d'Anthès could not be suspected of having been forced into an unwanted engagement because of cowardice. Pushkin, in withdrawing his challenge, was never far from believing that d'Anthès had in fact acted out of cowardice—though few of his contemporaries believed this. Another suspicion which now came to poison Pushkin's life was the unfounded belief that the anonymous letter had been the work of d'Anthès adoptive father, Baron Heeckeren, the ambassador of the Netherlands. (In 1927 a Soviet handwriting expert established that the letters were the work of a young aristocrat, Prince P. Dolgoruky.) Somewhat contrary to Pushkin's expectations, d'Anthès did marry Ekaterina Nikolaevna, on January 10, 1837. His motives for marrying her will probably never be fully understood, and were perhaps not fully understood by d'Anthès himself. But the marriage in no way affected d'Anthès' conduct toward Natalia Nikolaevna. While showing every tenderness to his bride, he continued his pursuit of Pushkin's wife, now his sister-in-law. The uneasy truce could never have lasted. Pushkin continued to snub d'Anthès in public, and d'Anthès' courtship of Pushkin's wife appeared at times an almost deliberate provocation, intended presumably to disprove any suspicion of cowardice, and motivated also, it would seem, by d'Anthès' growing dislike of Pushkin.

Pushkin's troubled domestic life had by late 1836 and early 1837 become an object of public gossip and amusement in Petersburg society. His abject situation was further aggravated by rumors—probably true—that the poet was carrying on an affair with his other sister-in-law, Alexandra Nikolaevna Gon-

charova. From 1834, Alexandra Nikolaevna, the second of the
Goncharov sisters, and Ekaterina Nikolaevna, the oldest, who
married d'Anthès, had been living in the Pushkin household.
Alexandra Nikolaevna, the only Goncharov sister to show an
interest in poetry, appears to have been infatuated with her poet
brother-in-law from the start of their acquaintance. The rumor
of a relationship between the two only rendered more ridiculous
the spectacle of the Pushkin mènage. Nor was Pushkin's own
conduct in public calculated to gain him sympathy. Undoubtedly under severe stress, as a result both of his growing feeling
of imprisonment in society life and, in particular, because of the
scandal focused on his personal life owing to the d'Anthès affair,
Pushkin's behavior in 1836 was extremely uneven. While at times
he appeared controlled, relaxed, and in good humor, there were
frequent occasions when he showed himself caustic, sardonic,
melodramatic, and rude. Among those who had never greatly
cared for him he was making himself more disliked than formerly, and among people who were genuinely well disposed toward him he was making himself something of an object of
ridicule. In his own mind he felt pursued, harrassed, and resent-
ful. His sense of honor was deeply wounded. And the score was
still to be settled with d'Anthès and Heeckeren.

The final showdown appears to have been sparked by a secret
rendezvous demanded by d'Anthès of Natalia Nikolaevna (under
the false pretense of discussing family matters), of which Pushkin was informed by an anonymous letter. Pushkin could no
longer afford not to take action, though indeed he was eager
enough to do so. On January 25 Pushkin wrote the following
insulting letter to d'Anthès' adoptive father, Heeckeren, whom
he had now come to hate almost more than d'Anthès:

Baron! Permit me to set down briefly everything that has happened.
The behavior of your son has been known to me for a long time past,
and I could not remain indifferent. I contented myself with the role
of observer, ready to intervene when I should consider it necessary.
An incident, which at any other time would have been extremely unpleasant to me, offered an excellent opportunity: I received the anonymous letters. I saw that the moment had come, and I put it to good
advantage. The rest you know. I obliged your son to play such an
abject role that my wife, amazed at so much cowardice and truckling,
could not refrain from laughing, and the emotion which she may per-

haps have felt for this great and lofty passion, was extinguished in cold contempt and deserved repugnance.

I have to confess, Baron, that your own conduct was not entirely seemly. You, the representative of your crown, acted as parental pimp for your son; it appears that his conduct (rather inept, by the way) was guided entirely by you. It was you, probably, who suggested to him all the pitiful things he related and the idiotic things he wrote. Like an obscene old woman, you lay in wait for my wife in every corner, in order to tell her of the love of your bastard, as he is reputed to be: and when, sick with the pox, he had to stay at home, you told her that he was dying of love for her; you would murmur to her: "Give me back my son."

You will agree, Baron, that after all this I cannot tolerate my family having any relations whatever with yours. It was on this condition that I agreed not to pursue this dirty business any further and not to dishonor you in the eyes of our court and yours—which I had the power to do and which I had intended to do. I do not care that my wife should continue to listen to your paternal counsels. I cannot permit your son, after his disgusting behavior, to have the effrontery to speak to my wife and, still less to tell her barrack-room puns and to play the role of a devoted and unhappy lover, whereas he is actually a coward and blackguard. I am obliged to address myself to you and ask you to put an end to all these intrigues, if you wish to avoid a fresh scandal, to which I will certainly not hesitate to expose you. I have the honor to be, Baron,

Your humble and obedient servant,

A. PUSHKIN

The inevitable challenge was issued on January 26. The duel took place between d'Anthès and Pushkin on January 27, at about four-thirty in the afternoon on the outskirts of Petersburg. Pushkin was mortally wounded and, after two days of considerable agony, died on January 29.

National sorrow at the death of Russia's greatest poet, struck down by a foreigner, was substantial enough for Benkendorf's department to fear popular demonstrations. The time and place of the funeral services were altered to avoid trouble, admission was by ticket only and—irony of ironies, since the diplomatic corps was probably that segment of society in which Pushkin was least popular—the service was attended almost exclusively by members of the diplomatic corps and the court. Pushkin's body was sent out from Petersburg on the road to Pskov—at midnight—in order, again, to avoid attracting attention, and on Feb-

ruary 6 he was buried in the Svyatogorsky Monastery near Mikhaylovskoe, beside his mother.

The works dealt with in the present chapter were, with the
exception of *The Little House in Kolomna* and *The Tales of
Belkin,* written during Pushkin's married years.

II   The Little House in Kolomna

The Little House in Kolomna is an unpretentious and slender
little work consisting of 40 octaves (it is written in *ottava rima*
in the manner of *Beppo* and *Don Juan*). The influence of Byron
has been noted frequently and justifiably, both with regard to
the "Southern poems" and to *Evgeny Onegin.* Nowhere, however, it is more in evidence than in this small work which was
written during the highly productive autumn of 1830 in Boldino.
Pushkin's digressions and their connection with Byron's works
have already been pointed out; but nowhere does Pushkin more
completely reflect the Byronic digression than in this poem,
where digressions, as in *Beppo* and *Don Juan,* lack the calculated precision shown in *Ruslan and Lyudmila* and *Evgeny
Onegin.* They approximate more to loose, relaxed, meandering
thoughts, which give the impression that the author is genuinely
unable to concentrate and to return to the topic at hand.

The Little House in Kolomna starts in rambling fashion with
Pushkin's thoughts on the caesura after the fourth syllable in the
iambic pentameter. This is, in effect, Pushkin's manifesto of
emancipation from the caesura—an emancipation which was
noted in connection with the "little tragedies." Along with meter,
the caesura and his preference for the caesura which he is
now discarding, Pushkin discusses the business of rhymes, which
are seen as soldiers lined up in array. After this preamble, the
poet gets down to the business of his slender story. In Kolomna
there is a widow living with her daughter. The two sew and
indulge in other feminine activities at their window. The daughter, though simply dressed, nevertheless attracts the attention of
passing guardsmen. Mother and daughter have been looked
after by an elderly cook who, however, now proceeds to die. The
mother bids the daughter to seek out another cook to replace
the late deceased. The daughter brings back a cook, who stipu-
lates no fixed wage—which is very pleasing to the mother—and

installs herself in the house. The cook proves highly inefficient. The dishes are broken, the meals are overcooked and oversalted. Nevertheless, the cook is cheap. On Sunday mother and daughter go, as is their habit, to church. Suddenly the mother is afflicted with suspicions about the cook; she wonders if the cook may not be stealing. Returning home early from the service, she discovers the cook shaving. The cook leaves without explanation and without demanding pay. The daughter returns somewhat later from church and is "horrified" to hear what has come to pass. The moral of this story, according to Pushkin, is that one should not try to hire a cook cheap or for nothing, and that someone who is born a man should not put on skirts, because sooner or later he will have to shave. This is a real "nonsense" poem, and as Pushkin says in his concluding lines, "there is nothing more that can be squeezed out of my story."

III   Angelo

Angelo is the only one of Pushkin's longer poems to be written in six foot iambics (with a caesura after the third foot). It is divided into three parts, consisting altogether of 535 lines. It is an adaptation of Shakespeare's *Measure for Measure*, with changes (Mariana is here Angelo's wife, whom he has put aside because her reputation was touched—though wrongly—by the breath of scandal), highly compressed (as must be evident from the number of lines), with everything discarded which was not central to Pushkin's main artistic goal—the delineation of Angelo's character, which clearly fascinated Pushkin. In expressing his preference for Shakespeare over Molière, Pushkin, we remember, called attention to Shakespeare's breadth in characterization as contrasted with the consistency and narrowness of Molière's creations, "personifications of a specific passion or vice." Shylock was on these grounds rated superior to Harpagon. So also Angelo to Tartuffe: "In Molière the Hypocrite runs after his benefactor's wife—hypocritically; assumes the guardianship of an estate—hypocritically; asks for a glass of water—hypocritically. In Shakespeare the hypocrite pronounces sentence with a self-satisfied severity, but justly; he justifies his cruelty on the well-reasoned grounds of administrative expediency; he tries to seduce innocence with powerfully persuasive sophisms, not with

a comic mixture of piety and gallantry. Angelo is a hypocrite—
because his public acts and statements are at variance with his
secret passions! But what depth this character possesses!"[1] Pushkin's interest in Shakespeare's approach to characterization and
in the complicated nature of human psychology provides a link
between *Angelo* and the "little tragedies." *Angelo* has, further,
in common with the "little tragedies" the same terseness and
elimination of all "non-essential" elements. It differs from the
latter in that it is not a drama. Although it contains (like *The
Gypsies* and *Poltava*) passages of dialogue, *Angelo* is basically
a verse narrative.

Angelo is for the literary scholar something of a problem. It
was rated very low by most of Pushkin's contemporaries. On the
other hand, we must try to take into account Mirsky's thought
that "*Angelo,* if not a masterpiece of the highest order, is for the
student of Pushkin and of his last manner [Mirsky has in mind
Pushkin's wish to write impersonally and objectively] one of his
most interesting works."[2]

The events presented in *Angelo* can be summarized very
briefly. The Duke of an Italian city has been too kindhearted
and lax in his enforcement of law and order. It is difficult to—
suddenly—turn the tide. The Duke therefore provisionally turns
over the reins of government to Angelo, "a man experienced, not
new in the art of governing, austere in his way of life," and the
Duke departs. Under Angelo, law enforcement immediately becomes stricter. One of the laws which under the Duke has not
been enforced is that against fornication, which has been going
its normal way, unimpeded by law. One of the first victims of
the new austere regime is the young patrician Claudio, who has
been caught fornicating with Juliet, whom, however, he intends
to marry. Claudio must therefore suffer the death penalty.
Claudio begs his friend, Lucio, to ask his sister, Isabella, to inter-
cede on his behalf. Isabella, who is on the verge of becoming a
nun, pleads with Angelo for mercy. Angelo, who conceives an
almost immediate lust for Isabella, makes her an obvious proposal—which, incidentally, Isabella is very slow to understand.
Isabella conveys this ultimatum to her brother, Claudio. Her
brother is much concerned with Isabella's honor, but he is not
reluctant to see her lose it, if only this will enable him to live.
Isabella is outraged by her brother's lack of moral fiber, but for-

gives him and still loves him. The Duke, who has meanwhile been masquerading as a monk and has overheard the conversation between brother and sister, then finds a solution: Mariana, the wife whom Angelo has put aside because of false rumors about her behavior, will replace Isabella at the night time tryst. The tryst is successfully consummated. But Angelo nevertheless orders the execution of Claudio. He is confronted and exposed by the Duke. Not lacking courage, Angelo asks that he be executed as soon as possible. The Duke forgives him.

Angelo is a rather depressing piece of writing. At the outset there is a certain "Byronic" lightness of touch; there is irony and the assurance that none of this should be taken too seriously. But then the atmosphere changes with the realization that Claudio will die. This is now a matter of life or death. The trouble—from the point of view of appreciation—is that the discussion between brother and sister, though well enough motivated, does not really move the reader very deeply; he is prepared for an easy way out. To oversimplify, it becomes more like a game of chess than a moving drama. Angelo's courage, expressed at the end in his request for death, does come through to the reader, and, as Pushkin would have wished, Angelo's "breadth" of character when he breaks his word to Isabella must be recognized. But the real impact, if any, of this narrative poem must be sought in Pushkin's demonstration of the fact that words mean nothing and principles change from one minute to the next: a brother who would fight for his sister's honor is willing to have her sacrifice that honor if only he can be kept alive! That is why—rated high or low—*Angelo* is a depressing piece of writing.

George Gibian, in an illuminating comparison of *Angelo* with *Measure for Measure* has shown convincingly that Pushkin, not so much by omissions (inevitable in so brief a poem), but by changes from Shakespeare's original, has revealed what he admired more and what less in Shakespeare's play. Citing several changes (e.g., the transfer of the action from Vienna to "happy Italy"), Gibian speaks of Pushkin's "lightening the mood." He sees in *Angelo* a Chaucerian quality. All this is valid. But it is precisely the lightness of the Chaucerian opening that renders more sordid what follows. And what follows is told so briefly, with the characters etched in so laconically, that the reader has, as it

were, no time to understand emotionally their motives and
actions. It is not, therefore, that the "immorality" of the story
and characters offend; if this were so, then much of Boccaccio,
Chaucer, and Pushkin would be offensive; it is, rather, the semi-
jocular opening leading abruptly to a revelation of human nature
at its least appealing—without the reader's sympathies being involved—which leaves behind a certain feeling of distaste for
human kind. To say this is not necessarily to diminish the value
of *Angelo;* it is to interpret it in the darkest of colors.[3]

IV   The Tale of the Tsar Saltan

The *skazki* (usually rendered in English as fairy tales in verse)
reflect two of the artistic preoccupations of Pushkin's later years:
his striving during the 1830's for impersonality and objectivity
and his increased interest in folk poetry. His completed *skazki*
are four in number: *The Tale of the Tsar Saltan* (1831); *The
Tale of the Fisherman and the Fish* (1883); *The Tale of the
Dead Princess and the Seven Heroes* (1833); and *The Tale of
the Golden Cockerel* (1834).[4]

Much of Pushkin's interest in folk poetry dates back to his
1824-26 stay in Mikhaylovskoe when he heard and wrote down
folk tales and poems recounted by his nurse, Arina Rodionova,
and others. If this period stimulated his interest, it also attuned
his ear to the folkloristic turns of phrase and intonational patterns which he was later to introduce into his own creations.
However, in his own *skazki* Pushkin did not faithfully reproduce
what he had heard at Mikhaylovskoe. Rather, he incorporated
what he had heard into his tales, making use of it where appropriate. He did not, in fact, feel bound by the Russian oral tradition. On the contrary, he felt free to turn to literary sources—
and, indeed, to sources of non-Russian origin, the Grimm
brothers and Washington Irving.[5]

This does not mean that his verse tales in any way lacked a
truly Russian quality. In order to understand this, we may recall
Pushkin's views on *narodnost'* discussed in connection with the
writing of Boris Godunov.[6] His view of *narodnost'* was not a
narrow one. He had the confidence to take what he wanted
where he wanted; it would be no less original, no less Russian
for that.

Of Pushkin's works the verse tales lend themselves, probably, least of all to interpretation for the non-Russian reader. This is because their content is slender indeed; there is no claim to profundity of thought; there are few theories or ideas to be discussed. Their greatness rests on their formal perfection, the rhythms, rhymes, repetitions, and variations which are bound to elude the non-Russian ear. For this reason little can be done in translation to convey the truly great merit of Pushkin's *skazki*. We shall content ourselves with recapitulating only one of his verse tales, that one which is generally regarded as his most perfect.

The Tale of the Tsar Saltan is written in four-foot trochees, with rhymed couplets alternating between masculine and feminine (i.e., 7-syllable rhymed couplets alternating with 8-syllable rhymed couplets), arranged in stanzas or paragraphs of varying length. It consists of 996 lines.

The tale opens with three sisters spinning at their window. Each speculates on what she would do if she were tsarina. The first would prepare a feast for the whole world; the second would weave an enormous cloth:

> "And if I should be tsarina,"
> Said the third of the three sisters,
> "I would bear a warrior-son,
> Bear him for my lord, the tsar."

This answer delights the tsar who has been listening from behind the door:

> "Thrive and prosper, lovely maiden,"
> Spake he, "thou shalt be tsarina,
> Thou shalt bear a warrior-son
> 'Ere September's days are done."

And to the other two sisters:

> "One of you shall work the loom,
> And the other be the cook".....
> And no time at all he tarried,
> On that very eve he married:
> At the marriage feast Saltan
> Sits with his tsarina young.....
> Raves one sister in the kitchen,

> At the loom the other's weeping,
> And they both great envy feel,
> Envy feel against the bride.
> And meanwhile the young tsarina,
> No long time at all she tarried,
> That first night she was with child.

Tsar Saltan then goes off to war. At the appointed time a magnificent boy-child is born. The tsarina sends off a messenger to
inform the father. But the envious sisters, with the help of the
scheming old woman, Babarikha, have the messenger inter-
cepted, and a false messenger reports to the tsar:

> The tsarina has brought forth
> Not a daughter, not a son;
> Not a mouse and not a frog,
> Some strange beastie she has born.

The tsar, mortified, wants to hang the messenger, but relents,
and sends him back with a written order to wait for the decision
which he will make on his return. The cunning women have the
returning messenger made drunk and substitute a different
order:

> Tsar Saltan his nobles orders:
> Secretly, with no delaying,
> The tsarina shall be cast
> With her offspring in the deep.

Reluctantly the nobles obey the order. Mother and child are
committed to the sea in a cask. The cask is washed up safely
ashore. The child who has been growing "not by the day, but by
the hour" has the strength to break it open. On the unknown
seashore the boy shoots and kills with an arrow a hawk who was
attacking a swan. The swan then, "in the Russian language,"
hails the tsarevich as her savior, tells him that the hawk was no
hawk but a magician, that she is no swan but a maiden, and
that she will repay his good deed.

Mother and son lie down to sleep. When they awake, they are
bewildered to see before them a magnificent city. They are
hailed by the citizens. The son is crowned and rules over the
city under the name of Prince Gvidon.

A ship sails by. The sailors are amazed to see on a familiar

island that a fine city has sprung up. They put in and are welcomed by Prince Gvidon who asks them what cargo they have
been trading and whither bound. They have been all around the
world and are now on their way to "the kingdom of the glorious
Saltan." The Prince tells them:

> Travel safely, goodly men,
> On the sea, upon the ocean,
> To the glorious Tsar Saltan;
> And to him my greeting give.

Prince Gvidon watches from the shore in sorrow as the ship departs. Suddenly the swan appears and asks him why he is sad.
He would like to see his father. The swan transforms him into a
mosquito, he flies, catches up with the ship, and is thus able to
visit his father's city. His father, surrounded by the three scheming women, is sad. He asks the sailors what they have seen beyond the seas, and they tell of the miraculous new city and of
Prince Gvidon's greeting. Tsar Saltan wishes to visit the city,
but is dissuaded by the women who tell of even greater wonders
more worthy of viewing. The mosquito in anger bites one of his
aunts in the right eye and flies away. This incident is repeated
twice more. Saltan again wishes to visit the new city, but on the
first occasion he is again dissuaded by the scheming women.
Finally, however, he rebels:

> "What am I? A child or tsar?"
> Says Saltan in earnest now:
> "Go I shall!" He stamped his foot,
> Walked away and slammed the door.

He sails his fleet to Gvidon's island, is reunited with wife and
son, embraces his beautiful daughter-in-law (the swan who was
in reality a princess), pardons the three wicked women, there is
a feast, after which Tsar Saltan is put to bed half-drunk, and
everything ends happily.

In mentioning the difficulty of conveying to the non-Russian
reader the beauty of Pushkin's *skazki*, it should also be noted
that Russian critics, while abundant in their praise of the *skazki*
—and most justifiably so—have very little to offer beyond gener-
alizations in the way of comment on the exact nature of their
esthetic qualities. The truth is that the *skazki* offer us art at its

most "playful," and at its best. The *skazki* are better read than
discussed, and better still read aloud.

V   The Bronze Horseman

The Bronze Horseman, completed in Boldino in the fall of
1833, is written in freely rhymed iambic tetrameters and consists of an *Introduction* and two "parts," 481 lines in all. It is
rightly regarded as one of Pushkin's greatest masterpieces. It is
also one of the most tangled webs ever woven by Pushkin. It is
composed of so many strands of a personal, literary, and political nature, there are so many facets and angles to this work, that
it is not surprising that various commentators have differed
widely in their interpretations of the poem, or at least in their
view of where its main emphasis lies.

The poem takes its name from Falconet's statue of Peter the
Great which stands in Petersburg near the banks of the Neva.
The historical incident around which the poem centers is the
devastating flood which hit Petersburg on November 7, 1824.
But the *Introduction,* consisting of 96 lines, begins many years
before that. Peter the Great is seen standing on the site of
what was to become Petersburg, looking out over the desolate
waters of the Baltic. The broad Neva River—on it a single small
craft—flows past. He sees only marshland and forest, with here
and there a poor Finnish hut. And then the fateful thought:
here shall be founded a city, whence Russia will threaten the
haughty Swede and "open a window onto Europe." There passed
one hundred years, and there from the dark woods and swampy
marshlands had arisen a prosperous, proud city, "the beauty and
wonder" of the North. Where formerly from the low shores the
lonely Finnish fisherman cast his dilapidated net into the unknown waters, now the lively shores are crowded with mighty
towers and palaces. Ships from the ends of the earth stream into
the rich wharves, and the Neva flows between walls of granite.
Famous are the lines:

> Before the new capital's bright blaze
> Dimmed is ancient Moscow's star,
> As before the new tsarina fades
> The aging widow of some tsar.

Here the theme of Petersburg becomes interwoven with the narrator's thoughts of his own activities and impressions. He loves Petersburg's austere harmony, the majestic flow of the Neva, "the transparent dark, the moonless gleam" of Petersburg's "pensive nights," when in his room he writes and reads without a lamp. He loves the motionless air and the frost of Petersburg's cruel winter, the sleds running along the banks of the broad Neva, the rosy flushed cheeks of the young girls, the glitter and stir and conversation at the balls, the sparkling wine and the blue-flaming punch of the bachelor party. And then his thoughts turn away from the more intimately personal impressions to embrace a larger, civic theme—the military reviews, the perfect precision of infantry and cavalry, the victorious standards tattered in the fray, the boom of cannon announcing the birth of a royal son or a new Russian victory. He concludes this paean of praise:

> Thrive, Peter's lovely city; stand
> Unshakable as Russia stands.
> Even the elements subdued,
> May they with you be reconciled....

And then an abrupt change! There was a terrible occasion. It is still fresh in the narrator's memory. He will tell about it, and "sad will be my story."

As *Part I* opens, it is a cold, dark, rainy, windy day in Petersburg, and the Neva is raging "like a sick man on his bed." It is dark and late as young Evgeny returns home. Let us call our hero Evgeny, the author suggests, since his pen was once on good terms with that name. The family name doesn't matter; it was once famous in the annals of Russian history, but is now a forgotten one. Evgeny undresses and goes to bed, but he is kept awake by his thoughts: he is poor, but he hopes by hard work to gain his modest share of financial independence and honor; he envies those unintelligent idlers who have life so easy. He thinks too of the rising river. If the bridges go down, he will be separated for two or three days from his Parasha who lives on one of the islands in the Neva. He sighs deeply and, like a poet, starts to dream. Marry? Well, why not? It will be difficult, of course, but he is young and healthy. And in his mind Evgeny sees the picture of a very modest, simple, domestic happiness.

Next morning Petersburg is flooded. The description of the

flood is among the most famous passages in Russian poetry. Everywhere there is chaos and destruction. Sad and troubled, the late Tsar Alexander I emerges onto his balcony and says: "Even tsars cannot master God's elements." He sits down and pensively, with eyes full of sorrow, gazes on the catastrophe. Meanwhile, Evgeny has sought refuge from the flood by seating himself astride a marble lion near the statue of Peter the Great. Evgeny is hatless and pale. He is in mortal fear, not for himself, but for Parasha and the little dilapidated house in which she and her mother live, and where the flood is raging with terrible intensity:

> They are there,
> Widow and daughter, his Parasha,
> His cherished dream. Could what he sees
> Be but a dream? Or is all life
> An empty dream and nothing more,
> Heaven's cruel mockery at earth?

The nearby statue is oblivious to Evgeny's torments:

> With his back turned toward Evgeny,
> High, mighty and unshakable,
> Towering above the raging flood,
> There proudly rides with arm outstretched
> The idol on the horse of bronze.

Part II opens with the Neva gradually subsiding, leaving behind death and destruction. Evgeny manages to hire a boatman to take him over to where Parasha lives. With difficulty they reach the shore. The scene is unrecognizable: houses twisted, collapsed, and strewn about by the flood; and all around bodies, as though on a battlefield. Evgeny rushes to where Parasha's house stood. Nothing! He walks round and round, talks to himself aloud, and suddenly, striking his forehead with his fist, he starts to laugh.

Very quickly life returns to normal. In their "cold callousness" people walk the streets as before. The civil servants return to their offices. The hucksters resume trading, trying to recoup their losses at the next man's expense. A minor court poet sets about describing the flood in "immortal verse."

But "my poor, poor, Evgeny," his mind gives way before the horror and the shock; his ears are filled with the rebellious roar of the Neva and the wind. He does not return home. His room is rented to someone else. By day he wanders around, sleeps by the wharves, feeds on what may be thrown to him through a window, his clothing is in rags, children throw stones at him, coachmen lay onto him with their whips if he gets in the way, but Evgeny seems not to notice. So he lives till summer is again turning to autumn. Then one night he awakes, and he remembers the full horror of his experience. He starts to walk about, to look around him, and there—

> There proudly rides with arm outstretched
> The idol on the horse of bronze.

He trembles and his mind grows terribly clear. He recognizes the place, the lions, the square, and that one whose bronze head rises immobile in the darkness, the man "by whose fateful will a city had been founded beneath the sea."

> How awesome in the mist is he!
> And 'neath that brow what thought is hid!
> What strength lies in that man contained!
> And in that steed what fearsome fire!
> Where are you galloping, proud steed?
> Where will your steal hooves come to rest?
> O mighty ruler of man's fate!
> Was it not thus that o'er the abyss
> On high with bit of iron you made
> The Russian steed to prance and rear?

Evgeny walks around the statue and confronts face to face the "ruler of half the world." Then, clenching teeth and fists, he hurls defiance at the statue, turns, and flees headlong! It had seemed to him that the face of the dread tsar had suddenly flamed with anger, and had turned toward him. As Evgeny flees through the streets of Petersburg, he hears the Bronze Horseman riding after him. From that night on, whenever Evgeny chanced through the fatal square, he would raise his battered hat, keep his eyes lowered, and pass well to the side.

The poem concludes with the mention of a small deserted

island, where sometimes a fisherman with his net puts in and
cooks his humble meal or where a civil servant may take his
boat on a Sunday outing. On this island a dilapidated little
house was washed ashore by the flood. Last spring it was removed by barge. It was empty and completely demolished. On
its threshold they found "my madman, and there in God's name
they buried his cold corspe."

In the writing of this poem Pushkin displays a complete mastery of technique. While employing the same meter throughout,
he changes his style to conform to the different moods, situations, and personalities. The majestic sonority of the lines describing Peter the Great and the might of Petersburg are in
marked contrast with the abrupt, jerky rhythms, and frequent
enjambments which convey perfectly all that has to do with
Evgeny: his humble dreams, his ineffectual actions, his harass-
ment, his panic. The poem contains a wealth of brilliantly de-
vised images which serve mainly to personify inanimate objects,
in particular the Neva and her raging waters, and to intensify
the sensation of constant movement and unrelenting restlessness
which pervades so much of *The Bronze Horseman.* Then, too,
there is the skillful use of onomatopoeia which permits the
reader to hear the echoing hoofbeats as the Horseman pursues
Evgeny. But it is impossible to treat exhaustively the many questions of style involved in *The Bronze Horseman.*[7]

The complexity of the poem lends itself to a variety of interpretations. We have, on the one hand, the affirmation of Peter's
great achievements and Russia's proud destiny; on the other, the
story of an average, insignificant young man who lost his fiancée
in a flood and went mad. And since Petersburg was founded, it
would seem, not in compliance with the logic of nature, but in
defiance of nature, at the bidding and through the iron will of
a dictator who was the embodiment of Russia's destiny and historical "mission," the poem clearly has as its theme the sacrifice
of the individual to "historical necessity." This has been frequently noted, but this explanation tells us little of the poem's
esthetic unifying principle. It is this principle that we must seek
to establish, or at least approach more closely.

What, to begin with, was Pushkin's personal attiude to the
dilemma of historical necessity and the welfare of the individual?
Pushkin's objectivity, his ability to see many conflicting sides

of a problem, and to hold the scales in even balance: this is a commonplace of literary scholarship devoted to Pushkin. But a closer look at the poet's subjective emotional attitudes, in this case as in others, helps to render the work more meaningful.[8]

One stimulus to the writing of *The Bronze Horseman* came from the great Polish poet, Adam Mickiewicz. Mickiewicz, then an involuntary guest of the Russian Empire, had become friends with Pushkin on the latter's return from exile in 1826. Mickiewicz had been allowed to leave Russia in 1829. There had followed the 1830–31 Polish uprising, during which—as we know—Pushkin had taken a strongly anti-Polish stand. After the defeat of the Poles, Mickiewicz wrote a cycle of poems (including especially "The Statue of Peter the Great" and "Oleszkiewicz") attacking the Russian autocracy, the lack of freedom in Russia, and the purposelessness of the vast Russian imperial mechanism. Pushkin's *The Bronze Horseman* is, in one of its aspects, a rebuke to Mickiewicz. Where Mickiewicz saw Asiatic inertia and aimlessness, Pushkin saw, embodied in Peter, dynamism and destiny. Highly critical though he was in many ways of his native land, Pushkin did not share the views of such thinkers as Chaadaev, who saw Russia as having contributed nothing to civilization and, in effect, lying beyond the pale of history and historical progress. Pushkin believed in Russia—although with gritted teeth. Thus the passages, mainly in the *Introduction*, praising Petersburg and Peter's achievements are perfectly sincere. In style and content these passages reflect the eighteenth-century tradition of the laudatory ode. At the same time Pushkin's attitude to Peter the Great was ambivalent. He was aware of the brutal methods employed by the tyrant to achieve his ends. Peter had used the "iron bit," forcing Russia to rear up on its hind legs. Peter had, other things apart, sacrificed over 100,000 Russian lives to the building of the strategically placed and beautiful city of Petersburg.

Against the background of these political evaluations Pushkin constructs the story of Evgeny. Evgeny is the victim of Peter's city. Evgeny is the prototype in Russian literature of a series of characters (found in the works of Gogol, Dostoyevsky, and others) rendered mad by the oppressive atmosphere of the "unnatural" city of the north. But it was not merely acute powers of social observation that enabled Pushkin to depict this emerg-

ing type—the victim of the indifferent metropolis—for Pushkin
was himself a victim of Petersburg. And in Evgeny there is a
great deal of Pushkin.

Evgeny, like Pushkin, came of formerly illustrious but now
impoverished stock. That in the final version of the poem
Evgeny, contemplating marriage, dreamed "like a poet" might
be dismissed as a piece of irony, but an earlier draft shows
Evgeny actually writing verse.[9] Far more important than these
superficial similarities between author and hero is the fact that
Evgeny's sense of injustice and persecution, and of his own
impotence, were Pushkin's own.

Andrey Bely, by taking quotations from Pushkin's letters to
his wife and from his diary, has demonstrated convincingly that
Pushkin's own pent-up feeling of imprisonment was expressed
in *The Bronze Horseman.* Pushkin was Nicholas' prisoner as
Evgeny was Peter's victim. Bely has also pointed out that the
lyric beginning "God grant that I not lose my mind," though the
dating is uncertain, was written at about the same time as *The
Bronze Horseman.*[10] In *The Bronze Horseman* Pushkin, as was
often his wont, concealed his most intimate feelings under the
cloak of objectivity. Recognition of this fact tells us a good deal
about Pushkin. More important, it gives a whole new perspective and undestanding of the poem. It renders Evgeny's misfortune, his madness, his defiance, and his irrational fear immeasurably more poignant and terrifying than they would otherwise
have been. Pushkin's own misery, transmuted into artistic terms,
is the esthetic unifying principle of *The Bronze Horseman.* This
would not be so were it not for the fact that, as so often with
Pushkin, the poet's personal emotions strike a deep chord in the
hearts of others.

There is another aspect to *The Bronze Horseman.* Even the
inadequate recapitulation above suffices to show that there is
some similarity between the scene at the poem's opening and
that at the end. In both scenes desolate nature, unmarked by
man's hand, predominates; even some of the same lexical items
are employed. Could it be that after all nature will triumph? As
the Tsar on his balcony remarked sadly, "even tsars cannot
master God's elements." Is this, perhaps, the thought, the un-
spoken wish of the poet that "unnatural" and oppressive Petersburg shall perish?

It has often been said of great works of literature that they lend themselves to varying interpretations from one generation to another. *The Bronze Horseman,* written in 1833, seems to have a clear message for the second half of the twentieth century, when millions of small individuals are confined in large cities, suffer from the heartless indifference of their surroundings, rise up in their ghettos in sometimes irrational anger and hurl defiance, and are consumed by irrational anxieties and fears —the more terrifying because they are not fully understood.

VI   *Prose Writings*

Pushkin, along with some of his contemporaries, realized early in his literary career that Russian prose had lagged far behind Russian poetry in its achievements. Furthermore, the floweriness characteristic of much Russian poetry had infiltrated the prose. As early as 1822 we find his commenting: "Voltaire may be regarded as an excellent example of sensible style.... Precision, tidiness, these are the prime matters of prose. It demands thought and more thought, brilliant expressions are of no use; poetry is another business.... Whose prose is the best in our literature? Karamzin's: this is no great praise."[11] Pushkin's intense interest in Vyazemsky's translation of Benjamin Constant's *Adolphe,* which he greatly admired, was motivated not only by the undoubted merits of the French original, but by Pushkin's feeling that Constant could point the way to what Pushkin felt was lacking in Russian literature, "metaphysical"[12] language as he termed it, by which he appears to have meant the language of abstract thought and of psychological analysis. In this connection Pushkin's thoughts were turned not only inward—to the needs of Russian literature, but outward—to the scene of world literature on which, he felt, only through prose writing could Russian literature win its right of citizenship. Thus Pushkin approached the problem of Russian prose writing—just as he approached the problem of the Russian theater—with definite theoretical views as to the needs of Russian literature and as to the correct path to be taken. As his remarks on Voltaire, cited above, indicate, it was essential that Russian prose be simple and to the point. It was essential that Russian literary prose be

sharply distinguished from poetry, should cast off the influence
which poetry had hitherto exterted on it, should free itself from
its Cinderella position and establish itself in its own rights. And
these theoretical views he sought to implement.

Pushkin himself was from his early days a master of Russian
prose. This can be clearly seen from his letters. We should not
forget that letter writing was in Pushkin's day, even when the
letters were intended for private consumption only, still considered as something of a literary genre. The clarity, precision,
and punch of Pushkin's letters show that he was quick to
acquire deftness and authority in wielding his native prose.
However, in the field of strictly literary prose, Pushkin was
slow to make his start.[13] His first serious attempt at literary
prose was in 1827, when he wrote his unfinished *The Moor of
Peter the Great.* His first completed prose works were written in
1830 at Boldino. But once started, Pushkin's prose output increased steadily. During the 1830's he wrote considerably more
in prose than in verse. The following comments can claim to do
little more than pay token tribute to his work as a prose writer
by discussing briefly three of *The Tales of Belkin, The Queen
of Spades,* and *The Captain's Daughter.*

The Tales of Belkin consists of five short stories purportedly
related to and recounted by the late Ivan Petrovich Belkin.
These are *The Shot, The Snowstorm, The Stationmaster, The
Undertaker,* and *The Lady Turned Peasant.* They were all written in the fall of 1830 at Boldino. In these seemingly simple and
unpretentious stories Pushkin follows rigidly the principles out-
lined above with regard to the necessity for drawing a sharp
distinction between prose and verse. The style is clear and concise, bereft of all ornamentation—to the point of deliberate
austerity. The syntax is straightforward and lean; there are few
subordinate clauses and few epithets. The narrative proceeds
logically and rapidly—with no attempt at psychological analysis
and with very few comments from the narrator.[14]

There is one aspect of *The Tales of Belkin* which is likely to
elude the modern reader and which also has to do with Pushkin's views on literature. *The Tales* are polemical in intent,
parodying the then-existing prose fashions. The parody is, in
general, achieved by taking a staple literary situation or character—and then adding a new twist, designed to expose the

artificiality of the literary cliché involved. Pushkin's "twists" point invariably in the direction of common sense. For example, *The Stationmaster* is a rebuttal of the Sentimentalist fallacy that poor girls are by nature innocent, that they are ensnared and deceived by rich young men, and that the results of their seduction or abduction are bound to be catastrophic. The polemical aspects of *The Tales* may well have little importance for today's reader and should not, in any case, be exaggerated. For this reader then, they will fall into perspective as straightforward light-weight anecdotes, well told, and with a touch of irony, and with no great literary pretensions.[15]

The hero of *The Shot,* Silvio, is a sardonic, "demonic," pseudo-Byronic character of about thirty-five years. His personality enables him to dominate the young officers (Silvio is a civilian) whose company he keeps in a small town where their regiment is stationed. One night, he is insulted at the gambling table by a newcomer, but to everyone's amazement, although he is an excellent shot, Silvio refuses to challenge the young officer. No one would have suspected Silvio of cowardice. And indeed the reason lies elsewhere. Six years earlier Silvio had received a slap in the face. He had been at that time a hussar, the hardest-drinking and fightingest in the regiment, and properly acclaimed therefor. But a new face, a new officer had joined the regiment —youthful, intelligent, handsome, gay, brave, of very high birth, immeasurably wealthy, and openhanded. Silvio's primacy had been challenged. He had sought the occasion for a quarrel. The brilliant newcomer's success with women—particularly one with whom Silvio had relations—was the last straw. A remark from Silvio at a ball, a slap in the face, and both men had drawn their sabers. Separated momentarily, the two were in place and ready to duel at dawn the next day—the young officer arriving late, his cap full of cherries which he was eating. After discussion the rivals drew for the first shot. Silvio's opponent won the draw, fired first, and put a bullet through Silvio's cap. His life was now in Silvio's hands, but Silvio's hatred would not be satisfied with killing a man who seemed not to care for life and continued to eat cherries and spit out the seeds. At Silvio's suggestion that his rival leave and take a meal, the latter agreed, saying that Silvio would be entitled to his shot at any time he chose to name. It was because of this incident that Silvio had retired from the regiment, had bided his time, and refused to duel with the drunken young officer who had insulted him.

The time for Silvio's revenge comes when his carefree rival gets married. Silvio arrives at the estate of his hated rival, the now married Count, and claims his shot. The Count, no longer so carefree and indifferent, in love with his wife and marriage, asks Silvio to fire quickly. But Silvio hesitates and insists they again draw lots. Again the Count wins. He fires and misses. How had he allowed himself to be persuaded to draw lots again? What dishonor! Silvio starts to take aim, when suddenly the Countess bursts in, the Count assures her that it was only a joke, Silvio continues to take aim, and then—when the Count begs him to fire quickly—Silvio, with the Countess at his knees, refuses! "I am satisfied," he says, "I have seen you looking bad; I have witnessed your timidity; I made you take the first shot, this is my satisfaction. You will remember me. I commit you to your own conscience." Silvio had later been killed fighting for the Greeks against the Turks, but he had had his revenge!

The Snowstorm is a designedly improbable story. The heroine, Maria Gavrilovna, has been brought up on French novels and is consequently in love. Her hero, Vladimir, is a poor army ensign. The parents are opposed to a match. The young couple decides to elope. Maria Gavrilovna is, according to plan, put in a sledge and brought to the church. Her hero (and this takes place in the countryside) loses his way to the church in a snowstorm. Maria Gavrilovna is returned home and becomes feverishly sick. Her parents decide that love is the cause and that—like it or not—she should marry her beloved. She recovers, but her beloved, Vladimir, in spite of the parents' willingness, refuses to enter the house. He leaves for the army (this is in 1812) and dies. Maria Gavrilovna's father dies. She inherits his property, moves, and is assailed by suitors whom she rejects. The 1812 campaign now being victoriously concluded, she—in spite of her lauded fidelity to Vladimir's memory—falls in love with the wounded returning veteran, Burmin, colonel in the hussars—and he with her. However, both are restrained in their courtship—by something undivulged. The problem, it turns out, is that both are married. On the fateful night when Vladimir had failed to show up, Maria Gavrilovna, without seeing the groom, had become married to someone else! That someone had been the then irrespon-

sible Burmin, also lost in the storm! The problem is therefore
no problem: they are already married!

The Stationmaster, as hinted above, tells of the abduction of
a poor girl, the stationmaster's daughter, by a rich young man—
in this case a young hussar. The poor girl, Dunya, is a flirt. The
hussar abducts her—with her full consent. The post station of
which the father is master boasts a picture of the Prodigal Son—
and the fallen returning sinner clearly forms a pseudo-ideologi-
cal background to the story. The father, when Dunya does not
return, falls ill. Recovering somewhat, he follows the pair to
Petersburg "to bring home his sheep that has strayed." The
hussar, Minsky, receives him after some delay, begs his forgiveness, tells him that he has no intention of returning Dunya, and
gives him some money. Somehow the stationmaster finds himself on the street. In conventional disgust he spurns the money,
throws it away, has second thoughts, returns—and finds that it is
gone! He makes one more unavailing attempt to penetrate
Dunya's new "home," and is ejected. He returns to the station,
becomes an alcoholic, and dies. Some time later a fine lady,
with a six-horse carriage and three children, arrives at the station, asks about her father, visits his grave in sorrow, and gives
money to the priest.

The Tales of Belkin are in some cases interesting for the insights they give us into Pushkin's intimate thoughts. The Shot,
for example, shows without doubt that Pushkin was, at the time
of writing, absorbed in the problem of the value of life, insignificant perhaps at one moment, but at another moment immeasurably enhanced by love of a woman.[16] The Tales are
interesting, too, for the possibility they afford of an understanding of his views on Russian prose and his quest for extreme
simplicity. They are of significance, though this has been exaggerated, for the development of Russian prose. But for today's
reader they are best taken for what they are—modest anecdotes
skillfully told.

Pushkin's The Queen of Spades (1834) is something rather
different, though here, too, its significance should not be overemphasized. Pushkin, as we know, loved to gamble. Pushkin
also, as we know, was a pioneer in describing the peculiar
madness induced by Petersburg. He was also familiar with the
works of E. T. A. Hoffman. Out of all this arose The Queen of

Spades. Critics have sometimes accorded to this story a profundity of thought that is not really there. Like *The Tales of
Belkin* it is really an anecdote, a good yarn. The characterization,
it is true, is somewhat more detailed. The mood, it is true, is
different. And the syntax shows a tendency to become more
complex and less austere—which is only another way of saying
that Pushkin's Voltairean prose simplicity and self-abnegation
could not be expected, in the long run, to weather the psychological complexities which were to be characteristic of nineteenth-century prose. *The Queen of Spades* shows where Pushkin himself as a prose writer would have had to go. It shows that
he could not have reproduced another cycle of *The Tales of
Belkin.*

The Queen of Spades opens with a scene of Russian officers
gambling. Hermann, the part-German hero, invariably watches,
but does not participate in the play. "Gambling is of great interest to me," he says, "but I am not in a position to sacrifice what
is necessary to me in the hope of acquiring a surplus." Hermann
is, Tomsky—one of the gambling Russian officers—opines, a good
German: "he is calculating, that's all there is to it." Tomsky then
proceeds to tell of his grandmother, who had lost catastrophically at gambling in Paris, but who had recouped her losses by
eliciting from a French nobleman a three-card formula which,
it seems, is *bound* to win but can never be repeated. Hermann
is bewitched by the thought of a three-card formula which
affords the possibility of a once-and-for-all-time coup.

The old Countess is still alive. In order to obtain her gambling
secret, the ruthless Hermann is willing to woo her woman companion, her ward, Lizaveta Ivanovna. By notes and other ploys
he succeeds in this. After a ball to be attended by the Countess,
Hermann will, it is agreed between him and the ensnared Liza,
install himself secretly in her room and await her return. But
no. After long, anguished waiting Hermann is not in Liza's
room, but—on the return from the ball—he is concealed near the
Countess's room. When the Countess is at last alone, her maids
departed, Hermann confronts her: Will she not give up a secret
which is useless to her, which would give him everything he
could ever have wished? The old lady is frightened and, as
Hermann perists, she panics and dies. Hermann, having lost the

chance of the three-card formula, turns to Liza and explains his duplicity. She guides him out of the house.

Hermann is present at the funeral of the old Countess. In the Orthodox tradition he approaches the corpse. At that moment he feels that the old Countess screws up one eye on him, and he faints. Later that night the Countess comes to him: "I have come against my own will," she says, "but I have to fulfill your wish. The three, the seven, and the ace, one after the other, will win for you—but on these conditions, that you never play more than one card in one day, and that you never gamble again. I forgive you my death on condition that you marry my ward, Lizaveta Ivanovna."

The three, the seven, and the ace. Hermann is frightened, but resolute. He is taken to the most exclusive gambling house in Petersburg, and is introduced to its owner, the distinguished Chekalinsky. Hermann asks to be allowed to play. When he announces the stake—47,000 rubles, his total ownings—excitement runs high. The three wins. Hermann leaves. On the following night he returns: 94,000 rubles, and the seven wins. On the third night his arrival is eagerly awaited by one and all. People abandon their own gambling and cluster round as Hermann approaches the table. Chekalinsky is pale, but he can summon up his habitual smile. The cards are played. " 'The ace wins,' said Hermann, turning up his card. 'Your queen loses,' said Chekalinsky gently. Hermann trembled: in very fact he did have not the ace but the queen of spades. He could not believe his eyes, could not understand how he had produced the wrong card. At this moment he thought he saw the queen of spades screw up her eyes and smile at him ironically. He was struck by a definite similarity. 'The old woman,' he cried out in horror."

Herman goes mad, repeating endlessly "three, seven, ace! Three, seven, queen!" Liza becomes happily and prospersously married. Tomsky is promoted and gets married. *The Queen of Spades* is an excellent, eery, suspenseful, well-told story.

The Captain's Daughter (completed in 1836) is a historical novel. The historical novel was very much the fashion at that time. Indeed, *The Moor of Peter the Great,* mentioned above, testifies to Pushkin's earlier interest in this genre rendered popular by Walter Scott. Pushkin's novel is—by comparison with those of Scott—told simply, without Scott's lengthy descriptions of person and place. The historical event on which Pushkin's novel is based is the uprising against Catherine II's regime headed by Pugachev (1773). The hero is a young officer loyal to Catherine. A multitude of events, in which Pugachev is sympathetically depicted, brings about various circumstances in which the young hero, Grinev, is now united with, now separated from his love, Maria Ivanovna, and eventually—owing to his meetings with Pugachev—arrested on a charge of disloyalty. A meeting between Maria Ivanovna and Catherine II results in Grinev's vindication, and everything ends happily—in the true tradition of the Sentimental Romantic novel.

It is difficult to make any valid comments on this—or for that matter on Pushkin's other prose works. Perhaps the most appropriate thing that can be said, in addition to the remarks made above, is—and this is surely no poor compliment—that none of his prose works makes for tedious reading, and that their sum total makes us wish that he could have written more in prose, makes us wonder if—had he lived longer—Pushkin would not have become one of Russia's great prose writers. But, as things are, the thought remains firmly implanted that Pushkin was first and foremost a poet.

CHAPTER 7

Lyric Poetry — 1820-1836

THE TERM *lyric* is sometimes used in Russian criticism to denote any poem belonging to the shorter genres—from the epigram to the elegy, from the personal theme to the patriotic or civic (anything, in effect, that can be listed under *stikhotvoreniya* or short poems, as opposed to the longer *poemy*). There is also the more limited and specific meaning of the word which envisages a *lyric* as a short poem in which the personal feelings of the author stand in the foreground: objective reality may well serve as a basis for such a poem, but it is the subjective feelings of the poet which receive the primary emphasis. It is in this latter narrower sense that Pushkin's lyrics are mainly treated in the present chapter. Our concern will be with those poems which most directly reflect his intimate personal experiences, reactions, moods, and outlook. And of these only a relatively small percentage can here be mentioned.

In speaking of the subjective and personal as characteristic of the lyric, it should be borne in mind that the lyric element was by no means confined to Pushkin's shorter poems. It found expression, as we have seen, in such diverse works as *The Prisoner of the Caucasus, Evgeny Onegin,* the "Little Tragedies," and *The Bronze Horseman.* So close was indeed at times the connection between his lyrics and his longer works—both narrative and dramatic—that, as early drafts show, short "lyric" passages were sometimes transposed into longer works, or excerpted therefrom to appear as lyrics.

At the same time, in Pushkin's case, the subjective and personal elements cannot be regarded as excluding wider issues of a political and social character. For not only was Pushkin's lyric poetry largely "autobiographical" in the broad sense that its many varied themes had as their focal, unifying point the author's own personality, but the author's moods and attitudes frequently reflected changes in the general Russian political climate, as well as the political hopes and disappointments not of

Pushkin alone, but of many of his contemporaries. In many cases, Pushkin's lyrics yield insights not only into the poet's inner world, but into the larger world of Imperial Russia in which he lived.

One question which occupies Pushkin scholars is how best to divide Pushkin's lyric output into periods. This is inevitably a difficult problem. Themes treated in adolescence reappear in his mature work. New themes are added at certain points in time —without, however, the old themes necessarily disappearing. Among literary genres, that of the lyric is one of the most tradition-bound. Thus, the borderlines between periods are hopelessly blurred. Recognizing, nevertheless, that in the course of his creative life changes in Pushkin's lyric writing are observable, it is possible to offer as a very rough guide the following breakdown:

(1) *1813–1820.* This early period begins with Pushkin's juvenile experiments in the ready-to-hand Classical and Sentimentalist genres, particularly those practiced by the *Arzamas* group. In 1816–17 his elegies sound a hitherto unheard note of despondency produced by unhappiness in love. In 1817–20 there is some change in his love poetry which would seem to reflect the greater firsthand experience of his Petersburg years. But the most important innovation of these three years consists in the writing of liberal verses betokening his opposition to the regime.

(2) *1820–1826.* 1820 marks the beginning of the powerful influence of Byronism which accords perfectly with Pushkin's own attitudes: his sense of betrayal by friends, alienation from society, unhappiness in love, and hopelessness with regard to his future. The impersonal liberalism of his Petersburg years comes increasingly to be blended in with more personal themes, and around 1823 a newfound skepticism begins to be heard with regard to the liberal movement in the West and in Russia. By 1823–24 Pushkin has developed a more mature, objective, and critical view of the "Byronic" hero. The period of his exile is marked by an abundance of love poetry—less "literary" by now and more closely reflecting actual situations and specific emotions.

(3) *1827–1831.* The poetry of these years, which includes some of Pushkin's finest and most moving love poems, is marked by a growing awareness of the poet's isolated position in society, a profound disquiet with regard to life's aimlessness, a preoccupation with the past, with the passing of youth, and at times,

with death. Pushkin's concern for the fate of the Decembrists also emerges in the poetry of these years, as do also his patriotic feelings prompted by the Polish uprising of 1831.

(4) *1831–1836*. In his last years there is a marked decrease in lyric output in general, particularly in lyrics devoted to intimate personal emotions; a tendency to "objectify" personal emotions is apparent; noteworthy is an increased interest in formal experimentation devoted to non-subjective themes and aiming at an extreme simplicity in style.

It cannot be overemphasized that this schema provides only the roughest of guides to thematic and stylistic development, not a series of watertight compartments.[1]

Pushkin's short poems written up to about 1820, as observed above, can, with a few exceptions, be treated as part of his apprenticeship. Elegance, technique, and feeling, although of a somewhat adolescent character, are clearly in evidence. But these early poems are, in the main, exercises in the literary tradition—both West European and Russian—in which Pushkin grew up. As Pushkin developed, he discarded many of the mannerisms of the *Arzamas* group, notably of Zhukovsky and Batyushkov. The formerly strong influence of Voltaire, Parny, and other eighteenth-century Classical poets diminished. The influence of André Chénier, Byron, and others was assimilated. Eventually, as we follow Pushkin's course, it no longer is meaningful to talk of influence. For though he continued all his life to experiment with non-Russian models, to borrow and to adapt, he reached a point where he was "using" models rather than "following" them, and his work became truly independent. But to this mature stage we shall come later.

The principal new important influence which Pushkin underwent in 1820 was that of Byron. This has been traced in Chapter 2 in connection with the "Southern poems." It made itself felt no less in Pushkin's lyric poetry. In fact, the first indication of Byronic influence occurs in a poem which in conception is undoubtedly indebted in some degree to Childe Harold's farewell to his native land (Canto I), and which Pushkin apparently wrote while sailing the Black Sea from Feodosia to Gurzuf:

> The frenzied love of former years I called to mind,
> And all I've suffered, all that's dear unto my heart,

And all the weary pain of thwarted hopes, desires. . . .
Fly on, swift bark, and carry me to distant lands
At the dread bidding of the e'er treacherous seas,
   Yet not, not to the gloomy shores
   That hem with mist my native land,
   The land where first fierce passion's fire
   Awoke, inflamed my youthful heart,
   And where on me the tender muses secret smiled,
   Where, battered by life's early storms,
   My youth decayed, my youth was lost,
Where light-winged joy and happiness deceived, betrayed,
Marked, doomed to suffering my heart, benumbed and cold.
   I go to seek new sights and sounds;
   Far, from you I flee, my native land. . . .

And Pushkin goes on, in a vein with which we are familiar from the "Southern" poems, to deplore the follies and mistakes of his youth, and the young women who deceived him, all forgotten now; only not forgotten are the deep wounds of love inflicted on his heart, which nothing has been able to heal.

The corrosive "Byronic" skepticism, which leads to a negation of all positive values in life, is described in "The Demon" (1823):

   In those past days when new to me
   Were all the sights and sounds of life—
   The maiden's gaze, the tree leaves' rustle,
   At night the nightingale's sweet song—
   When feelings noble, lofty, proud,
   When freedom, glory, yes, and love,
   And when the arts' winged inspiration
   So strongly made my blood to pulse—
   Then was it that some evil spirit,
   Casting upon my hopes and joys
   A sudden shade of grief and pain,
   Would come and sit alone with me.
   Sad were the meetings 'twixt us two:
   His smile and, yes, his beauteous gaze,
   His venom-laden, biting words
   Streamed a cold poison in my soul.
   With calumny upon his lips
   He tempted, challenged Providence;
   Beauty he called an idle dream;
   And inspiration he despised;
   Did not believe in freedom, love;

He looked with mockery on life—
And for no thing in all the world
One word of blessing would he speak.[2]

The considerable number of poems written to different women
during the first half of the 1820's show a wide range of feeling:
grief at parting; jealousy; sorrow at the imminent death of a girl;
the poet's reluctance to divulge the story of his mad passions and
sufferings to the innocent and uncomplicated woman who has,
for the moment, made him happy.

The theme of love is for Pushkin sometimes related to the
theme of reborn inspiration: after a period of spiritual flatness
and boredom the poet is reawakened by his meeting with a
woman, he experiences an almost Dionysiac *Lebensfreude,* his
heart is unlocked, reopened to joy and sorrow, his whole being
comes alive again, and he feels once more the urge to create.
This is the theme of his famous lyric to Anna Petrovna Kern.
Pushkin had been strongly impressed by her in a brief meeting
in 1819 in Petersburg. In 1825, while Pushkin was in exile in
Mikhaylovskoe, Anna Petrovna visited her relatives on the
neighboring estate of Trigorskoye. The following poem was the
fruit of the second meeting:

The wondrous moment I recall
When you appeared before my view;
You came, a dream ephemeral,
The spirit of pure beauty, you.

Through hopeless sorrows, somber, drear,
Through life's vain follies, whirls, alarms,
For long your gentle voice I'd hear,
And call to mind your tender charms.

Life's gusting storms—the years passed by—
Dispersed my dreams, and I forgot,
Forgot your gentle voice and I
Your face's heavenly charms forgot.

Remote, in gloomy isolation,
My days dragged by, the months, the years—
Without a god or inspiration,
With neither love nor life nor tears.

Thy soul, my soul to life recall!
Before me you appeared anew!
You came, a dream ephemeral,
The spirit of pure beauty, you.

And my heart beats in wild elation,
My spirit waked takes wing above;
Reborn are god and inspiration.
Reborn are life and tears and love.

But Pushkin's lyrics during the first half of the 1820's were not confined either to the theme of love or to the depiction of ennui and disillusionment. Pushkin is still the voice of Russian liberalism. In a verse epistle to his fellow poet Gnedich (1821), Pushkin compares his situation to that of Ovid in exile, but unlike the latter, "I to Octavius, in blind hope,/Pour forth no prayers of flattery." In his most famous political poem of this period, "The Dagger" (1821), Pushkin treats this weapon as a just means of retribution against tryanny and injustice. "The Dagger" is indeed a more outspoken, belligerent, and vengeful poem than the 1817 "Ode to Freedom." However, it is not, in this sense, entirely typical of the political verse written by Pushkin in the South and in Mikhaylovskoe. During the years 1820–25 two important changes are discernible in Pushkin's political verse. First, the narrowly political themes of 1817–20 are treated more broadly. The poet is, "The Dagger" excepted, no longer content to inveigh against tyranny, injustice, and serfdom, as though the setting right of these abuses would solve life's problems. These abuses are now viewed in the wider context of more general problems such as the processes of historical change, the meaning of life, and the destiny of man. At the same time these broader questions become interwoven with the personal emotions and reflections of the poet, and there occurs a fusion between the political theme and the truly lyric element in Pushkin's poetry. Secondly, from about 1823 a new note of skepticism is heard, skepticism both as to the successful outcome of any revolutionary attempt and as to the genuine determination of the people to achieve freedom.

This skepticism was undoubtedly induced in large measure by the failures in these years of the revolutionary movements in Portugal, Spain, and Naples. Pushkin's misgivings may also have arisen to some extent as a result of his contacts in the South with various members of the Russian revolutionary secret societies. His political skepticism is also to be seen as one facet of the tendency, noted above, to broaden the narrowly political theme, since it is applied not merely to political developments but to human nature in general. It is also tied in with the more specifically personal theme, since the poet complains that his call for freedom falls on deaf ears. This disillusioning dilemma, which seems to have provoked a spiritual crisis, is expressed in the following poem (1823), based on the parable of the sower:

> Sowing the seed of freedom I
> Early went forth, before the dawn,
> Into the wilds and with pure hand
> In furrows dark with slavery
> Freedom's life-giving seed I cast—
> I cast in vain; 'twas waste of time,
> Of labor and of noble thought . . .
> Graze on in peace, ye peoples, graze!
> You sleep and hear not honor's call.
> What use have herds for freedom's gifts?
> The butcher's or the shearer's knife
> Were better—and from age to age
> The yoke, the harness bells, the whip.[3]

"To the Sea" (1824) exemplifies perfectly Pushkin's growing tendency to combine the problem of freedom, presented now on a broad, almost philosophical base, with the problems of his personal life. Actually, this lyric started out as a meditation on the sea and the poet's destiny. The opening stanzas were written shortly before Pushkin's enforced departure from Odessa. The sea is seen as a symbol of freedom and power, and the poet recounts his own failure to carry out the plans he had nursed during the Odessa period—to escape from Russia by sea. The thought of Byron's death caused Pushkin, who had meanwhile arrived in Mikhaylovskoe, to enlarge his original theme to embrace both Byron, identified with the sea, as a symbol of freedom, and Napoleon.[4] Thus, in its final form, "To the Sea" is a lyric poem, which focuses on the poet's subjective emotions, but which defines these emotions by reference to the sea and to the world arena from which had recently passed two figures who had in different ways dominated the age:

Farewell, thou freedom's element!
For the last time before my gaze
Thy blue waves rise and surge and sink
And sparkle, beautiful and proud. . . .

Alas, I wished but never left
The dull and tedious earth-locked shore
To hail thee with enraptured joy
And through thy troughs, atop thy crests
To speed full-sail a poet's flight!

And thou didst call . . . but I was chained;
In vain my soul was torn and rent:
Held back by passion's powerful spell,
Alas, I stayed upon the shore . . .

Oh why regret? And whither now
My carefree steps can I direct?
One point in all your vasty wastes
Would make an impress on my soul.
One sea-swept rock, proud glory's tomb . . .
There memories of majesty
Waned and turned cold, were laid to sleep:
'Twas there Napoleon sank to rest.

There with his grief Napoleon lies.
And in his steps, like the storm's roar,
A second ruler of men's minds
Has sped away beyond our ken.

Has gone—and Freedom mourns his death—
Leaving the world his poet's wreath.
Surge waves, storm seas, and thunder gales:
He was thy bard, he sang of thee. . . .

The world's grown empty . . . Whither now,
Great ocean, could'st thou bear me? Where?
Man's fate is everywhere the same:
Where life seems blessed, there lies in wait
Man's petty sway or tyrant's tread.

Farewell, thou sea! I'll not forget
The solemn beauty of thy waves;
Long after this I still will hear
Their crashing roar at eventide.

> Into the silent, lonely woods
> I'll carry in my memory
> Thy cliffs, thy headlands and thy bays,
> Thy sunlight, shades and sound of waves.

In this poem Pushkin bade farewell not only to the sea, not only to his life and loves in Odessa, but also in some measure to the early Byronic Romanticism which had taken such strong hold in 1820 at the start of his Southern exile. "To the Sea" expressed his regretful conviction that with the passing of such gigantic spirits as Napoleon—his ambition and despotism notwithstanding—and Byron, the poet of freedom, the world had somehow become a smaller and emptier place. It also expresses (in the last stanza but two) a certain skepticism, which was to reappear in Pushkin's work, as to the benefits which were allegedly to be obtained by replacing despotism by more liberal forms of government. At the root of this skepticism is the poet's suspicion that no form of government can make men free and happy, and that the essence of man's freedom and happiness lies outside the sphere of government—elsewhere, in some spiritual independence which Pushkin himself never achieved.[5]

One problem which was to preoccupy Pushkin throughout his creative life had to do with the role of the poet in society. Does the poet have a social mission to perform? Can the criteria of utilitarianism be applied to his work? Does poetic art have laws of its own, purely esthetic laws, independent of any message that may be propagated? What about art for art's sake? Is the poet answerable to himself alone for what he writes? And how does the poet fit into the outside world of society? A fair number of Pushkin's finest lyrics are attempts to deal with one or the other aspect of this broad problem. Over the years, as will be seen in the following pages, his answers were not entirely consistent, or, more precisely, there occurred shifts in his emphasis, dictated by his own circumstances and moods. In "The Prophet" (1826), perhaps the best known of all his short poems, the poet's role is seen as a highly dynamic one. Endowed through inspiration with an understanding of life's essence, the poet is charged to go forth like a biblical prophet and transform the heart of man:

With fainting soul athirst for Grace,
I wandered in a desert place,
And at the crossing of the ways
I saw the sixfold Seraph blaze;
He touched mine eyes with fingers light
As sleep that cometh in the night:
And like a frighted eagle's eyes,
They opened wide with prophecies.
He touched mine ears, and they were drowned
With tumult and a roaring sound:
I heard convulsion in the sky,
And flights of angel hosts on high,
And beasts that move beneath the sea,
And the sap creeping in the tree.
And bending to my mouth he wrung
From out of it my sinful tongue,
And all its lies and idle rust,
And 'twixt my lips a-perishing
A subtle serpent's forked sting
With right hand wet with blood he thrust.
And with his sword my breast he cleft,
My quaking heart thereout he reft,
And in the yawning of my breast
A coal of living fire he pressed.
Then in the desert I lay dead,
And God called unto me and said:
"Arise, and let My voice be heard,
Charged with My Will go forth and span
The land and sea, and let My Word
Lay waste with fire the heart of man."[6]

"The Prophet" was written in the late summer of 1826. At that time the sentencing of the Decembrists (five hanged and many exiled to Siberia) must have loomed large and fresh in the poet's mind. His very use of biblical style and imagery (see Isaiah 6) is in conformity with a Decembrist poetic tradition which depicted the Old Testament poet-prophet as scourging injustice and tyranny. This is not to impose on "The Prophet," as some have sought to do, a narrowly political message. This poem lends itself rather to a broader, more general, almost philosophical interpretation. It has its roots in the distinction—already noted and a constantly recurring theme in Pushkin's work—between the poet in moments of inspiration and the poet reduced to

mediocrity by the toils and snares of everyday petty preoccupations. The poet's superior wisdom and loftier view is granted
him by virtue of his inspiration. This concept would appear to
have something in common with the pantheism of Schelling
which commanded support among Moscow intellectuals at that
time. True, "The Prophet" reflects a basically Romantic view of
the role of the poet. But Schelling's ideas on life and art were in
essence alien to Pushkin's earthy outlook. Just as it is a mistake
to see "The Prophet" in narrowly political terms, so also it would
be wrong to read into this poem either Schellingian "other-
worldliness" or any specifically religious appeal. The poet's inspiration is the foundation and keynote of the poem. With all
this, "The Prophet" remains a challenging call to the poet to
maintain the integrity of his vision and to speak out loud and
clean on the side of truth and justice.[7]

The failure of the Decembrist uprising had important reper-
cussions for Pushkin's political thinking. A nascent political skepticism was, as noted above, already apparent some time before
December 14, 1825—in the short and bitter poem in which Pushkin likens himself to the sower in the New Testament parable,
and in "To the Sea." After December 14 it was obvious to Pushkin and to others that the liberal cause had been defeated and
that Nicholas I intended to rule with a firm hand. The poet's
reaction was not, however, one of simple resignation. His interest in Russian history, exemplified in his work on *Boris Godunov,*
which was completed about a month before the Decembrist
debacle, had been growing. He was beginning to ask himself
the question, which was to preoccupy so many Russian minds
in the nineteenth century, as to whether the Russian path of
historical development had necessarily to follow along lines
observed in other countries, particularly West European, or
whether peculiarly Russian conditions might not demand peculiarly Russian solutions.

More specifically, Pushkin was conversant with the views of
the Russian writer and historian, Karamzin, whose conservatism
found its justification in the indisputable fact that progress and
enlightenment had come to Russia not through the efforts of
society or the people, but as a result of deliberate measures imposed by Russia's autocratic rulers, in particular Peter the Great.
Add to this general line of speculation the gratitude Pushkin felt

owing to his reprieve from exile, and it is not difficult to understand how Pushkin came to hope—and he was not alone in this
hope—that, notwithstanding the brutal suppression of the Decembrist revolt, rational reforms would be forthcoming. But,
these reforms would be introduced from above, as indeed the
Tsar appears to have carefully stipulated in the September 8
interview in expressing to Pushkin his concern for the welfare
of the Russian people. It is also understandable how Pushkin at
times tended to draw a parallel between Nicholas I and Peter
the Great. "Stanzas," written in December 1826, at the outset of
Nicholas' reign and shortly after the poet's reprieve, conveys
Pushkin's initial optimism:

> In hope of happy days, renown,
> With confidence I gaze ahead:
> The start of Peter's glorious reign
> Was marred by risings crushed with blood.
>
> But he with truth won minds and hearts,
> With learning tamed the savage breast,
> Let Dolgoruky speak his mind,
> Saw not rebellion in his words.
>
> Boldly, with autocratic hand,
> He sowed the seeds of knowledge far
> And wide throughout his native land:
> Russia's proud destiny he knew.
>
> Now scholar and now man of war,
> Now carpenter, now mariner,
> His mind and hand encompassed all;
> A sovereign, he asked no rest.
>
> His the proud line from which you stem;
> Be proud, and follow in his steps:
> Like him, work tirelessly, be firm,
> Nor harbor rancor for what's past.

These noble sentiments bear testimony to Pushkin's delusions as
to the amount of influence a poet's voice might be expected to
have on his imperial master. The poem is also an appeal for
clemency for the exiled Decembrists. Furthermore, as already
noted, the poet's optimism was shared by others at the time. Yet
this poem marks the beginning of a problem which was to

plague Pushkin increasingly: it was widely regarded, even by some of the poet's friends, as a betrayal of his former convictions and an attempt to flatter the Tsar. It was, in fact, a compulsion to rebut charges of sycophancy which prompted Pushkin to write in 1828 a thirty-two line poem, "To My Friends," which begins:

> No flatterer I when to the Tsar
> I freely write a poem of praise:
> I speak sincerely, unrestrained,
> I speak the language of the heart.

Pushkin goes on to say that he feels a genuine warm affection for his Tsar, who has returned him from exile and "liberated my thoughts." The real flatterers are those who would counsel the Tsar to repress a natural instinct for mercy, to despise the people, and to distrust enlightenment as the seed of depravity and rebellion. He concludes:

> Woe to the land where round the throne
> Only the slaves and flatterers stand,
> And where the poet, heaven's elect.
> Stays silent, with his eyes cast down.

"To My Friends" was submitted to Nicholas I, who caused to be conveyed to Pushkin his satisfaction, together with his wish that the poem not be published.

Pushkin's position with regard to the Decembrists, if not a particularly comfortable one, was natural enough. Pushkin was, of course, shocked and despondent. Many of the Decembrists had been his friends. But there was absolutely nothing he could do to help them now. He had been lucky not to be involved himself. He had himself asked the Tsar for pardon. He had made, roughly speaking, his peace with the regime. Sympathy with the exiles' sufferings, the exhortation to bear adversity with courage, and hope for the future was all that he or anyone else could offer. In January 1827 he handed to one of the Decembrist wives, who was leaving Moscow to join her husband in exile, his "Message to Siberia":

In the depths of your Siberian mines
Preserve your courage, patience, pride;
Your toil, your burden's not in vain,
Your noble vision shall not fail.

True sister of misfortune, hope
Shall in your gloomy dungeons keep
Your spirits high and bring you cheer,
Your long-awaited day will come:

The call of friendship and of love
Will penetrate your gloomy bars,
As my free voice now reaches you
Within your dark and somber lairs.

The heavy chains shall fall away,
Your prisons crumble—and in joy
Freedom shall greet you at the gate,
And brothers hand to you the sword.

Pushkin's return from exile brought obvious blessings. It ended his enforced isolation and reopened to him the pleasures of companionship and society. At the same time it complicated immeasurably his emotional life. Not only had the Decembrist affair left him with a feeling of unease, but it had removed from Moscow and Petersburg a goodly number of former friends, whose very names could now be mentioned only with caution. The reader is already familiar with other aspects of Pushkin's situation in the bachelor years following his reprieve. The freedom granted by the Tsar on September 8, 1826, was proving to be, at best, only partial. There were the constant pinpricks of Benkendorf's Third Section, and there was the grave threat of the *Gavriiliada* incident. In general, it soon became impossible to substantiate Pushkin's contention that the Tsar had "liberated my thought." But the most serious threat to Pushkin's peace of mind lay within him. By Pushkin's own admission, the dissipations of his early Petersburg years (1817–20) had brought him more distress than happiness. Now he was again exposed to similar temptations: his gambling was near-compulsive and costly. The companionship of men and the attractions of women were time-consuming, as was also his emotional need to cut a figure in society. If these types of distraction caused distress in 1817–20, when Pushkin's age might have seemed to justify the sowing of wild oats, it is not difficult to understand their more serious effects on a man who was now approaching thirty and felt that his youth, which he regarded as largely misguided and misspent, was slipping out from under him. He was afflicted by a sense of aimlessness: he seemed to have no niche and no purpose; either life in general was a futile exercise, or his own individual life had gone astray. Benkendorf's supervision and Pushkin's own weaknesses formed a ring of encirclement from which it was difficult to break free.

Such were, loosely speaking, the circumstances which provided the backdrop for some of Pushkin's finest mature lyrics. One particular aspect of a more general unease has to do with the problem, already mentioned, of the position of the poet in society. In "The Poet" (1827) Pushkin makes the distinction—referred to above—between the poet inspired and the poet immersed in the trivialities of everyday living:

> Until Apollo summons him
> Unto the sacred sacrifice,
> Weakly the poet gives his heed
> To life's vain cares and futile round;
> And silent is his sacred lyre;
> Cold and unfeeling sleeps his soul,
> And 'mid the worthless of this world
> More worthless still, perchance, is he.
>
> But once Apollo's call divine
> Reaches the poet's eager ear,
> Like an eagle roused and taking wing,
> The poet wakened soars in flight.
> An alien to the world's vain joys,
> And shunning man's society,
> Before the idols of the crowd
> He proudly keeps his head unbowed;
> Austere and wild, the poet flees,
> Yes, filled with strange alarms and sounds
> Flees to the shore, the lonely waves,
> Flees to the pathless, soughing woods.

In "The Poet and the Throng" (1828) Pushkin vehemently denies any obligation on the part of the poet to feed neatly packaged moral truths to the public. He concludes with the following quatrain:

> Not for life's tumult and alarms,
> Nor for life's struggle, nor for gain,
> No, we were born for inspiration,
> For prayer, and for harmonious sound.

The poor reception accorded to his *Poltava* and, in general, a feeling of being harassed by his critics caused Pushkin to emphasize increasingly the poet's independence. In "To the Poet" (1830) he insists that the poet pay no heed to the praise or foolish abuse of the public; he must go his own way without expecting any reward; he is his own "highest judge," answerable only to himself. Pushkin's poetry in the last five or six years of his life met with less and less understanding from the public, and the feeling of disaffection expressed in "To the Poet" was to become a more or less stable part of his attitude.

The disquiet which began to oppress Pushkin after his return from exile was both general and specific. Anxiety over the consequences which could have ensued from the *Gavriiliada* investigation is expressed in "Foreboding" (1828):

> Once again above my head
> The calm sky fills with clouds of bane
> And envious fate with evil tread
> Stalks my footsteps once again.
> Can I still my fate deride?
> Shall I still to fate oppose
> The staunchness of my youthful pride
> Unbowed before her sternest blows?
>
> Bruised, battered by Life's cruel wind,
> The storm, indifferent, I await;
> Perhaps, saved even now, I'll find
> Some port of refuge from my fate.
> But parting's dread hour—I feel 'tis true—
> Looms near, forbidding, merciless,
> For the last time I haste to you,
> And your hand, my angel, press.
>
> Serene and gentle at the last.
> Angel, bid a quiet farewell;
> Let eyes uplifted or downcast
> Tenderly your sorrow tell.

> And your memory inside
> For me the heart's lone flight will wage,
> Replace the hope, the strength, the pride,
> The daring of my youthful age.

The woman from whom Pushkin seeks courage in this poem is
A. A Olenina, whom Pushkin was at the time courting with a view
to marriage, but by whom he was rejected.

As we know, it was Natalia Nikolaevna Goncharova to whom
Pushkin was eventually to become engaged and then married.
His attitude to marriage and to his fiancée was extremely complicated psychologically. On the one hand, there was the hope of
genuine happiness and spiritual rejuvenation; on a less ambitious
level, there was the desire to organize his life on a firmer, more
stable, more conventional footing. On the other hand, there were
his grave misgivings and his doubts as to whether happiness
could ever be his. At times he cast reluctant, at times nostalgic
backward glances at his past and thought of the women he had
once known and loved, still loved perhaps; and there was the
sorrowful feeling that his youth now lay behind him. This stock-
taking and the knowledge of the imminent change in his way of
life gave rise to some of his most moving lyrics. "Remembrance"
was written in 1828:

> When the loud day for men who sow and reap
>   Grows still, and on the silence of the town
> The unsubstantial veils of night and sleep,
>   The meed of the day's labour, settle down,
> Then for me in the stillness of the night
>   The wasting, watchful hours drag on their course,
> And in the idle darkness comes the bite
>   Of all the burning serpents of remorse;
> Dreams seethe; and fretful infelicities
>   Are swarming in my over-burdened soul,
> And Memory before my wakeful eyes
>   With noiseless hand unwinds her lengthy scroll.
> Then, as with loathing I peruse the years,
>   I tremble, and I curse my natal day,
> Wail bitterly, and bitterly shed tears,
>   But cannot wash the woeful script away.[8]

The pangs of remorse revealed in this poem were (as the unpublished continuation indicates) connected in the poet's mind with memories of past idleness and dissipation, of false friends, and of two women, now both dead, the remembrance of whom inspires in him—why, is not clear—feelings of guilt.

The realization that the time had come to adjust to a less exhilarating, more sober, and responsible way of life was not always expressed in the somber tones of "Remembrance." In a delightful verse epistle to Yazykov (1828), a fellow poet, Pushkin regrets that he is unable to join Yazykov and a mutual friend, N. D. Kiselev, in Derpt. His debts, incurred mainly by gambling, keep him in Petersburg:

> For long I've wished to join you in
> That German town whose praise you've sung,
> To drink with you, as poets drink,
> The wine whose praise you've also sung. . . .
> Oh youth, brave, carefree days of youth!
> I watch your passing with regret.
> In youth, when to my ears in debt,
> I'd give my creditors the slip,
> Take to my heels, go any place;
> But now I go to importune
> My debtors who are far from prompt,
> And staid and prudent how I curse
> The heavy weight of debt and age!
> Farewell, dear bard! Make merry, feast,
> May Venus, Phoebus bring you cheer,
> Heed not the pomp, conceit of rank,
> Heed not your debtors' honied words,
> Nor pay your debts: this is, you know,
> A Russian noble's inborn right.

The lighthearted touch of the Yazykov epistle is, however, not characteristic of this period. The following short, famous poem (1828) reads like an act of painful renunciation:

> I loved you once: love even now, maybe,
> Love's embers still within my heart remain;
> But trouble not; no, think no more of me;
> I would not cause you sorrow, bring you pain.
> I loved in silence, without hope, design;

Now shy, now jealous, torn by deep distress;
So tender and sincere a love was mine:
God grant some other love you no whit less.[9]

The sense of aimlessness and frustration which afflicted Pushkin at the time, produced moments in which the thought of
death amounted almost to an obsession. There exists no more
famous illustration of this mood than the following poem written
in 1829, which was a far from happy year:

When'er I walk on noisy streets,
Or watch the crowd that throngs the church,
Or sit and feast with reckless youth,
Then to my mind come brooding thoughts.

I think: the years will swiftly pass
And, many though we now may be,
The grave's eternal vaults await,
And someone's hour is now at hand.

I see, perchance, a lonely oak,
I think: this forest patriarch will
Outlast my petty span as he
Outlasted those who went before.

A dear, sweet infant I caress,
At once I think: farewell! farewell!
To you my place on earth I yield:
For you shall bloom, while I decay.

To every day and hour I bid
Farewell and speed them on their way,
Wondering which day shall prove to be
The anniversary of my death.

And where will fate send death to me?
In battle, travel, on the sea?
Or will a neighboring vale receive
Me when I turn to earth's cold dust?

And though the unfeeling body knows
Not where it's laid, where it decays,
Still I would rather take my rest
Near places which I once held dear.

> And at the entrance of the grave
> May youthful life laugh, romp and play,
> And may unheeding nature there
> With everlasting beauty shine.

The productive autumn of 1830, when a cholera epidemic confined Pushkin to the Boldino estate, was shot through with nostalgic moods. Ekaterina Vorontsova, the wife of the governor-general of Odessa, has been one woman to leave a profound and lasting impression on the poet. It was with her in mind that on October 5 of that year he wrote "Farewell":

> For the last time I dare embrace
> In thought your image dear to me,
> To have my heart relive its dream
> And with despondent, shy desire
> To recollect once more your love.
>
> The changing years pass swiftly by,
> Bring change to all, bring change to us,
> And for your poet you are now
> Cloaked in sepulchral shade, while he—
> For you—has vanished from the scene.
>
> And yet accept, my distant friend,
> A farewell greeting of my heart,
> Just as some widowed wife might do,
> Or friend embracing silent friend
> Before the prison door is closed.[10]

His "Elegy," written one month earlier on September 8, professes a desire to live and experience, but the mood is clouded and somber, the fragile pleasures and fleeting moments of inspiration he anticipates are outweighed by ominous forebodings, even the love he still hopes for will be flawed with the sadness of decline:

> The extinguished merriment of madcap years
> Weighs on me like a hangover's dull ache.
> But—as with wine—the sadness of past days,
> With age its strength increases in the soul.
> My path is dark. The future's troubled sea
> Holds little for me, mostly sorrow, toil.

> But no, my friends, I do not wish to die;
> I wish to live that I may think and suffer;
> And I know too that pleasures will be mine.
> Amid my troubles and my tribulation:
> At times again the Muses will delight,
> Creation's work will cause my tears to flow;
> Perhaps once more my waning star will shine
> Beneath the fleeting, farewell smile of Love.

One outgrowth of the increasingly tragic view of life expressed in Pushkin's lyrics at this time was a more devotional frame of mind. Pushkin was still capable of the irreverence of his *Gavriiliada* days. But more characteristic of the period around 1830 is a newfound respect for purity and sanctity. This is not, in the narrow sense, a religious feeling. It is, as always with Pushkin, partly esthetic, but it is also partly ethical in its aspiration for something pure and unchanging. A famous poem (1829) describes a poor knight who, after seeing an image of the Virgin Mary, will no longer look upon women or speak to them, but spends entire nights weeping before the image of the Virgin. Returning from Palestine, where he has fought bravely as a crusader, the knight secludes himself in his remote castle: "Still adoring, grieving ever,/And unshriven there he died." The Devil wishes to claim his soul, since the knight had neither prayed to God nor observed the fasts, and had adored unseemingly the Mother of Christ, but the Virgin intercedes and admits "her paladin" to heaven. Among other stimuli contributing to the makeup of this poem there is undoubtedly an underlying eroticism.

The same sublimated eroticism is clearly evident in Pushkin's "Madonna" (1830). In this poem, inspired by a painting of the Madonna and Child, as a letter written to his fiancée on July 30 of that year confirms, the Madonna of the poem is linked in the poet's emotions with the image of Natalia Nikolaevna.

The poet's marriage in February 1831 coincided with an abrupt change in his lyric output. Compared with the highly productive 1827–30 period, 1831 was a lean year: of only five lyrics with serious pretensions, three are devoted to patriotic themes and reflect both Pushkin's support of Russia against Poland and his temporarily improved relationship with Nicholas I. Nor in the years that remained (1832–36) was Pushkin ever again to achieve that high level of productivity which characterizes his last bachelor period. Undoubtedly the social round interfered with his work and almost certainly, there were poems of a highly intimate nature which did not survive. Then, too, Pushkin was in his last years directing his efforts more and more to prose. But it is also reasonable to assume that Pushkin's pleasures and anxieties as a married man did not lend themselves as well by their very nature to lyric expression as had been the case in the 1827–30 period. An opposition as simple as that between happiness and unhappiness is not here involved—Pushkin was never very happy for very long. Nor should it be implied that unhappiness is the essential stuff of good poetry. It is, rather, that the problems which beset Pushkin in 1827–30, though very much his own, are also universal problems which inevitably beset grown thinking men. And it is this that makes this period, judged on quality and quantity, a highwater mark in his career as a lyric poet. After Pushkin's marriage, either these problems were less often in the foreground of his mind, or he felt inhibitions about writing about them—and certainly about publishing. Yet the less abundant poetry written in 1832–36, where it deals with the poet's intimate emotional life, reveals no falling-off of his powers. The relatively few personal poems of these years must rank among his finest.

One interesting illustration of the difficulties that can beset the married lyric poet is a small poem almost certainly inspired by Pushkin's wife, published posthumously, of uncertain date, but probably written early in his marriage:

> Abandon's pleasures are not dear to me,
> Frenzy, voluptuous rapture, ecstasy,
> The young Bacchante who with groans and cries
> Writhes in my grasp and with hot ardor tries
> Her burning touch, her biting lips to lend
> To haste the shudd'ring instant of the end.
>
> How far more sweet the meekness of your kiss;
> With you I know O what tormented bliss,
> When yielding to long prayers, you tenderly
> And without rapture give yourself to me.
> Modestly cold, to my elation's cry
> Heedless of all, you scarcely make reply
> Then passion wakes, burns, blazes hotter, till—
> You share at last my flame—against your will.[11]

Whenever Pushkin did permit himself to vent his personal feelings during the last years, the tragic impasse into which his married and social life had plunged him, is revealed with an appalling starkness. In one poem, written in 1833 or later, Pushkin—the epitome of intellectual sanity, balance, and retraint—is seen toying with the temptation of madness:

> God grant that I not lose my mind.
> Better the beggar's staff and pouch;
>   Or better hunger, toil.
> I do not mean that reason I
> Now hold so dear; nor that with it
>   I'd not be glad to part.
>
> If only they would leave me free,
> How swiftly, gaily would I flee
>   Into the darkling woods!
> I'd sing, delirious, possessed,
> And lose myself enraptured in
>   Chaotic, wondrous dreams.
>
> And I would harken to the waves,
> And I would gaze, in happiness,
>   Up in the empty skies;
> And I would be so strong and free
> Like to a whirlwind cutting swathes
>   Through fields and forest trees.
>
> But here's the rub: if you go mad,
> Then men will fear you like the plague,
>   And, fearing, lock you up,
> And they'll attach you with a chain,
> And come and through the cage's bars
>   Torment you like some beast.
>
> And so by night I would not hear,
> Not hear the nightingale's clear voice,
>   The rustling of the trees—
> I'd hear my comrades' shouts and cries,
> The cursing of the nighttime guards,
>   And shrieks and sounds of chains.

It was to this poem that passing reference was made in our interpretation of *The Bronze Horseman*.

An unpublished excerpt, written probably in June 1834, reflects the poet's extreme weariness with the life of the capital and his longing to retire to the country. This excerpt is clearly an appeal to his wife:

> 'Tis time, my friend, 'tis time! the heart has need of peace—
> Days follow swiftly days, and each hour bears away
> Some fraction of our being—while we all unawares,
> Imagining we live, in life we are in death.
>
> Happiness none knows—but calm, and freedom: these can be.
> An enviable lot has long since been my dream,
> Long since, a weary slave, I've contemplated flight
> To some far-off abode of work and simple joys.

The manuscript contains Pushkin's plan for this unrevised and apparently unfinished excerpt: "Youth has no need of an *at home* [in English], mature age feels horror at *its own* isolation. Happy the man who finds a woman to share his life—he should make for *home*. Oh, shall I soon transfer my Penates to the country—fields, garden, peasants, books; poetic labors—family, love etc.—religion, death."[12]

But for Pushkin there was to be no escape. A visit to Mikhaylovskoe in September 1835, did not bring the hoped-for relief. In a somber poem Pushkin laments that his nurse, Arina Rodionovna, is now dead. He notes that young pines are beginning to grow up near the three tall pines he so often rode by. He himself will not live to see the young ones fully grown, but he hopes that his grandchild may see them and remember him.

As early as 1824, in his poem "To the Sea," Pushkin had expressed some doubt as to the relationship between different forms of government and the true happiness of the individual. "Man's fate is everywhere the same," he had written. Now in 1836 he restates this thesis more explicitly in his poem "From Pindemonte." The poem, translated here only in part, gives also a clear picture of the sense of confinement and imprisonment which had taken hold of Pushkin, of the desperate need for the independence of mind and body which he craved in vain, and of those things which in his despair he treasured most and identified most closely with happiness:

I set not too much store by those high-sounding rights
Proclaimed so loud by some, which dazzle some men's minds....
For these, I understand, are *words, words, words,* no more...
Dependence on a tsar or on the people's will:
It's one and the same thing. These are not rights. To have
To give account to none; to seek how best to serve
And please oneself alone; neither for power nor pomp
To bend the neck or compromise one's plans;
As one's own fancy bids, to wander here and there,
Gaze on the sacred gifts, the beauty Nature gives,
And wonder at the fruits of art and inspiration
With trembling joy, delight, enraptured adoration,
These things are happiness and freedom's rights...

Beset by marital problems, at odds with society in which he
was cutting an even sadder figure, and suffering from a neglect
of his literary genius—which made him feel that as a writer he
was regarded as having outlived his days of glory—the poet,
through much of 1836, is plagued by a foreboding of imminent
doom. A poem, written for the October 19, 1836 lycée anniversary, begins:

There was a time: 'twas then our youthful feast
Shone, noisy, gay and garlanded with rose,
The clink of glasses mingled with our songs....
This is no longer so: our rakish feast,
Like us, has with the years now run its course,
It has grown tamer, quieter and more staid,
The toasts and clinking glasses ring less loud,
Less playfully the conversation flows,
Some seats are empty, sadder now we sit,
More rarely 'mid the songs is laughter heard,
More often now we sigh, and silence keep....

What may be called Pushkin's final will and testament is a
poem entitled "Monument" (1836). This poem is Pushkin's con-
tribution to a longstanding literary tradition which, including in
Russia Dershavin and Lomonosov, extends back to Horace's
Exegi monumentum. The poem presents a sort of balance sheet
of the poet's past achievements. It is born of that sadness caused,
as noted above, by the lack of recognition accorded to his work
during the 1830's—a lack of recognition which, added to his personal tribulations, and compounded by the journalistic polemics

directed against him, embittered his last years. It is also the
poet's last assertion of his freedom and independence.

> I've raised a monument no human hands could build
> The path that leads to it can ne'er be overgrown,
> Its head, unbowed, untamed, stands higher from the ground
>   Than Alexander's column stands.
>
> Not all of me shall die: in verses shall my soul
> Outlive my mortal dust and shall escape decay—
> And I shall be renowned so long as on this earth
>   One single poet is alive.
>
> My hallowed fame shall spread through Russia's mighty land,
> And each and every tribe shall venerate my name:
> The proud Slav and the Finn, the still untamed Tungus,
>   The Kalmuk, dweller of the steppe.
>
> Long after this my name shall warm the people's heart,
> Because my lyre has sung of feelings good and kind
> And in my cruel age I sang blessed freedom's praise
>   And for the fallen mercy begged.
>
> Be thou obedient, Muse, to the command of God!
> Not fearing hurt nor wrong, seeking no laurel crown,
> Remain indifferent to calumny and praise,
>   And do not quarrel with the fool.

Undoubtedly, Pushkin was right in predicting his own lasting
fame. He was right, too, in the sense of timing which prompted
him to write this poem—concealing beneath its traditional sur-
face a mass of suffering—six months before his death.[13]

What, in conclusion, can be said of the best of Pushkin's lyric
poetry? The sounds—in translation—elude us. Those to whom the
privilege of reading Pushkin in the original is denied must take
on faith that the sound patterns in his lyrics, though seldom
obtrusive, are not only beautiful but also functional in that they
harmonize with and contribute to the sense. The same must also
be said, specifically, of the rhymes which play an important part
in most of the lyrics—not merely as embellishments or line-mark-
ers but also as structural factors which shape the syntax and
point up the thought, to which they are subordinated.

The themes and thoughts of Pushkin's lyrics speak largely for
themselves. But some further understanding of his outstanding

achievement as a lyric poet may be gained by comparing the best poems of his mature years with what he wrote in his youth. When, for example, in his 1816–17 elegies Pushkin speaks of unrequited love, of sorrow, and of death, though he is certainly sincere, one is aware that these are the moods of despair which sometimes beset the very young, moods which respond to the treatment of experience and adjustment, moods also, let it be said, which reflect a literary era. When in his mature work he speaks of such things, he speaks with his own voice, with a freshness, directness, and immediacy that give the impression that such emotions have not been treated in literature ever before. He speaks for himself in such a way that the natural and simple words he uses seem to emanate directly from the specific experiences and impressions of one man—experiences and impressions which could be precisely conveyed in those words alone. At the same time the balance, sense of proportion and self-restraint impart to his writings a universal quality. For Pushkin's writings are characterized—in form as well as content—by that self-restraint in dealing with deeply felt emotion which life demands of all men. Furthermore, this very self-restraint renders intelligible and doubly poignant to others the sufferings and tribulations which motivated Pushkin in writing of himself. And he wrote of things which are the common lot of grown man everywhere, of the limitations which life imposes on each and all, limitations which impart to life a tragic element which cannot be overlooked.

CHAPTER 8

Conclusion

THE FINAL questions remain—for Pushkin as for any other writer. What is the peculiar nature of his appeal? Can some unity be discerned in his writings? Are there certain specific qualities which make up a whole and which would justify our speaking of Pushkin's own poetic world? What is the sum total of his achievement? Any attempt to answer such questions is beset with pitfalls. There is the legitimate doubt as to whether these and similar questions should be posed at all. The difference in values and attitudes between one age and another must be reckoned with. Personal tastes and preferences are involved. There is the inherent disadvantage of trying to discuss on one plane—the critical and analytical—questions which bear on a different plane—the imaginative and poetic. And there is the certain knowledge that no judgments are final.

An obvious starting point is Pushkin's time and the circumstances, literary and otherwise, of his life. The world into which he was born was an apparently secure one: aristocratic, in some ways and on some days elegant, refined, literary, in seeming harmony with the cultural values and interests of French Classicism which so early and so profoundly influenced Pushkin. Yet as a result of the generally unsatisfactory nature of the Pushkin family relationships and, in particular, the lack of maternal affection, Pushkin was denied some of the normal feelings of childhood security. This deprivation was reflected in a certain unevenness of temperament and behavior which manifest itself during his lycée days. The lycée, for all that, did provide Pushkin with a feeling of home: it satisfied one obvious need by giving recognition to his special talents; it gave him comradeship; it permitted him to identfy with a young elite to whom no avenues in future life would be closed; and, for six crucially formative years, it postponed full awareness of his family's straitened finances which were to make it virtually impossible for him to hold his own among his chosen elite.

187

The full extent of Pushkin's unpreparedness for the demands of adult "aristocratic" life is revealed in the vagaries of his three Petersburg years (1817–20). With little or no sense of family, and with insufficient money for the role he would have liked to play, Pushkin was quickly at odds with himself. Courting different milieus (conservative, literary, gay blade, and liberal), but never fully identifying with any one, Pushkin placed himself to some extent in the position of the outsider whose need is for recognition—this notwithstanding his ever growing reputation as a poet and as the voice of liberalism. He wanted many things, but was committed to no fixed goal. His enforced but perhaps subconsciously sought transfer to the South and the period of exile in Mikhaylovskoe inevitably increased his feelings of isolation and alienation. And these attitudes, born of the tribulations of his personal life, found an almost perfect parallel in the pessimistic Romantic tendencies which in 1820 so strongly influenced his literary activities.

This combination of personal and literary factors was, I believe, to a large extent decisive for Pushkin's emotional makeup throughout the remainder of his life. Pushkin was never to achieve a feeling of security or identification. His 1826 return from exile provided no solution. The meaninglessness of much of his bachelor existence and the constant harrassments of a suspicious regime made him long for escape and produced the moods of despair reflected in his lyrics around 1829. Finally, his choice of a marriage partner merely compounded his unease: his relationship with his wife, redeeming features notwithstanding, was basically unsatisfying. He failed to occupy in society the position he held his due, and he lacked the determination to brave the Tsar's and his wife's displeasure by withdrawing from society. He was plagued by increasing financial insecurity. He was tormented by jealousy, and, meanwhile, even in the sphere of literature, he found himself partially denied the recognition which had at one time been so freely and generously accorded. His duel with d'Anthès, whatever the justifications and provocations, was, also, an attempted escape—which was, in a sense, successful.

To dwell thus on the less happy aspects of Pushkin's life is not to wish to depict him as some lachrymose melancholic who wore his heart in a sling. It is rather an attempt to emphasize the often underplayed fact that Pushkin was all his life insecure and extremely, as it were, vulnerable, and that this emotional vulnerability accorded perfectly with his literary Romanticism.

There is also the other side of the coin: Pushkin's gaiety and ebullience, the sanity and balance of his intellect have been many times—and justifiably—emphasized. Nor do we forget, since our focus is literary, that Pushkin did not stop short at Romanticism—certainly of the Byronic variety with which he became acquainted in 1820. This is not to place him in the literary school of Realism. The strongly Realist vein in Pushkin's mental outlook was, as much as anything, a result of the formative influences of French Classicism and a part of the poet's personality. The fact remains that Pushkin's mature work drew its sustenance from a variety of genres and schools, and that to label him a Romantic would be no more justified than to label him a Realist. Romanticism did, however, in the final analysis, serve as an emotional point of departure for many of Pushkin's finest creations. It is in what Pushkin did with Romantic moods and problems that much of his achievement lies. The poetic world of his most outstanding serious writings reflects the tension between a Romantic-type emotional attitude and an intellect which was constantly brought into play to moderate and transmute the excesses, the subjectivity, and the limitations which were often a concomitant of the Romantic *Weltanschauung*.

Pushkin's poetic world is striking by its pluralism and multiformity. One strong vein in his work is that of humor. This is evidenced in many of his short poems and verse epistles to friends. It is displayed at its best in such works as *Ruslan and Lyudmila, Gavriiliada, Count Nulin,* and certain portions of *Evgeny Onegin*. This trait has its literary inception in the eighteenth century (Voltaire first and foremost) and parallels in its development the early nineteenth-century humor of Byron's *Beppo* and *Don Juan*. We have here a Pushkin who can be witty, ironic, irreverent, zestful, gay, and sometimes bawdy. We have also—and this is, alas, all too often forgotten—Pushkin at his very best. It is a sad mistake on the part of some content-hungry, development-obsessed critics to pluck profundity from certain Pushkin poems while dismissing as delightful trivia such masterpieces as *Ruslan and Lyudmila* and *Count Nulin*. They contain no profundity, for no profundity was sought. Their emotional range is limited, for such was the author's intent. But in their own way they approach perfection as nearly as anything Pushkin ever wrote. As Byron once put it in his defense of Pope, "the poet who *executes* best is the highest, whatever his department," and again, "a good poet can imbue a pack of cards with more poetry than inhabits the forests of America." Pushkin's humorous poetry must rank very high in any assessment of his achievement and must be accounted for in any attempt to define his poetic world.

At the opposite pole there is the Pushkin of the "Southern" poems—humorless, disillusioned, nostalgic, antisocial, acquainted with love's torments and with despair. There is also the Pushkin of 1829 and 1830, preoccupied with the thought of death. There is the Pushkin, weary, persecuted, and shackled, of *The Bronze Horseman* and some of the later lyrics. And there are other facets to Pushkin's genius: his patriotism, his intense interest in the processes of Russia's historical evolution, his liberalism, his conservatism, his delight in formal perfection displayed, for example, in his graceful fairy tales in verse. And finally (though not in time) there is *Evgeny Onegin*, which weaves together so many strands of Pushkin's thoughts, feelings, and moods, which, more fully than any other work, reflects the diversity of his poetic world, and which—with all due respect to other opinions—is not only his most popular but his greatest achievement.[1]

In his perceptive booklet, *The Hedgehog and the Fox*, Isaiah Berlin distinguishes among writers between the "hedgehogs", "who relate everything to a single central vision, one system less or more coherent or articulate, in terms of which they understand, think and feel" and, on the other side, the "foxes", "who pursue many ends, often unrelated and even contradictory . . . . seizing upon the essence of a vast variety of experiences and objects for what they are in themselves. . . ."[2] Pushkin, as Berlin points out, clearly belongs to the "foxes." But even the most free-roving, wide-ranging of foxes will inevitably seize upon experiences which, for some overt or covert reason, are of particular interest to *him*. And it is this process of selection and treatment, conscious or unconscious, which can be expected to yield insights into the writer's, perhaps unformulated, view of life. Pushkin is no exception. He did not simply choose to write about Don Juan out of idleness or caprice; his choice of the Don Juan theme and his manner of handling it were dictated from within. In fact, here and elsewhere, he injected into allegedly "objective," third-person situations his own most intimate thoughts, feelings, and problems. It is, therefore, in the recurrence of certain themes, preoccupations, notes, and moods in Pushkin's writings that we seek a unified, though not specified, view of life, a point of reference for Pushkin's poetic inspiration, and some insight into the nature of the appeal which his poetry exerts.

Pushkin's "foxlike" diversity or, in Berlin's words, his "protean genius" would appear as an obstacle to any attempt at establishing unity. Yet it is precisely here that a start must be made. For the absence of a "central vision" is no less significant than its presence. The central vision of a Dante or a Dostoevsky posits the existence of some point of anchorage in the endless, shifting sea of life, some stable point of reference to which life's vagaries can be related. The very lack of this in Pushkin accounts for a great deal. Pushkin's was a pragmatic mind, concerned primarily with the immediacy of life on earth. At the same time Pushkin became and remained intensely aware of Death, to which, indeed, he at times seemed irresistibly drawn. It is Pushkin's feeling for Death that provides a key to many of his feelings for the experiences of life. Lacking a "central vision"—specifically a Christian central vision—he could not feel Death as a prelude to some continued existence or life hereafter; for him Death simply rang down the curtain on the final act of life here below. And this almost pagan view of Death's inevitability and finality imbues with added poignancy what he wrote about our earthly existence—which is indeed his sole concern. Life's unrelenting ebb, the irretrievable passage of time, the unpredictability of Fate—the vulnerability of man's destiny, a metaphysical despair—these are some of the preoccupations and moods which go hand in hand with and accentuate the more dynamic sides of Pushkin's passionate nature: his zest for life, his wit and humor, his pursuit of love, his intense feeling for beauty in many forms. There is in much of Pushkin's work an exuberant, uncomplicated, almost sunlight quality. But his view of the world is, in the final analysis, somewhat bleak and tragic.

It is, I believe, on this ontological foundation that Pushkin's poetic achievement rests. But this is not his achievement. His achievement lies in the individual poems, concrete images, and specific words which he composed. It is not unusual, in the writings of some critics, to find Pushkin hailed as a brilliant and profound thinker. This approach is misleading and inaccurate. There is nothing radically original in the view of life which emerges from Pushkin's poetry. The originality lies in the poems themselves. In one sense only can Pushkin justifiably be considered pre-eminent as a thinker—in the sense that *content* and *form* are one and indissoluble, and that therefore Pushkin's *thought* was his *poetry;* for, as T. S. Eliot reminds us, "the meaning of a poem exists in the words of the poem, and in those words only."[3] Moreover, the "words" of which Eliot speaks are—in Pushkin's case—Russian words. Their sounds, meanings, associations, and sequences can never be rendered perfectly in any language other than Russian. This is what distinguishes them from the words of the abstract thinker, the technological expert, or the pamphleteer. Herein lies their extra dimension. They defy paraphrase and they defy, at the very last, stylistic analysis. A poem's meter, rhythm, alliterations, assonances, and other qualities can be discussed. In the final analysis, however, it cannot be explained why a sensitive reader like Maurice Baring was so struck and so deeply moved by the simple enough line from *The Covetous Knight. "I more, gde bezhali korabli"* (And the sea where ships were scudding free).[4] There are many such lines in Pushkin's writings—some charged with thought, some completely unpretentious in this respect. I will take the liberty of citing four lines from *Ruslan and Lyudmila,* which have always impressed me both by their complete lack of "profundity" and by their perfection:

> *Ja kazhdy den' vosstav ot sna*
> *Blagodaryu serdechno Boga*
> *Za to, chto v nashi vremena*
> *Vol'shebnikov uzh ne tak mnogo.*
> (Each single day when I awake,
> I give my heartfelt thanks to God
> For having so arranged it that
> We've fewer wizards in our age.)

For Pushkin then as for other poets, it is meaningful to talk of his poetic world in terms of his psychology, his ideas, the outlook on life which emerges from his writings, but we bear in mind that his achievement and his appeal are to be found in the manner in which he gave concrete expression to this poetic world.

Notes and References

All references to the large seventeen-volume Soviet Academy of Sciences edition of Pushkin's works (1937–1959) are abbreviated below as *Ak. nauk,* followed by the volume in Roman numerals, and the page reference given in the normal manner, e.g., *Ak. nauk,* V, 397.

Chapter One

1. Thirty-eight introductory lines in the first canto were written later, around 1824.

2. Pushkin was also indebted to the Russian tradition. Noteworthy are two eighteenth-century comic-epic predecessors, V. I. Maykov, author of *Elisey,* and I. P. Bogdanovich, author of *Dushen'ka,* the latter himself strongly influenced by La Fontaine. Further, a wealth of Russian sources for Pushkin's poem have been indicated; see V. V. Sipovsky, "*Ruslan i Lyudmila* (K literaturnoy istorii poemy)," *Pushkin i ego sovremenniki,* IV, 59–84. However, not only will the comparison with Ariosto and Voltaire be more meaningful to the Western reader, but—it is safe to add—this comparison was in 1817–20 more meaningful for Pushkin himself. Voltaire, in particular was greatly admired by Pushkin, and in two previous uncompleted attempts to write comic epic ("The Monk," 1813, and "Bova," 1814), Pushkin had specifically paid tribute to him.

3. For a discussion of these *Arzamas* attempts on the epic, see A. L. Slonimsky, "Pervaya poema Pushkina," *Pushkin: Vremennik pushkinskoy, komissii* (Moscow-Leningrad, 1937), III, 183–202.

4. The probable relationship between Zhukovsky's projected *Vladimir* and *Ruslan i Lyudmila* is discussed by L. N. Nazarova, "K istorii sozdaniya poemy Pushkina *Ruslan i Lyudmila,*" *Pushkin: Issledovaniya i materialy* (Moscow-Leningrad, 1956), I, 216–21; also B. Tomashevsky, *Pushkin* (Moscow-Leningrad, 1956), I, 299–302.

5. L. N. Nazarova, *op. cit.,* p. 221.

6. B. Tomashevsky, *op. cit.,* I, 456ff., is inclined to place unnecessary emphasis on the contemporary quality of *Ruslan and Lyudmila* which he quite correctly links with the narrator's digressions and a certain lyricism in Pushkin's poem. Tomashevsky's insistence appears to be motivated by the desire to set Pushkin off clearly from Ariosto and Voltaire. But Ariosto and Voltaire were in their own day and way equally "contemporary," and though Voltaire's anti-clerical satire is entirely absent from *Ruslan and Lyudmila,* the link between Pushkin's poem and *La Pucelle* is nevertheless a strong one.

7. Pushkin eventually removed from his poem some of the erotic details which appeared at this point in the first edition. For an even more outspoken description of a roughly similar situation, see *Orlando Furioso*, VIII, stanzas 49 and 50, with which Pushkin was familiar. In two other places, changes made by Pushkin were also dictated by modesty.

8. The situation in which a man finds himself obliged to make love to an old crone is found also in Chaucer, Dryden, and in Voltaire's "Ce qui plaît aux dames." However, with these three poets the old crone turns out to be a beautiful maiden in disguise, and everything ends well. Pushkin has, so to speak, reversed this situation in the most delightfully telling way; particularly effective is Finn's oversight with regard to the passing of time.

9. See "Oproverzhenie na kritiki," *Ak. nauk*, XI, 144.

10. This is not the place to go into the extremely complicated and often disputed critical question as to the nature of the poetic world created in *Orlando Furioso;* we can, however, say, in very general terms, that Pushkin's lightness of touch in *Ruslan and Lyudmila* conveys an impression similar to that conveyed in certain episodes of *Orlando Furioso*.

Chapter Two

1. The connection between the 1816–17 elegies and Pushkin's subsequent "Byronism" is well made by B. V. Tomashevsky, *op. cit.,* I, 120–21.

2. The outstanding work on the Byron-Pushkin literary relationship during Pushkin's Southern exile is that of V. M. Zhirmunsky, *Bayron i Pushkin* (Leningrad, 1924).

3. For a summary of these views, which he rejects, see Tomashevsky, *op. cit.,* I, 644–46.

4. See letter to V. P. Gorchakov, October–November, 1822; also "Oproverzhenie na kritiki," *Ak. nauk*, XI, 145.

5. "Oproverzhenie na kritiki," *Ak. nauk*, XI, 145.

6. From a letter to A. I. Turgenev, December 10, 1822; see *Ostaf'evsky arxiv knyazey Vyazemskikh;* here quoted from Tomashevsky, *op. cit.,* II, 430.

Chapter Three

1. The details of the audience are taken from various sources. The following are in English: H. Troyat, *Pushkin* (New York, 1950), pp. 250–53; E. J. Simmons, *Pushkin* (Cambridge, Massachusetts, 1937), pp. 252–55.

2. This is in the final version which was not only worked over by Pushkin, who excluded two scenes, but also suffered some change at the hands of the censor.

3. It is true that Pushkin was reading Shakespeare in the spring of 1824 in Odessa. This is clear from a letter written in April or the first half of May, 1824; see *Ak. nauk*, XIII, 92. However, this does not alter the fact that the influence of *Beppo* and *Don Juan* preceded that of Shakespeare. The point that Byron's later works were instrumental in "emancipating" Pushkin from his "Southern Byronism" is well made by V. Zhirmunsky, "Pushkin i zapadnye literatury," *Pushkin-Vremennik pushinskoy komissii* (Moscow-Leningrad, 1937), III, 77.

4. See W. N. Vickery, "Parallelizm v literaturnom razvitii Bayrona i Pushkina," *American Contributions to the Fifth International Congress of Slavicists* (The Hague: Mouton, 1963), pp. 371–401.

5. *Ak. nauk*, XI, 141.

6. *Ak. nauk*, XIII, 197.

7. *Ak. nauk*, XII, 159–60.

8. V. Belinsky, *Polnoe sobranie sochineniy* (Moscow, 1953–56), VII, 505.

9. V. P. Gorodetsky, "Dramaturgiya," *Pushkin: Itogi i problemy izucheniya* (Moscow-Leningrad, 1966), p. 446.

10. *Ibid.*, p. 453.

11. *Ibid.*, p. 449.

12. See note 5.

13. *Ak. nauk*, XI, 419.

14. *Ak. nauk*, XI, 40.

15. See I. Vinogradov, "Put' Pushkina k realizmu," *Literaturnoe nasledstvo*, XVI–XVIII, 84; however, the views expressed by I. Vinogradov in this article do not command general sympathy among Soviet Pushkinists.

16. *Ak. nauk*, XI, 67. It was also somewhat surprisingly entitled a "comedy." See *Ak. nauk*, ten-volume edition (Moscow-Leningrad, 1949), V, 597.

17. I. V. Kireevsky, *Polnoe sobranie sochineniy v dvukh tomakh* (Moscow, 1911), II, 45.

18. Affinities between Boris and Pushkin's apathetic "Southern" Byronic heroes, especially Aleko, are noted by D. Bernstein, "Boris Godunov," *Literaturnoe nasledstvo*, XVI–XVIII, 223.

19. The play originally ended with the crowd obediently echoing: "Long live Tsar Dimitry Ivanovich!" This ending could not have been interpreted as a happy one, since only an instant earlier the crowd maintained a horrified silence on hearing the news of the death of Boris' widow and son. The present accepted ending—with the crowd again maintaining silence—reflects a change, thought at one time to

have been dictated by the censor, but now regarded as almost certainly Pushkin's own. The crowd's silence is seen as a stronger ending, indicating the people's moral condemnation of the killing of Boris' widow and son, and the people's potentially menacing attitude. See M. P. Alekseev, "Remarka Pushkina 'Narod bezmolvstvuet,'" *Russkaya literatura* (1967), No. 2, pp. 36–58.

20. An interesting comparison in the manner of handling Boris' death is provided by Musorgsky's opera *Boris Godunov*, in which the dying takes longer and the Tsar's sickness seems more closely connected with his feelings of guilt.

21. (Zametka "O grafe Nuline."), *Ak. nauk*, XI, 188.

22. *Ibid.*

23. *Ibid.*

24. See P. E. Shchegolev, "Iz razyskany: v oblasti biografii i teksta Pushkina," *Pushkin i ego sovremenniki* (Saint Petersburg, 1911), XIV, 176–81.

25. See B. Koplan, "Poltavsky boy Pushkina i ody Lomonosova," *Pushkin i ego sovremenniki* (Leningrad, 1930), XXXVIII–XXXIX, 113–21; also A. N. Sokolov, "*Poltava* Pushkina i *Petriady*," *Pushkin: Vremennik pushkinskoy komissii* (Moscow-Leningrad, 1939), IV–V, 57–90.

26. Lines 345–68 in the first canto (starting *Kto pri zvezdax*....) were in an early variant written in the trochaic meter, which was sometimes used in Russian for ballads. See *Ak. nauk*, V, 28–29 and 215–18.

27. See V. V. Vinogradov, *Stil' Pushkina* (Moscow, 1941), pp. 237–39.

28. For contemporary criticisms and Pushkin's views see *Pushkin: itogi i problemy izucheniya* (Moscow-Leningrad, 1966), pp. 25–27 and 385–88; see also *Ak. nauk*, XI, 158–60 and 164–65.

Chapter Four

1. Often included among the "Little Tragedies" is "The Water-Nymph" (1832) which remained unfinished and is not dealt with in this book.

2. S. V. Shervinsky, *Ritm i smysl* (Moscow, 1961), pp. 157–58.

3. L. Polivanov, quoted here from Shervinsky, *op. cit.*, p. 158.

4. Noted by V. Setschkareff, *Alexander Puschkin* (Wiesbaden, 1963), p. 152.

5. Shervinsky, *op. cit.*, p. 218; and Tomashevsky, *Pushkin i Frantsiya* (Leningrad, 1960), pp. 266–81.

6. See V. Setschkareff, *op. cit.*, p. 155.

7. The link between *The Covetous Knight* and *Mozart and Salieri* is pointed out by D. D. Blagoy, "Pushkin—Master psikhologicheskogo analiza," *Literatura i deystviteľnost'* (Moscow, 1959), pp. 366–400.

8. For a fuller treatment of Pushkin's relation to his hero and of other ways in which his personal life influenced this work, see the extremely perceptive article by Anna Akhmatova, "*Kamenny gost'* Pushkina," *Pushkin: Issledovaniya i materialy* (Moscow-Leningrad, 1958), pp. 185–95.

9. *Ibid.*, pp. 194–95.

10. "L'originalité du *Convive de Pierre* de Pouchkine," *Revue de Littérature Comparée* (Paris, 1955), XXIX, 48–71. See also, Leo Weinstein, *The Metamorphoses of Don Juan* (Stanford: Stanford University Press, 1959), pp. 92–93.

11. "Pushkin and Don Juan," *For Roman Jakobson* (The Hague: Mouton, 1966), pp. 273–84.

12. O. Mandel, *The Theatre of Don Juan* (Lincoln: University of Nebraska Press, 1963), p. 449.

13. The passages "translated" here are (with the exception of the "Hymn to the Plague") from John Wilson's original.

Chapter Five

1. Onegin's letter to Tatiana in Chapter VIII was written in October, 1831.

2. For a complete critical discussion of the "tenth" chapter, see B. Tomashevsky, "Desyataya glava 'Evgeniya Onegina,' (Istoriya razgadki)," *Pushkin* (Moscow-Leningrad: Ak. nauk, 1961), II, 200–244.

3. Pushkin seems to have toyed with the idea of continuing his poem as late as 1835; see, for example, V. Nabokov, *Eugene Onegin* (New York; Pantheon, 1964), III, 376ff.

4. The final version, as approved by the poet, is that of 1837; this edition does not, however, for reasons of censorship, include a number of passages which are normally considered part of *Evgeny Onegin* and which do appear in the Academy of Sciences edition (Vol. VI, 1937). The differences are, for present purposes, negligible.

5. R. D. Waller, quoted by E. Boyd, *Byron's Don Juan* (New Brunswick, 1945), p. 51.

6. This viewpoint has become so firmly established in one form or another that it is impossible to associate it with any one particular critic. In the introduction to his *Evgeny Onegin: Roman v stikhakh* (Moscow, 1957), N. L. Brodsky declares (p. 7) that "Belinsky saw in *Evgeny Onegin* first and foremost a Realist novel." Brodsky then proceeds (pp. 7–8) to the effect that with his *Evgeny Onegin* Pushkin

"wrote the first Russian Realist novel." Brodsky also enlists (p. 10) in support of the Realist cause D. D. Blagoy who "correctly reminds us that *Evgeny Onegin* was the first genuinely great Realist work in all of nineteenth-century world literature, since it preceded in time the generally recognized models of European Classical Realism, the novels of Balzac and Stendhal, which appeared at the beginning of the thirties, at a time therefore when Pushkin had already completed all of *Evgeny Onegin*." The tendency of Brodsky and like-minded critics is, further, to equate Realism with social protest. This in turn leads to a quite disproportionate stressing of Pushkin's allegedly negative attitude to his own class. The ridiculous lengths to which this approach has been pushed can be clearly seen in L. Grossman's treatment of the subject. In his *Pushkin* (Moscow, 1960), p. 387, Grossman suggests that the peasant masses emerge as more noble than their masters and, as an illustration, quotes some rather sentimental phrases uttered by the authoritative Belinsky on the subject of Tatiana's nurse; it must surely be clear to any unbiased reader not only that Tatiana's nurse is obtuse and senile but that the significance of her role in *Evgeny Onegin* is minimal.

7. See L. N. Stilman, "Problemy literaturnykh zhanrov i traditsii v 'Evgenij Onegine' Pushkina," *American Contributions to the Fourth International Congress of Slavicists* (S-Gravenhage: Mouton, 1958), pp. 321–67; and A. A. Akmatova, " 'Adol'f' Benzhamena Konstana v tvorchestve Pushkina," *Pushkin-Vremennik pushkinskoy komissii* (Moscow-Leningrad, 1936), I, 91–114.

8. E. Boyd, *op. cit.*, p. 34.

9. Henry Fielding's oft-quoted statement that "a comic romance is a comic epic poem in prose" (Preface to *Joseph Andrews*) is more revealing in connection with *Don Juan* than *Evgeny Onegin;* however, it does have application in the present context, if only for the attention it draws to the tendency of different genres to coalesce.

10. Individual portions of *Evgeny Onegin* can, it has been pointed out, be identified as germane to the idyll, ode, satire, parody, epigram, or even drama; see Vsevolod Setschkareff, *Alexander Puschkin: Sein Leben und sein Werk* (Wiesbaden: Otto Harrassowitz, 1963), p. 125. The generally valid statement that *Evgeny Onegin* and *Don Juan* derive from the same literary tradition requires some qualification. As Setschkareff points out (*ibid.*, p. 124), while Pushkin's work has affinities mainly with the eighteenth-century Sentimental novel and the modern psychological novel (as an example of which he cites *Adolphe*), Byron's is more closely linked with the picaresque novel and the burlesque epic of the Renaissance. Actually, the strands of tradition are so intertwined in both works that even the distinctions made by Setschkareff can legitimately be further modified. Thus,

while Pushkin's narrative technique owes some debt to Fielding and Sterne, the Haidée episode in *Don Juan* reflects the influence of Rousseau.

11. D. Cizevsky, *Evgenij Onegin: A Novel in Verse* (Cambridge, 1953), p. xxviii.

12. See L. N. Stilman, *op. cit.*, pp. 351–52.

13. For a discussion of symmetry in *Evgeny Onegin*, see V. Nabokov, *op. cit.*, I, 15–20, and the analysis of the work's structure in the following pages.

14. L. N. Stilman, *op. cit.*, p. 360, speaks of this aspect of the poem as a "deviation" and a "departure" from Romanticism: "This does not yet constitute the triumph of Realism, but it is a move in the direction of Realism."

15. My interpretation here is, I believe, basically in accord with that given by D. S. Mirsky (who, by the way, has pointed out that Tatiana's conduct in the final chapter was partly determined by Pushkin's desire to provide his future wife with a model of correct and loyal behavior). In *A History of Russian Literature* (New York: Vintage Books, 1958), p. 92, Mirsky writes: "The greatness of Pushkin in the creation of Tatiana is that he avoided the almost unavoidable pit of making a prig or a puritan out of the virtuous wife who coldly rejects the man she loves. Tatiana is redeemed in her virtue by the sadness she will never conquer, by her resigned and calm resolve never to enter her only possible paradise, but to live with never a possibility of happiness."

16. See note 7.

17. For the view that Pushkin condemned both Onegin and Lensky, see, e.g., N. L. Brodsky, *op. cit.*, pp. 8–9. Brodsky considered Pushkin basically hostile to the society which produced these two characters. Brodsky does, however, show his awareness of Pushkin's sympathy for Onegin and Lensky. The difference here between my view and Brodsky's is really one of emphasis—but this, in an attempt to arrive at a critical appreciation of the work, is an all-important difference.

18. "I am always glad," he wrote in the first chapter, "to note the difference between Onegin and me."

19. Pushkin's willingness to defend Lensky's naïve idealism emerges even more clearly from some stanzas which he originally included in his characterization of Lensky (Chapter II).

20. See R. F. Gustafson, "The Metaphor of the Revolving Seasons in *Evgenij Onegin*," *Slavic and East European Journal*, VI (1962), pp. 6–20.

21. E. LoGatto, *Pushkin: Storia di un Poeta e del suo Eroe* (Milan: Mursia, 1959), p. 38.

22. *Ibid.*, p. 30.
23. In this respect Pushkin's work differs markedly from Tchaikovsky's opera; in the story of the opera it is the actions of the main characters which are all-important.
24. Boyd, *op. cit.*, p. 31.
25. See Cizevsky, *op. cit.*, pp. 256–59.
26. See note 13.

Chapter Six

1. *Ak. nauk*, XII, 160.
2. D. S. Mirsky, *Pushkin* (New York, 1963), p. 207.
3. George Gibian, *"Measure for Measure* and Pushkin's *Angelo,"* PMLA, LXVI (1951), 426–31.
4. Also basically completed was the earlier (1830) *The Tale of the Priest and His Worker Balda.* Censorship considerations prevented Pushkin from putting it in final form. A mutilated version was published in 1840 by Zhukovsky, who replaced the priest with a merchant. In later editions the priest was reinserted. It is of considerable interest to the student of versification, since its lines lack regularity both in the number of syllables and the number and positioning of the stresses; its only technical regulating principle is rhyme.
5. See further M. K. Azadovsky, "Istochniki skazok Pushkina," *Pushkin: Vremennik pushkinskoy komissii* (Moscow-Leningrad, 1936), I, 134–63; also S. A. Bugoslavsky, "Russkie narodnye pesni v zapisi Pushkina," *Pushkin: Vremennik* (Moscow-Leningrad, 1941), VI, 183–210.
6. See Chapter 3, notes 13 and 14.
7. See R. Jakobson in "The Kernel of Comparative Slavic Literature," *Harvard Slavic Studies,* I (1953), 16; L. V. Pumpiansky, "Medny vsadnik i poeticheskaya tradiditsiya XVIII veka," *Pushkin: Vremennik pushkinskoy komissii* (Moscow-Leningrad, 1939), vols. 4–5, pp. 91–124; W. N. Vickery, " 'Mednyj vsadnik' and the Eighteenth-Century Heroic–Ode," *Indiana Slavic Studies,* III (1963), 140–62; P. Call, "Pushkin's *Bronze Horseman*: A Poem of Motion," *Slavic and East European Journal,* XI (2) (1967), 137–44.
8. The best-documented and most illuminating study of this poem is by W. Lednicki, *Pushkin's Bronze Horseman* (Berkeley and Los Angeles, 1955).
9. See Lednicki, *op. cit.*, p. 69; also *Ak. nauk*, V, 445.
10. A Bely, *Ritm kak dialektika i "Medny Vsadnik"* (Moscow, 1929), pp. 266–79. Unfortunately, Bely goes too far in subscribing to the rather widely held view that Nicholas I rather than d'Anthès constituted the real threat to Pushkin's marriage. As I have stated in

this book and elsewhere, I consider this improbable. It is in any case unnecessary to Bely's perfectly convincing thesis. We know that Pushkin resented the Tsar flirting with his wife. And there may perfectly well have been some analogy in Pushkin's mind between the Tsar's flirtatiousness and Peter's "robbing" Evgeny of his Parasha. But the main point is that Nicholas, in Pushkin's mind, intruded into Pushkin's life by forcing him to live in Petersburg and to lead a life that was frustrating, degrading, and confining. Pushkin felt himself to be Nicholas' prisoner. Nicholas seemed omnipresent, just as the will of Peter the Great was omnipresent in the life of Evgeny.

11. *A. S. Pushkin: o literature* (Moscow, 1962), p. 23.

12. *Ibid.*, pp. 67, 173.

13. Actually, he started writing his autobiographical memoirs as early as 1821. However, most of this material he burned after the catastrophe of December 14, 1825. Only relatively recently have attempts been made to "reconstruct" this early autobiographical undertaking which is known to have occupied a great deal of Pushkin's time during 1824 in Mikhaylovskoye. See I. Feinberg, *Nezavershennye raboty Pushkina* (Moscow, 1955).

14. For a more detailed study see B. O. Unbegaun, *Tales of the Late Ivan Petrovich Belkin* (Oxford, 1947).

15. For a more detailed study of the polemical aspects of *The Tales of Belkin* see V. Setschkareff, *Alexander Puschkin* (Wiesbaden, 1963), pp. 165–72.

16. *The Shot* can reasonably be compared with *Mozart and Salieri* and also with *The Stone Guest*, both written during the same 1830 fall period at Boldino. The comparison suggests itself for two reasons: (1) the problem of envy of another person who appears to have or acquire things without effort; (2) the question of when life is easy to sacrifice, and when not, in particular the added meaning that may be given to life by love or marriage. See A. A. Akhmatova, "'Kammeny gost' Pushkina'," Pushkin: *Issledovaniya i materialy* (Moscow-Leningrad, 1958), II, 185–95.

Chapter Seven

1. See also B. P. Gorodetsky, *Lirika Pushkina* (Moscow-Leningrad, 1962), p. 29, and Gorodetsky, "Lirika," Pushkin: *itogi i problemy izucheniya* (Moscow-Leningrad, 1966), pp. 408–13.

2. "The Demon" was widely interpreted as being a psychological portrait of Alexander Raevsky, a Russian "Byron" and a member of the family which had taken Pushkin to the Caucasus and Crimea in 1820, and introduced him to Byronism.

3. This poem, unpublished during Pushkin's life, was prompted by

the failure of the Spanish uprising which was suppressed by French troops.

4. For details concerning the composition of this poem see N. Izmailov, "Strofy o Napoleone i Bayrone v stikhotvorenii 'K moryu,'" *Pushkin: Vremennik pushkinskoy komissii* (Moscow-Leningrad, 1941), VI, 21–29; also N. L. Stepanov, *Lirika Pushkina* (Moscow, 1959), pp. 310–26.

5. "From Pindemonte" (1836), discussed later in this chapter, expresses more plainly the poet's misgivings as to the relationship between different forms of government and the true nature of human freedom and happiness.

6. Translated by Maurice Baring, *Have You Anything To Declare?* (London, 1936: William Heinemann Ltd.), p. 246.

7. The views here expressed on the ideas informing "The Prophet" are, in large measure, a condensation of N. L. Stepanov's evaluation. See N. L. Stepanov, *op. cit.*, pp. 347–63.

8. Translated by Maurice Baring, *op. cit.*, p. 244.

9. The woman to whom these eight lines were addressed remained unknown for many years, and her identity has still not been established with complete certainty. However, convincing evidence points to Karolina Soban'skaya whom Pushkin first met in Kiev or Odessa in 1821 (while on leave from Kishinev) and with whom he again became embroiled in Petersburg after his return from exile. See M. A. Tsyavlovsky, *Rukoyu Pushkina* (Moscow-Leniningrad, 1935), pp. 179–208. At the same time, it seems probable that Pushkin copied this same poem into the album of A. A. Olenina who in 1828 rejected his marriage proposal; see T. G. Tsiavlovskaya, "Dnevnik Olenina," *Pushkin: Issledovaniya i materialy* (Moscow-Leningrad, 1958), II, 289–92.

10. See B. P. Gorodetsky, *op. cit.*, pp. 289ff.

11. The dating of this poem is uncertain. Gorodetsky (p. 359) gives it as January 19, 1830. On the assumption, which I am strongly inclined to accept, that it was addressed to Pushkin's wife, this date would be impossible. His wife's copy was dated 1831, and the poem may not have been written till 1832.

12. *Ak. nauk*, III, 517.

13. For an excellent study of this poem see M. P. Alekseyev, *Stikhotvorenie Pushkina "Ya pamyatnik sebe vozdvig . . ."* (Leningrad, 1967).

Chapter Eight

1. It should be mentioned that many Pushkin lovers would disagree with this assessment. *The Gypsies, The Bronze Horseman,* and

the verse fairy tale about Tsar Saltan have all been rated above *Evgeny Onegin* at various times. It is, in the end, a matter of personal taste.

2. Isaiah Berlin, *The Hedgehog and the Fox* (New York: Simon & Schuster, 1953), p. 1.

3. T. S. Eliot, *On Poetry and Poets* (London: Faber & Faber, 1957), p. 225.

4. "Introduction," *The Oxford Book of Russian Verse*, 2nd ed. (Oxford, 1948), xliii.

Selected Bibliography

Primary Sources

Boris Godunov, tr. by A. Hayes (New York: E. P. Dutton and Co., 1918).

Eugene Onegin, ed. and tr. by Vladimir Nabokov (New York: Bollingen Foundation). 4 vols.

Eugene Onegin, tr. by Walter Arndt (New York: E. P. Dutton and Co., 1963).

Eugene Onegin, tr. by Babette Deutsch (New York: Limited Editions Club, 1943).

Eugene Onegin, tr. by Oliver Eton (London: Pushkin Press, 1937).

Mozart and Salieri, tr. by R. M. Hewitt (Nottingham, 1938).

Poems by Alexander Pushkin, tr. by I. Panin (Boston: Cupples and Hurd, 1888).

Poems, Prose and Plays of Alexander Pushkin, ed. by A. Yarmolinsky (New York: Modern Library, 1943).

Polnoye sobranie sochineniy, ed. by M. A. Tsyavlovsky (Moscow-Leningrad: "Academia," 1936–38), 6 vols.

Polnoye sobranie sochineniy, (Moscow-Leningrad: Akademiia nauk, 1937–59).

Pushkin's Poems, tr. by Walter Morison (London: Allen and Unwin, 1945).

The Captain's Daughter, ed. by N. N. Sergievsky (New York: International Universities Press, 1946).

The Captain's Daughter and Other Tales, tr. by Natalie Duddington (New York: E. P. Dutton and Co., 1933).

The Golden Cockerel, tr. by E. Pagany (New York: Nelson and Sons, 1938).

The Prose Tales of Alexander Poushkin, tr. by T. Keane (London: Bell and Sons, 1896 and 1914).

The Russian Poets: Selections from Pushkin, Lermontov and Tyutchev, tr. by V. Nabokov (Norfolk, Conn.: New Directions, 1944).

The Works of Alexander Pushkin, ed. by A. Yarmolinsky (New York: Random House, 1936).

Three Tales: The Snowstorm, The Postmaster, The Undertaker, tr. by R. T. Currall (London-Toronto: Harrap, 1943).

Translations from Poushkin in Memory of the Hundreth Anniversary of the Poet's Birthday, tr. by Charles E. Turner (London: Marston and Company, 1899).

206 ALEXANDER PUSHKIN

Secondary Sources

BLAGOY, DMITRIY D. *Masterstvo Pushkina* (Moscow: Sovetskiy Pisatel', 1955). Placing sometimes exaggerated emphasis on sociological factors, this study nevertheless contains valuable materials relevant to individual works and their relationship to each other.

BRODSKY, N. A. S. *Pushkin. Biografiya* (Moscow, 1937). A competent critical biography, which, however, overstresses sociological factors.

GERSHENZON, M. *Mudrost' Pushkina* (Moscow, 1919). A stimulating, but often onesided attempt to evaluate Pushkin's "philosophy."

GORODETSKY, B. P., ed., and others. *Pushkin: Itogi i problemy izucheniya* (Moscow-Leningrad, 1966). An excellent survey, from the Soviet standpoint, of Pushkin scholarship. While many of the views expressed by different collaborators are questionable, this survey covers much ground and gives indispensable bibliographical sources.

LAPSHINA, N., I. ROMANOVICH, B. IARCKO. *Metricheskiy spravochnik k stikhotvoreniyam A.S. Pushkina* (Leningrad, 1934). Although now somewhat outdated, this is an invaluable guide for those interested in Pushkin's metrics.

LEDNICKI, WACLAW. *Pushkin's Bronze Horseman; The Story of a Masterpiece* (Berkeley and Los Angeles, 1955). A well-written, sometimes biased, but stimulating account of the political and personal factors which formed a background for the writing of this poem.

LO GATTO, ETTORE. *Pushkin: storia di un poeta e del suo eroe* (Milano: Mursia, 1959). The attempt in this study to tie in much of Pushkin's biography with *Evgeny Onegin* is sometimes forced. Carelessly written, the book nevertheless contains valuable insights.

MIRSKY, D. S. *Pushkin* (New York: E. P. Dutton and Company, 1926, 1963). A critical biography. Unsatisfyingly brief in its treatment of many works and dogmatic in some of its views, Mirsky's work shows much perception in its insights into Pushkin's psychology and the esthetic merits of his writing.

SETSCHKAREFF, V. *Alexander Puschkin* (Wiesbaden: Otto Harrassowitz, 1963). A skillfully constructed critical biography. Covers a great deal of material, but briefly. Lacks notes.

SHAW, J. THOMAS, ed. *The Letters of Alexander Pushkin* (Bloomington, Indiana, and Philadelphia, 1963). 3 vols. The only work available for those reading Pushkin's letters in English. Excellently annotated with a valuable biographical index.

SIMMONS, ERNEST J. *Pushkin* (Cambridge, Massachusetts: Harvard

University Press, 1937). A well-written and well-documented account of Pushkin's life. Its views of Pushkin's tragic end may be sometimes open to question. Makes little attempt to discuss his works.

SLONIMSKY, ALEXANDR L. *Masterstvo Pushkina* (Moscow, 1963). A sensitive examination of many of Pushkin's works.

Slovar' yazyka Pushkina (Moscow-Leningrad, 1956–1961). 4 vols. This four-volume dictionary is of interest only to the more serious Pushkin scholar, for whom it is essential.

TOMASHEVSKY, B. *Pushkin* (Moscow-Leningrad, 1956–1961). 2 vols. The first volume is an authoritative and, on the whole, fair account of Pushkin's creative development up to his exile. Its continuation was prevented by the author's death. The second volume is a miscellany of posthumously published articles on various subjects relating to Pushkin.

———. *Pushkin i Frantsiya* (Leningrad, 1960). The most complete study on Pushkin's relationship to French literature and culture.

TROYAT, HENRI. *Pouchkine* (Paris, 1936). English abbreviated translation: *Pushkin* (New York, 1950). An interesting critical biography—the abridged New York edition is mainly confined to biography, and is unannotated.

TSYAVLOVSKY, M. A. *Letopis' zhizni i tvorchestva A. S. Pushkina*, I (Moscow, 1951). A chronicle of Pushkin's life, work, and background events, unfortunately extending only to 1826. Interrupted by Tsiavlovsky's death. Further volumes are expected.

TSYAVLOVSKY, M. A. and others. *Rukoyu Pushkina* (Moscow-Leningrad, 1935). Contains interesting materials for the Pushkin specialist—documents, notes, etc., not available elsewhere.

VERESAYEV, V. *Pushkin v zhizni* (Moscow, 1936). 2 vols. A collection of background materials and comments on Pushkin by contemporaries. The selection has been criticized for its emphasis on the more piquant sides of Pushkin's life and personality. Nevertheless it is of great value, if judiciously used.

ZHIRMUNSKY, V. *Bayron i Pushkin. Iz istorii romanticheskoy poemy* (Leningrad: "Academia," 1924). The most thorough comparative study of Byron's influence on Pushkin's "Southern" poems. Also touches briefly on *Poltava*, and even more briefly, on *Evgeny Onegin*.

Serial Publications

The following are serial publications containing many valuable articles on Pushkin's life and work:

Literaturnoe Nasledstvo. 16–18 (Moscow, 1934) and 58 (Moscow, 1952).

Pushkin. Issledovaniya i materialy (Moscow-Leningrad, 1956–1967). 5 vols.

Pushkin: Vremennik pushkinskoy komissii (Moscow-Leningrad, 1936–1941). 6 vols.

Pushkin i ego sovremenniki (Petersburg-Leningrad, 1905–1927). 39 issues.

Index